AF700680

THE Freedom TO Live WITHOUT Fear

Mission Center
826 Valencia Street
San Francisco, CA 94110

Tenderloin Center
180 Golden Gate Avenue
San Francisco, CA 94102

Mission Bay Center
1310 4th Street
San Francisco, CA 94158

826valencia.org

Published May 2020 by 826 Valencia | Copyright © 2020 by 826 Valencia

Program Manager | Ryan Young

Program Coordinators | Yareli Arreola, Stina Perkins

Program Associates | Diego Hernandez, Hannah Johnson

Program Interns | Nico Vallone, Tarryn Warn

Editorial Board

Volunteer Editors | Tess Canfield, Katie Cugno, Maura Kealey, Anne Sloper, Tarryn Warn

Student Editors | Virginia Coello, Jackie Hernandez, Ezrealla Laudenorio, Kimberly Hernandez T.

Volunteer Tutors | Kanya Abe, Yareli Arreola, Eedit Bareket, Paolo Bicchieri, Skylar Burkhardt, Sara Bursavich, Tess Canfield, Kevin Cranfill, Reginald Cruz, Katie Cugno, Dory Culver, Lila Cutter, Melissa Dittrich, Sarah Duncan, Sharon Elswit, Renata Espinosa, Ana Medrano Fernandez, Darci Flatley, Rebecca Fox, Nina Gannes, Cristina Giner, Paul Glantz, Sophie Goethals, Anne Guaspari, Thomas Hatfield, Diego Hernandez, Hannah Johnson, Maura Kealey, David Kirp, Ellie MacBride, Naomi Marcus, Michael McNamara, Kevin Meehan, Katey Mokelke, Jake Murphy, Molly Parent, Lucie Pereira, Stina Perkins, Bill Poole, Conan Putnam, Karen Rhodes, Johann Schiffer, Michele Sloat, Anne Sloper, Maria Elena Urquico, Nico Vallone, Tarryn Warn, John Weil

Partner Teacher | Catherine Reyes

Design Director | Brad Amorosino

Publications Project Manager | Meghan Ryan

Designer | Molly Schellenger

Illustrator | Azul Quetzalli

Copyeditor | Christopher Keilman

ISBN 978-1-948644-47-1
Printed in Canada by Prolific Graphics
Distributed by Ingram Publisher Services

826 Valencia and its free programs are fueled by generous contributions from companies, organizations, government agencies, and individuals who provide more than ninety-five percent of our budget. Our Young Authors' Book Project and this publication are made possible in part by grants from the Dow Jones Foundation, Norman Raab Foundation, Sam Mazza Foundation, San Francisco City & County: Department of Children, Youth & Their Families (DCYF), and The Walther Foundation.

FREEDOM TO LIVE WITHOUT FEAR

Written by twelfth-grade students at Mission High School with a foreword by Nikky Finney

The views expressed in this book are the authors' and do not necessarily reflect those of 826 Valencia. We support student publishing and are thrilled that you picked up this book.

Contents

Foreword

▮ NIKKY FINNEY

Geography is the study of the physical features of the earth and its atmosphere, and of human activity as it affects and is affected by these . . .

I arrived at Mission High School, in San Francisco, in the winter of the new year 2020, to meet a new world of young writers that I had never met before. I didn't know the terrain but I trusted the map used to get there as well as my newly introduced and passionate guides, the older writers and teachers of our young people who are often the great unsung navigators of our youth across the great flowering deserts of our planet.

Even before I met them I knew I wouldn't have enough time with them and I had no idea how to get to know them as well as I wanted to know them, in only one afternoon of legend and mapmaking. I wondered as I walked to their door if they were feeling what I had been feeling of late about the quality of the hot air coming from so many of the adults standing in the lights of cameras and microphones speaking glibly of what the world was quickly becoming.

In their electric presence I talked about the weather and wondered if they might be able to see the tide pools between their own emotions and some evocative weather words. I lost my place because they were so beautiful sitting there in their high-altitude poetry and prose space suits ready for whatever I had to offer them. We spent the afternoon in love with words and ways of saying. We talked about the world and looked directly at each other and said true things and hard to say things in that way people who fall in and out of love often do.

And later that day before we left each other for good, like people in love sometimes have to do, we came to a quiet mountain climbing understanding that what we had shared, in that sun-filled space, was something akin to discovering a mighty new world, one whose golden fields of grain weren't just promotional advertising for a world that might one day be. But were instead a kind of real food—that fed each of us sitting and standing there together. The recognition of our kinship made us plump and invincible for the world we knew we would soon have to reenter without the other. There was a gravitational pull in the room—for any of us who allowed our hearts to listen and lean in. I thought of the other high schools and the other young writers all across the San Francisco city nesting more young wordsmiths I would not get to stand before and listen to.

I flew back to the land from which I had come, patiently waiting to see what their great hearts might lay out before the sandy page.

Unequivocally. These young writers are riders of the big wave, conquistadors and matadors and watchful grandmothers of the ocean of the heart. In their writing they tell what they know of what it means to be alive. They lead us to their magnificent "little circles of families hanging outside their residences" and they allow us to hear how fiercely they hold on to all of who they are.

These young writers have worked their air tubes into the seven layers of the Earth's atmosphere and have found their purest breath. They have dug their pens down deep into the good soil in order to teleport us back to a magical time when they were standing in the plazuela with their "crazy uncles" and everyone was wearing a red jersey and waiting for the moment to ride through the mud together. And how in that moment "they looked like a field of roses all packed in one place."

I am now three thousand miles away from this new human planet of young writers. I swallow easy and hard at what they are writing about their place on this Earth at this time. I turn the pages carefully in order to not to miss one word of what they feel. I hear them say that we do a lot of standing on the Earth and how we need to make more time to listen to what it has to tell us. I hear them say the American dream is over there somewhere. I hear them speak of growing up Jewish and not wanting to be firebombed while in synagogue. I hear them speak of being proud of their abuelitas and their grandfathers that outlasted slavery and what they know of being the only black kid being raised by a black father.

These young writers and their stories are unwilling to be viewed as outsider or alien anything. The black and green and cornflower blue planet is their home. They don't whisper the word immigrant or other and they know who built America and they are only willing to be called explorers—of their own mountains and valleys and flatlands and city parks and low riders. Do not ask them to un-see the kneeling football player speaking his truth with hair rising into the nitrogen-rich air like a garden of tiny clenched fists inspiring her to circle her own truth then speak it aloud.

These young people with pens and pencils will tell you they have gotten into a few fights and have gotten over the twin peaks of heartache and heartbreak. They know what the 13th, 14th, and 15th Amendments guarantee and have memorized both the geography of oppression and the spectacle of invisibility. They are young people who are alive and willing. They are inclusive. They have walked through the explosive landmines of homelessness and the northern lights of motherlessness and fatherlessness and they have found their heroes inside the walls of that sacred active volcano better known as the community library.

They get it. They give it. They want it. They are our living geography and I bow to their writhing writing hands in search of the rest of the great atlas of their lives.

Nikky Finney
Columbia, SC
March 27, 2020

La Niña with the Big Dreams

LARISSA CHACON

Sitting back on the bench, under the same tree over and over again, I finally took the courage to open my memory box, full of moments I had never had time to open. I dove into it, and the first thing I saw was my tassel from graduation back in high school, and it suddenly began.

I took myself into my journey to find the "freedom." Crazy to think that I was going to be free, but there I was, back in my chair in a school where I was full of dreams, full of goals, and joy; however, the same question came up over and over again. *Do you have freedom? What is freedom?* The question of freedom that came around always caused me to lose myself in thought, from my grandmother back in my homeland, El Salvador, to my middle school counselor, all the way to my senior days. There were always people trying to stop me and place limits on me, making my idea of freedom its own paradox.

My grandmother and her sayings, "LAS NIÑAS NO ANDAN EN LA CALLE," *girls don't play in the street,* because you are "UNA MUJERCITA," *you are a young lady!*

To the "You really think they will accept you at the best public high school in San Francisco?" of my middle school counselor.

To the high school teacher who looked at me skeptically when I said I was applying to University of California, Los Angeles and University of San Diego. I have always had to leap over the obstacles to live a life of freedom. I finished that thought in my head and pulled out pictures of my family and those who I once considered friends.

The day went by and I was still on the same bench. I felt like the time had stopped and it was just me and the pictures. How can you be free or claim to be free when you are afraid of being yourself, of making observations without your "friends" judging you? When they completely forget the promise of "never leaving your side?"

I took a deep breath and stopped myself for a minute. I looked at my family picture. Even though they were all I had, I felt confused, confused about the way they wanted me to be . . . again to limit me from being who I am today!

Now myself, I went home again, a place where, now, I was stuck. Full of sadness and sorrow after that moment at the park, I emptied my box and looked at everything in it . . . and suddenly I thought, *Why do I have all of this? Why do I keep on tying myself to these memories and events?* And so there I was, making of myself and my life its own trap. A trap in which I again became the prisoner of my own and I no longer felt like a pretty bird, free and unaware.

The mix of movie tickets, pictures, flowers, letters, and more, made me realize everything I had been through and how little I remembered! I put everything in the box and laid on my bed. I took a deep breath and finished what I had from work . . . As I finished, I said, "I need a break!" I sent a request for a week of break, that it was crucial, that I didn't tend to ask for a break, but now I felt like I deserved it. I tried to fall asleep while thinking about my own traumas and what worried me . . . and suddenly I began to cry. Personally, I don't often do this, but this time was different. I cried until I went to sleep. I really had forgotten what it was like to cry yourself to sleep, and I did feel like my childhood memories came back again. The beautiful days, running, playing, laughing, no worries, and a life full of good moments . . . but in the moments of hardship, I cried myself to sleep as a form of relief.

I received my week off and the first thing I did was call my mom and tell her, "Get ready, because tomorrow we are going out." It was just a matter of time. My boyfriend was at work, so I planned on going with my mom and then surprising him to go on a date. I saw my mom after a long week of work and maybe about three months had passed since I had last seen her. I totally felt like I had abandoned her.

I grabbed some orchids for her and picked her up. The first thing she said was, "Why are you not at work?"

She was too surprised to see me on a weekday, but I took it in a good way and told her, "Can we not talk about me and work, and focus on having a nice time together?"

She just smiled. I drove us to the restaurant and got seated at the table. I usually went all by myself. While talking to her, some things just came to my head . . .

"So how are you? How is your relationship?" she questioned me. "Is everything going okay? Is there anything you want me to know?"

I just looked at her and said, "Well, that is going just fine, and about telling you, it might only be the feeling of confusion and disappointment!"

"Ay hija, confundida por qué?" *Why babe, what is confusing?*

I answered and told her everything from the day before. I felt my eyes get watery, my palms started to sweat, and my heart felt like a massive elephant was sitting on top of it, trying to ignore the knot built up in my throat.

"Ay mi niña como que aun no cambias, así eras de pequeña . . . Feliz hoy y enojada en un par de segundos." *OMG babe, that has always been you. One moment you are happy, and next thing you know you're really pissed.*

We started to eat and laugh because she was reminding me of my childhood, how I used to worry so much to get everything to match, from the bottom of my shoes to the top of my head! Or when I hated her braiding my hair before school or just didn't let her do my hair. I apparently was a really hard child! I totally felt the struggle of my mom. And not to mention she was just twenty years old when she had me!

"But still I see that en tus ojos, hija. It feels like there is something you want to say but you can't? ¿O estoy mal?"

I loved my mom a lot and something that had always surprised me about her was how well she knew me, but I felt like not telling her yet. We were just starting, but she kept on asking, so I told her . . .

"Well, there is something . . . and it's just that I have been remembering things of my childhood and there is a question. I totally forgot until two days ago. While I cleaned my house, I was trying to throw away things, and [illegible] box where I keep a lot of memories. I spent a good time remem- [illegible] and thinking about everything inside of it." I asked her, "How do [illegible] free? Or have you ever questioned yourself about whether or not [illegible] re free?"

[illegible] y mom said that she does feel free . . . but *there was a little pause.*

I then started to ask her, "How do you define freedom, or how do you think that changed when you were younger while being instructed by my grandmother? How or what do you feel towards freedom?"

She then suddenly started to tell me, "Wow, I actually feel like I'm free because no one is putting limitations on me, but now that you talk about my mom, I can actually picture or visualize my childhood."

We both started to talk about Grandma, about the culture of El Salvador and the American culture, about the big factor of whether you are free or if it is just an illusion. I had heard the stories so many times about how strict and sexist the rules were back then when my mom was a teenager. How could this still resonate with me? Maybe because my grandmother raised me during my most important years.

My mom started sobbing while talking about her experiences and also reflected on what it was like to get pregnant at a pretty young age. She mentioned a keyword, "NO TODAS SOMOS IGUALES." She said, *We are not all the same,* which for everyone has a different meaning. At least for me it was that I was born to make a change, and no one would understand me, even if I explained myself more than once.

In the end, my mom and I came to the conclusion that, if it wasn't for our culture, we would still be in a very machista (sexist) community, unfair and full of contradictions!

We finished eating and then we had a good time updating each other while shopping and talking.

After the day with my mom, I went to my boyfriend's work, and told him I was going to wait for him so we could have dinner together. He was so happy about it and told me to wait just half an hour. I then took the time to stay in the car, while thinking about the entire day with my mom. How all this just made me picture my days back in middle school, those days full of joy and hope.

I never thought that someone could ruin or kill my spirit. I never questioned my counselor or confronted him on how he behaved towards some students. It only took some words to kill a part of me: "Do you really think that you will get placed at Lowell High School?" One little sentence for such a big response. I trapped myself like a vulnerable, wild animal, who comes and falls into a trap, ready to be killed or to be exploited. It might sound exaggerated but, how would a young woman, who is barely starting to see the other face of life, feel getting slapped this way, treated and shut down like I was? How would you feel? Wouldn't you feel confused in these thoughts of, *Maybe I deserve it? Maybe I was not meant to come this far? Maybe I don't belong here?* This made me totally question my freedom until I was older.

The seasons flew by and the years passed, and the situation happened again but now with a teacher, a teacher who was not a bad person, just not so wise to see that his words and the little things he did did matter, or at least for me. At the time I was someone unstoppable, ready for the Nos and the Yeses of life, but I was not ready to be shut down one more time.

This teacher asked us what colleges we were applying to. I wanted to keep it to myself, but he had to call on me and ask me! Still today, I really don't even see the point of why he called on me, but when I answered, he looked at me skeptically and mentioned, "Someone tried to apply before and got denied. Y'all should know it is a hard school to get in, and some students at Mission are not ready." This for me was really hard to process. "I don't know why Mission kids . . ." and with just that I felt like my dreams were being taken away one more time. I definitely questioned myself on why. Wasn't I free to think, to create, to imagine, to innovate, to be the first one, to be WHATEVER I WANTED TO BE?

"*Aghhh,*" I exhaled, but then the door of the car opened . . .

"Hi babe! How are you?"

I answered with a soft tone, "I'm fine."

We left and had dinner together. We laughed and had a good time, like the old days back in high school. I then went home and laid down again, this time with a different feeling. The talk with my mom opened new doors for me, to actually think deeply and just analyze what I was feeling. I ignored everything completely; I just smiled and thought of all the good memories instead.

In the end, freedom is within me. I might be still tied down, I might be still trapped, without feeling free. Because I'm stuck in this world in which now all that matters is the vanity of making money and stressing over all my debts. The stress of having food on my table and my mom's table, the stress always being all about work instead of what I want.

I now can say that when I talk about freedom, it is also my freedom in my language, culture, story, community, and even more. The need to always try to fit in, always making me insecure about myself, is a constant obstacle. But what if I tell you that in the end all that matters is that you validate everything in your life, because no one else will do it?

Like James Baldwin once said in "A Talk to Teachers," "If I am not what you say I am, then you are not who you think you are," which I now can definitely understand. Freedom, or should I say, libertad! The liberty that I need to fight and work hard to be happy. In the very end, the bench where I always sit to think has been the one that brought my feet to the ground to think, to explore, to talk, to smile, to cry, to do anything! As long as you are happy, freedom will come no matter what. Freedom is something that will always be deep inside you.

"I used to think that I was the strangest person in the world but then I thought there are so many people in the world, there must be someone just like me that feels bizarre and flawed in the same way I do. I would imagine her, and imagine that she must be out there thinking of me, too. Well, I hope if you are out there and read this and know that, yes, it's true I'm here, and I'm just as strange as you."—Frida Kahlo

Larissa Chacon was born in El Salvador and moved here back in 2014. She is eighteen years old. She likes to do art, like dancing, drawing, and listening to music. She loves cooking and her culture of being a young Latina in San Francisco. One day, she hopes to become an immigration lawyer. She is a coordinator of the Organización Latinoamericana Estudiantil and the creator of the Immigrants Rising Club at Mission High School. She loves to teach about empowering voices who need it the most.

“Freedom is something that will always be deep inside you.”

Larissa Chacon

The Undefeated Horse

■ JASMINE THOELECKE

Society is a whirl of judgment, but why?

As a society, we should have the freedom to associate with one another and live through a simplistic lifestyle without having to just survive. From committing to daily tasks and rushing through life like it is survival mode, many of us feel restricted, as if we are a burden to society. Running through a maze, constantly hitting dead ends that are dominated by oppression, feeling like we can't escape. Often feeling like we need to conform to humanity's calling, just so we can be accepted.

I

Society erupts like a volcano.

I was born in the year of the horse, which represents speed and freedom. When I was younger, I grew up living by horoscopes, which can be stereotypical, especially within an Asian household.

As a horse, I am told to be fierce, decisive, and aggressive with my decision-making. When I was in my junior year of high school, I was brought down to the counselor's office and asked to select my classes for senior year. Knowing I hadn't thought about this topic prior to the conversation with him, I felt pressured with a sense of anger towards myself. When the counselor offered to message my parents, letting them know I should think about my choices, I instantly felt bothered by the idea. A sense of vulnerability and fear ran through my veins as I knew the topic of my zodiac would be discussed.

When going home, my mum met me with dark eyes, causing my body to tense as I felt my face redden. As expected, I was told off about not making decisions quick enough and dragging things out, which would lead to more trouble. Throughout the conversation, I felt insecure and upset. Upset as to why she couldn't understand me, as a high school student who was having trouble finding my path to "success." I felt out of my element. Miscategorized. Trapped, needing to conform to a stereotype. At that moment, I didn't feel like a horse. Going back to my room, I sat quietly, reviewing all the classes with a weighted feeling on my shoulder from the pressure all around. I felt defenseless. Incapable. Lost. Trapped in a horse's stable with only one way to escape. An escape I couldn't decode. My schedule.

Throughout the process, I realized that the choice was mine and I had control of what classes I wanted to take. I used the pressure as a source of motivation to help me make a decision. Thinking back to my long-term passion for working in business management, I finally settled my schedule in time, which brought a feeling of success.

You

You are a sponge.

Water is your self-worth. It gets squeezed out.

Trapped. Every time you suspect judgment.

People label you as three things. Shy. Reserved. Good at math. Nothing else. Feeling trapped in your own body, constantly trying to conform to the way people perceive you, thinking there is no way to escape.

Classroom. A place that is supposed to bring a feeling of comfort and safety.

Imagine yourself as an Asian girl, supposedly good at math and allegedly good at everything concerning numbers. As the teacher goes over an equation with the class, a quizzical thought clouds your mind while flashes of questions pop up within you.

"Are there any further questions? Ask them NOW." The teacher's voice pierces through your body like a needle poking your skin. Knowing you need to ask the question now to prevent being told off causes every inch of your body to tense. In a panic for answers, you scribble the question on paper with shaky hands before practicing the line over and over.

Finally developing the courage to raise your hand, the teacher points at you, causing eyes to dart towards you. Looking down at your paper, you pick the side of your sweaty hands while feeling your face burn.

Once stuttering your question out, the nearby snickering creates a desolate feeling as everyone surrounding you is now talking amongst one another. **"I already answered that question."** The teacher shoots a glare, causing your eyes to avert down at your paper with an ashamed nod.

You instantly feel the same numb feeling as before you asked. The numbness in your body, where you feel like you can't feel anything but dullness. Happiness and satisfaction seem so foreign, causing you to feel so far away from becoming better.

The feeling of losing value and the burden of feeling as if you don't belong, as if you are not conforming enough. Ghost-quiet silence fills the air as the tense atmosphere surrounds you, as if everyone in that room is tugging on an elastic band, stretching it as far as possible, but not enough to break it. It's like you are in the middle and everyone is pulling away from you.

You feel a sense of insecurity, like you don't belong. Your hands sweat and you yell to yourself to continue walking. Your id and superego speak on behalf of you, battling with each other, trying to figure out what to do. Telling yourself to keep your head down and focus on a specific spot on the paper in hopes to distract you.

The feeling of doubt never leaves.

Judgment once again. More drops of water are being released.

She

Life is like a maze.

Constantly running into dead ends while feeling your surroundings enclose on you. Just trying to escape.

As a horse, we are told to be fierce, decisive, and aggressive with our decision-making.

After her morning run, she stepped into her local café, causing the door bells to chime, making heads turn from all directions. Looking around the café for potential seats, people gave nasty stares upon her sweaty form, as if they were digging into her soul. Her face began to burn as she screamed to her inner self not to make eye contact with anyone. The atmosphere around her grew tense as her teeth gritted and her mouth grew bitter from nervousness. Stepping forward to order, her hands began to sweat as the waiter eyed her forehead, making insecurity grow within her. Hesitating with her words, she let out a sigh while waiting for her card to be processed by the machine before stepping away.

Standing awkwardly in the corner, a white man stood beside her, eyeing her outfit up and down, causing an unwelcome feeling of distress to run through her veins. The sirens ran through her head as the word "judgment" rang in her ears, causing an overwhelming sensation of adrenaline to flush upon her bright red face.

Looking down at her feet, her name was called, causing her to flinch from the loud noise, which led to more stares from nearby tables. Her heart began to race as she grabbed her drink before navigating through the tables, keeping her head toward the ground, trying not to slip. Heading out, she found a sense of relief, as if she had survived another maze.

You are now the horse, choosing to run away from the fear of judgment. Judgment that is unknown, yet known.

Perfection is darkness.

Foreign. Unknown.

Perfection can be another word for common. The same. If everyone were "perfect," no one would be different. But if everyone were perfect in their own way, it wouldn't need to be foreign nor unknown. We wouldn't need to feel the need to judge others.

Jasmine Thoelecke is a seventeen-year-old girl who was born in Anhui, China, a small province south of Beijing. She finds joy in fictional writing and walking through nature for a source of inspiration. Valuing the art of creativity holds importance in her life and comforts her when in need of escaping reality. The youthful feeling of communicating with peers has developed her intent for a future job in business.

Hunters Point, My Home

RJ LOVELESS

If you walk deep into my neighborhood, you'll probably notice that hip hop/ rap music is playing outside from the car speakers. People, from little kids to adults, all dancing, lip-syncing, and shaking what their mama gave them and having fun. The good smell of barbecue ribs and soul food flowing through the air. Other people who aren't outside having fun are inside having the same kind of fun. And for the people who are inside, they're either blasting music, making food, or playing video games. Everybody knows everybody, so there aren't any problems or chaos.

This is my neighborhood. This is Hunters Point. I've lived here for more than half of my life. The people who live in this neighborhood are simply just regular humans who want to see the youth, who are the future of our community, do better and make better life decisions than they did when they were younger. Some of the people out there are coaches from Pop Warner football and AAU basketball teams, who push kids to not only be great on the field or the court, but in the classrooms as well, and to be both a student and an athlete. Other people who make an impact in our neighborhood are the people who started after-school programs and other things of that nature to keep youths off of the streets and take them out to the movies, amusement parks, etc. Places that do this are the Bayview Teen Center, the 100% Club, the YMCA, and many more. All these places give teens a safe place to do productive things and succeed. Lastly, people who make an impact in my neighborhood are just ourselves. Every day you can find someone learning, or teaching somebody else, to find a way to earn money, to change their life, or to start a business of some sort. I love my neighborhood because it's not all violence and chaos; there's more to Bayview than what people may hear. I've heard people say things like, "That's a bad neighborhood to live in. All the people that live there will end up being drug dealers and killers and won't get anywhere in life but jail." The Bayview is what makes me feel free and more open. This is my home, my sanctuary, my throne, and I wouldn't change it for anyone.

Walking onto the football field chanting and shouting just before kick off is something that I've always enjoyed about football. The butterflies in my stomach flowing as the referee blows his whistle to let everyone know that it's game time. Every game day, the coaches make us take a knee, touch a teammate around us, and pray. At halftime, the cheerleaders go to center field and have a dance battle against the other team's cheerleaders. All the parents shouting and cheering us on as we battle the other team from the first kickoff to the last whistle. The lessons we learn from our mistakes and doing better the next play. Losing a game and staying strong and coming back the next week with a win. The brotherhood all of your teammates make by the time of the second or third game. Everybody has everybody's back. All these things are what I truly cherish and love about football.

My neighborhood isn't the only thing that makes me who I am today. Football took my life over and I fell in love with it at an early age. Growing up, I always would go to the field and play touch football with my cousins, but I never took it very seriously because I was very little and usually played basketball.

One summer afternoon, I was about eleven years old and my cousin had football practice at the time. He told me to tag along so that I wouldn't be bored. We were in practice and the coach came up to me and asked for my information, and told me to ask my mom if I could play for his team. Unfortunately, the coach who asked me to play was from Vallejo and I didn't get to play because my mom said no, but I still felt good because I had found out how important I could be on a team. Some weeks went by and I was back home with my mom, and my uncle had told me about the SF Brown Bombers. From the first day I started playing with the Bombers, they made me feel needed and welcomed. Luckily I knew most of the players on the team from the neighborhood, so I was basically right at home where I needed to be. Being on the Bombers for three years and being with friends and coaches on the team made it seem like one big family. Whether we won or lost, we always stayed loyal.

When I got to Mission High School, the first thing I asked one of the older students was, “Where do I go after school for football?” The first person I talked to when I got to football practice was Coach TB. He told me that he knew my dad and that he was gonna take care of me until I graduated high school, and that’s exactly what he did and still does. My coaches from the Bombers to high school made sure everything was okay at home, at school, etc. Not only did they care about me playing football, but they saw that I had the potential to be a leader.

RJ Loveless was born and raised in Bayview–Hunters Point, San Francisco, California. He grew up playing sports, hip hop dancing, and being the life of the party. In sixth grade, RJ found his love for the game of football and continued to play it throughout the years of middle school and high school. When RJ got to high school, his English teacher noticed his hidden talent for free writing and poems. RJ spends his time going to school, playing football, interacting with friends, listening to his favorite artists, NoCap, Polo G, and Radwave, and writing his own songs.

Not a Pretty Feeling

■ YDALIA MORALES-MILLER

To me, having no freedom means I have no breathing room.

It feels like I always have people breathing down my neck.

I don't feel like myself, like I've been swept off my feet.

People see me, but that's all. They don't listen or hear me. They don't know me.

Being free means I don't have to worry.

I don't have to worry about being followed.

I'm on BART with my cousin and a man comes up to us. He says we're pretty. He says we should smile more. He says, "I'd tap that." We just want to get to our grandma's house. We get on the train and it is super crowded. I look over and see the man from earlier. He is staring at us and then quickly looks away. I realize that he is following my cousin and me. My heart starts pounding so fast it feels like it will pop out of my chest at any moment. I immediately text three people where I am and where I am going. He starts to follow another girl and that's when I see the opportunity to go to a different car. We finally get to our stop and before going any farther, I look around to make sure he isn't there so he won't follow us.

This is what it's like for me on public transportation in San Francisco.

It means I don't have to worry about being catcalled.

I'm fourteen. It's my first day of work. I just got off the bus and I'm on my way to St. Peter's. As I walk down 24th Street, there is a group of men standing on each side of the sidewalk. It makes it so I have to walk in between the group of men. The closer I get, the more uneasy and uncomfortable I get. It feels like I have all eyes on me. As I walk by the group, a man says, "Hey, little mama, that's a nice a— you got there. We should go chill somewhere." I freeze. This is the first time I've ever been catcalled. I walk to work, but now my day has been ruined by their words and eyes.

This is what it's like to walk through San Francisco.

It means I don't have to worry if I'm going to be raped or harassed.

All I can say about this is trauma sticks with people . . .

It means I don't have to worry about what people have to say about me and my body.

I'm in middle school. I sit in bed, bored, and I decide to start scrolling through Instagram. All of a sudden I get a DM from a random person I don't know. I go to check what it says. This person decided it was a good idea to call me an "anorexic b—" and that "I should eat more." Once I read that I feel that lump in my throat like I am about to cry. I sit there wondering why someone would say this to someone. I get up to get some water and I walk past a mirror and look. I don't like what reflects back.

This is the effect of social media on some people, including me.

It means I don't have to worry if what I wear is too revealing.

I'm sixteen. It's summer, and my family and I are going on a trip to the lake. I throw on my bathing suit and on top I put on a cardigan and some shorts. We all pack our things and get in the car. My dad pulls into the parking lot of the 16th St. Safeway. I had no idea that we were going to Safeway to get some lunch. I say to myself, *It will be quick and there's nothing to worry about.* I walk in and immediately feel eyes on me. I start to feel uncomfortable. I close my cardigan and cross my arms to hold it close. While walking, a group of men walk by and say, "The things kids wear these days." This uncomfortable feeling gets even worse and all I want to do is get back in the car.

This is what it feels like when you're judged for your clothing choices.

It means I don't have to worry if what I'm doing is enough.

I've always wondered if I'm doing enough to please other people. This thought has been with me for a long period of time now. That is the definition of my old self. Now I wonder if I'm doing enough to keep myself safe, physically and mentally.

It means I don't have to worry.

Ydalia Morales-Miller was born in San Francisco. She is seventeen years old. Her parents were born and raised in San Francisco and she has a little brother, Iban, who was also born in San Francisco. She loves to design, paint, draw, dance, and just be out and about with the people she cares about. Her favorite movie is *10 Things I Hate About You.* She currently doesn't have any plans for the future except to get into college, specifically University of California, Santa Cruz. Her goals and dreams are to make a change in our society, in our country, and hopefully one day, in the world.

Seikatsu

ALEXIS MALDONADO

Freedom is a way you don't feel trapped and overflowed with things to do. Right now I don't really have free time, which means I have a lot of responsibilities, like school, work, and other things that I have to do after school, like soccer and college programs, which I used to go to to prepare myself for work. I don't feel that stress when I go out of the country; I feel free. It's just leaving your responsibilities for a while. To me, it's having fun and not being bothered by other people. To me, it's my parents; they want me to have good grades, to fulfill all my responsibilities, and to never forget to do anything. They also ask me to do things even if I'm busy, but it's kinda calmed down now.

There is a lot of traffic here at times. For example, I go to school in the morning and then work (which is pretty hard for me since work is always busy), then I have soccer, and then homework after soccer, and it takes up all my time until pretty late. Usually, I don't go to sleep until 1:30 a.m.

On school days, I have to get up at 7:00 a.m. When there is no traffic, the buses take forever. They are like twenty minutes apart, which is a lot. When there is traffic, it takes me like an extra twenty minutes to get to where I want to.

For school, I have a lot of classwork and homework, and I have to worry about a test that we may need to study for the next day. Work is so tiring because of how busy it is and how my manager questions me about how I do things every week. All this is hard to do, but it's necessary to have a good life and be successful, and since I have a lot of responsibilities, I don't have time to have fun.

In Mexico, there is this thing called Las Posadas. It's a tradition that has lasted for a very long time, and it's mass and a small ceremony and then a dance. Everyone usually comes for the music because everyone loves to dance and there are really well-known bands. The bands are the type that have a keyboard, tuba, trumpet, and guitar and are dressed in unique types of suits. They are pretty funny sometimes when they make jokes and act like clowns. They play different types of music and it really gets you in the mood. If you don't have a partner, you can just go to anyone and ask them to dance.

Every February, there is another celebration called Carnaval and it's a town thing. It's at the end of the month. Although I have never been to one, I have seen them in videos and my cousins tell me all about it, since it's really fun for them. In our family, there are people that are in charge of setting it all up and getting all the things that are needed. I have a couple of uncles that already have done it, and this time it's my uncle Miguel's turn. They go from oldest to youngest and I have already had like four uncles do it. It goes from my Uncle Fello, the oldest, Uncle Uba, Uncle Rojelio, Uncle Juan, Uncle Miguel, Uncle Angel, Uncle Leonardo, and my mom, Gloria. I helped my uncle Miguel a bit in December with some of the items he might need. I have spent a lot of time with my uncles, even as a child, since they used to live in San Francisco, but Uncle Miguel is one of the ones I spent more time with. He is one of many of my short uncles; he is pretty dark and a really chill guy, with a wife and two kids. We went to go pick up a lot of wine and it was in big boxes; we had gotten about 160 bottles. Usually in a Carnaval there is food and there is music and some celebration. Now, for the dance part, which is everyone's favorite part, as I was told, there is a pole in the middle of where they have the dance and some ropes on it that people grab. The reason it's fun is because everyone wears a costume and dances in a circle around the pole and everyone just has fun; the main part is that all the costumes are custom made, something they designed way before the festivities. There is probably way more stuff to say about Carnaval, but I'm not sure what it may be and I have to check more into it.

I had fun when I went to Mexico and met up with a few of my cousins and we planned to go to Teco late at night. Teco is like a city where everyone goes to hang out. It has more stores than the towns that people like me are from. It's a nice place with shops, parks, and a small flea market some days. My cousin Uba and I went to go see a girl I was talking to. My cousins Johnny and Angel were with their girls and went for some tacos, which we would take to eat in my room. The tacos looked really good. Half were bistequeso (steak and cheese) that were amazing with the hot, melted cheese, and the others were al pastor (pork with some spices), which were so juicy when you took a nice big bite and got that sweet hint of the pineapple.

Now, as for my cousins, it's not good to list a favorite, but Johnny is the cousin I get along best with, since we have a lot in common. We like to go around and have fun and do the most we can, do new things, and go to events far or close. He is a couple months older than I am, a bit shorter, like 5′7″ tall, pretty light skinned, and he has the same body type as me, skinny with some mass. He likes to dress like a cowboy and dance to Mexican music. All my cousins are around my age, but I have only two at the moment in Mexico that are older than me. They are really Mexican, like in the way they talk, the songs they listen to, and their attitude of being hardworking while finding ways to have fun, like me. This is why I consider myself Mexican.

They also don't have freedom: they have work, which is like one-and-a-half hours away, and they also have to go to school, which is equally as far, but their classes are shorter. They may have extra activities to do, so they don't really have time to have fun. They also always have a lot of homework and projects, which take up all their time. The only real time they relax is on vacation or when I come by. It's fun because we do a lot of things together. Every time I talk to them or go to Mexico, we get closer and closer. We understand each other and it's like sometimes we just think the same things. The very first time that I met my cousins was in 2015, and I was kinda jet lagged, but excited when I finally got there. I'm a kinda shy guy, but when it comes to family or someone I want to know, I'm really confident; I immediately said hi to them as if I knew them, and I guess they saw that because we just hit it off and hung out a lot. I bonded with all my cousins really well, but especially well with my cousin Johnny: we just act the same way, goofy and immature at times, but mature at others, and we think the same way over things like experiences and things we should say to girls and stuff. We both also prefer to go out as much as we can, like going swimming, eating, exploring, and more.

I talked to this girl I'm really interested in the last time I went to Mexico and started talking to her. She is pretty short with long hair and is very light. She was the best friend of my cousin Angel, and she was one of the many girls that my cousin tried to present to me who I was interested in. We were together for about an hour since it was the first time we saw each other for a while. After, my cousin Johnny and the others came to the place in a taxi. We headed home after I said bye to her and her mom, and on our way home we decided to get snacks and drinks. We got off near our houses, and without realizing it, I lost my wallet and my cousin Angel lost his phone. We went to my room and had a little fun and talked and the night ended.

It's overall a fun time, especially if you have a family you can hang out with. You could go to swim in rivers, go on quad bikes in hills, motorcycles in dirt, and a lot more. I don't really do these things here because I don't really have time. At times, I go with a cousin that lives all the way in Antioch. We go ride dirt bikes and have fun doing donuts and going off hills. I wish I could do more, but it's very limited, which is another reason that I myself feel less free here, while my freedom feels almost unlimited in Mexico.

A step to take that would not make me feel restricted would be exploring. I'm going to buy a motorcycle when I go to Mexico and ride around. I'm going to see new places and try new things without problems or worries. Also to have that feeling of the air when you're riding and that feeling of excitement for the new place you are going to. I have these same feelings all the time when I go to new places and explore. I have felt the feeling when I went swimming and looked around at the beauty of nature around me in the rivers. I would jump off the rocks into the river and feel the thrill of free falling, the rush and then the impact of the water, and just be filled with happiness of what just happened and where I was. It's really something. You just want to try and try again. It's all the new things, the times that you have no worries, that you feel free and you can relax and enjoy life.

Right now, I can't really think of any plans for trips in the future. It's normally after I come back from one that I plan one. I have permanent plans in mind for when I go to Mexico. I really love Mexico, I would prefer to live there, and I am planning to move there when I finish my career. I will try to work over there and here in America. Before finishing my career, I plan to take a quarter/semester off to study abroad. I want to do this because I can learn a lot more about cultural stuff, since I want to be an architect. It would help me understand what people may want when I start working. I want to do a lot over there and enjoy life with my family in a place I feel free.

Alexis Maldonado was born in San Francisco. He is seventeen. He loves to draw anime. He loves soccer and going on quad bikes. Alexis wants to be an architect to build his home and help those in need. Alexis's favorite foods are pambazos, tacos, and pasta.

A Home

■ ELI CALABRESE

"We're moving," my dad said to me as I rubbed the sleep from my eyes.

"What?"

"We're moving," he said, annoyed that he had to repeat himself.

"Why?" I asked as I struggled to find my shoes in the shadows of the small room we shared. I was about twelve at the time, and I had only really moved once before, but I was already numb to the feeling of lost freedom. He gestured to the cramped room, its size making everything louder.

"Why not? Look at this place. It's so small. Who would want to live here forever?" He paused for a second, then said a bit quieter, "That, and Sharon says we can't live here anymore."

Ever since my parents' divorce a year or so prior, my dad had struggled to find a place to live. My earliest memories of the divorce involved us visiting open houses all around the Bay Area, always leaving when we realized that we couldn't afford the listing. It was because of this that we lived with his old friend Sharon, in her house out in Walnut Creek. While we at least had a place to stay, it was far from ideal. My dad, my sister, and I would share one cramped room together next to the kitchen, while the rest of the house remained mostly unoccupied. I was young at the time, but already I realized that I would never have the freedom I had before my parents divorced. My dad would move around a few more times after we left Sharon's, but none of the places we moved to truly felt like "home" to me.

Many people would consider my frequent moving to be a freedom, but it certainly didn't feel free. We never had any control over when we moved, why we moved, and for the most part, where we moved. Everywhere we lived was only temporary.

During our few years living in Walnut Creek, I felt isolated. In the rich, suburban neighborhood that surrounded us, we were the only family who didn't own the house they lived in. I noticed that the people around me had a freedom I didn't; they had the freedom to have a place to call home. Home was a permanent place for them, one they could associate positively with. I felt no such connection. While we were cramped into a single room, everyone around us had more space than they knew what to do with. While we would endure hours in my dad's cramped Honda, driving from home to school, the kids I knew could just wake up in the morning and walk to school right next to their house. My life juxtaposed against the lives of the kids around me in every way. They had freedom that I didn't.

When my dad moved from Sharon's to our new apartment out in Pacifica, the neighborhood we were around was drastically different. Out were the rich, suburban houses of Walnut Creek and in were the undeveloped, mountainside apartments of Pacifica. My neighbors went from upper-middle-class families to struggling single parents. There weren't many kids my age in the complex, but I would frequently talk with the group of adults who would converse outside in our shared driveway. We wouldn't have all that much in common, but our stories of how we ended up in this apartment complex were mostly the same. We all lived in San Francisco at one point, and we all were forced to move after some financial issue and ended up in Pacifica. This felt freeing in a way. After so many years of being surrounded by people who had no idea what I was experiencing, I was finally able to meet others who had experienced the same things as me. While they seemed to be able to accept Pacifica as a home and permanent residence, I still had a feeling of uneasiness that prevented me from sharing this feeling. We had a home, but it was by no means a stable one. It was plagued with issues that our landlord refused to fix since the day we moved in, rent kept rising, and I was still afraid we could lose it at any time. Even though I was at least friendly with my neighbors now and we had a living space to ourselves, my dad's Pacifica apartment failed to give me that sense of belonging that I had sought before.

Over the years of moving, I kept searching for something similar to my living situation before my parents divorced. Then, I had a stable home, a place I knew I could go back to whenever and feel safe, somewhere that I knew we wouldn't have to move from in a few years, somewhere I could truly call home.

One day when we were driving back to our apartment in Pacifica, my dad informed me that we had an offer to move back into San Francisco. The only issue though was that we would be living with my old preschool teacher. Initially, I was skeptical. I hadn't loved living in Pacifica, but moving again to a new home just to potentially go through all the same things I had gone through while living in past houses didn't seem appealing. Unfortunately, my dad didn't give me much say in the matter, and soon after the announcement, we moved. While my original skepticism and paranoia that this new house wouldn't last for long lingered for the first few months of living in our new residence, these fears dissipated quickly. This new place we lived actually felt similar to what my living situation was like before the divorce.

Today, after living with my old preschool teacher for close to a year, I realized that it is pointless to chase that old feeling of what a home is because I'll never have a living situation similar to before the divorce, at least for the time being. My mom never moved from where she settled after the divorce, so in that unique sense, I had a "stable" home to go to. However, due to her many jobs in the medical field, she was largely absent from my home life, and I only spent half my time with her anyway. I won't have a perfect ending, but very few people do. Maybe my family will end up moving again, and maybe we won't, but for now, I can at least get a taste of what it's like to have a home.

Eli Calabrese is a seventeen-year-old San Francisco native who attends Mission High School. He likes to listen to music as well as write his own. He doesn't have many plans for the future.

Mission to Dream

■ KRISTINA ARROYO

One gloomy Tuesday night, my six-year-old cousin told the family that white people and black people had to be separated. One word stuck out to me as much as it did to my family: *had.* At first, I was angry; we all were. He was upset because we told him it wasn't true, so he thought he did something wrong. He pulled me aside to tell me his teacher taught him that. We found it was all a misunderstanding and that he heard the teacher wrong. I explained to him that black people *had* to be separated because of laws created by the government, *not* by nature.

"What's government?"

"The government holds *a lot* of power to make, change, and take away laws." As I said those words, I didn't know how to explain the government to a six year old.

The next night, I had just finished showering when my six-year-old cousin wanted me to read him a book about dragons before going to bed. He stopped me from reading the story about dragons.

"KC, Martin Luther King Jr. had a dream," he said.

It took me a minute to comprehend what he was saying due to his speech. The way his eyes lit up when he continued to talk about MLK made me excited. He absolutely loved to talk about how it wasn't right for people to be separated. I could see the passion and the knowledge was making him feel empowered. It was like seeing a child in a candy store: they never know where to begin!

"KC, it was bad because people would die and not be treated good. Black people had separate fountains, bathrooms, and food. They would even get spat on."

It was ultimately a beautiful, freeing feeling to know that my six-year-old cousin was learning about the civil rights movement. Here he was, in the first grade, being exposed to an essential part of history. In the moment, I was proud, even relieved, that children were being taught the struggles instead of being kept in the dark.

When I brought up the Delano grape strike, he was beyond excited. I taught him that Filipinos were also not treated well.

"Filipino, like us?" he asked.

We often give credit to Cesar Chavez for leading the Delano grape strike. But the leadership of Larry Itliong, Philip Vera Cruz, and several Filipino workers was equally important. Itliong organized strikes and marches demanding better wages. It wasn't until a week later that Cesar Chavez joined the fight. It was a remarkable moment in history. Latinos and Filipinos uniting and creating the nation's first United Farm Workers union. Leaders such as Martin Luther King Jr. and Larry Itliong did the impossible.

My cousin desired to know more about the people who looked like him. He admired them because he viewed them as heroes. The power of knowledge—the passion that rises—brings me hope. I have the freedom to spread knowledge and the privilege to teach my six-year-old cousin the history of his people.

"I have a dream too, KC."

Despite having no memory of our first home, my family liked to tell me stories about the house.

"Our neighbors were Filipino. One of them became your godmother. The others became our close family friends, and we even had another family living with us!"

I never knew that's how friendships blossomed. Hearing how great their lives were in that home, I wondered why they decided to leave.

"One day, we came home to the gates of our own home, locked," my mom told me.

I was still just a gumdrop-shaped baby when my family was forcibly removed from our first home in the Mission District, after migrating from the Philippines. Too busy packing belongings, we couldn't celebrate the holidays. Instead of presents underneath the tree, there were boxes and empty spaces where our furniture once was. No photos documenting the kids opening their gifts that year. Filipinos have a superstition that we need to have twelve round fruits on the table to represent each month of the year for good luck, but we had nothing except a heavy heart. How can this be luck, if the bank had locked our home and forced us to immediately leave?

Instead of celebrating and embracing the New Year, my family was lugging in furniture and unpacking belongings into our new home in Crocker Amazon, just outside the city. They were eating McDonald's on the boxes they were unpacking. The roof was a dark, dirty red, with white paint fading away.

The sun doesn't glisten as much as it did at our old home. We have two stoves that don't work, leaking sinks, and many holes in the wall. Even with three bedrooms, there isn't enough room for ten people. My neighbors like to blast music at night and rev the engines of their motorcycles early in the morning.

As much history as there is in my home, I wish to move. I wish for my family to move into a more stable home. I walk through 30th and San Jose: my first home. The homes are freshly painted, the neighborhood silent, and the sun shines more here. My home is barely recognizable, until I see the brick exterior. It is the only part of the house the owners didn't change. Tourists, unaware of those who came before, are stuffing their faces with San Francisco's beloved Mitchell's ice cream.

"I have a dream too, KC," echoed in the back of my mind.

Hearing that teachers are explaining a complex subject to young kids builds hope for the future. Since I didn't have the privilege of learning the true history that young, I want my cousin to continue asking questions and be more invested in it.

San Francisco is not what it was before; the culture is being pushed out of the city. Being raised in San Francisco, I've had a front row seat to the drastic changes. Neighborhoods are not what they once were. I didn't have the privilege of learning hardships as young as my cousin, but being older and having this knowledge of people's stories, I realized something: the same way black people and white people have been separated, Filipinos have been too. San Francisco used to be a place where Filipino migrants were welcomed; but over time, the government has taken homes from thousands of migrants.

Their message was clear: we weren't welcomed. Today, many families and people of color are being displaced due to the lack of affordable housing.

Breaking free is a long process. Learning the truth is a difficult transition. The path to freedom isn't easy. Freedom. I dream that the next generation will bring us closer to a brighter future. A future of people of color making their hopes and dreams come true. I'd like to believe that the future begins with my story.

Kristina Arroyo was born in San Francisco and is seventeen years old. She loves to bake. Stepping out of high school, she hopes to help people by becoming a psychiatrist. Living in a rich city, she dreams that she'll buy a home for her family.

"I dream that the next generation will bring us closer to a brighter future. A future of people of color making their hopes and dreams come true."

Kristina Arroyo

Conscious

▌EDWARD HUMPHREY

I understand /
I comprehend /
I do it all /
Zone from within /
Man of my fate /
I hold the reigns /
I am the God /
God of my ways /

I understand, you gotta grow /
Growing my freedom, in all, every note /
Singing my soul, as my soul release /
I will keep vibing until I just cease /

You walk in a room, it's just all black /
But with every emotion, colors attract /
Mixing, turning, making a beautiful throng /
That's what I feel when I write a song /
I ease the pain /
When I just write /
All of the pain, leaking out of my life /
That is a time when I'm feeling free /
And I'm feeling free, almost constantly /

What is my song, what is my way /
What do I feel /
On a normal base /
I have the feel of a young flame /
Who started a forest fire and took all the blame /
When I walk through life, I am alone /
But my life is growing, but I need a loan /

Cutting people off just to move on /
Trying to find my way around phenomenons /
Just wanna climb, climb to the light /
Leaving all darkness, goodbye to the night /

Freedom comes with the biggest cost /
The cost of a balance /
In which you exhaust /
My mind's at a curve /
My mind's not straight /
Does my writing make me free /
Or am I enslaved to the pen in ink /
Using my writing just to cope /
With a reality where there's low-to-minimal hope /

Kunta Kinte man I was in chains /
Kunta Kinte my life was pure pain /
Isolated, my soul was contained /
My mind's a plantation, Harriet showed the way /

I understand /
I comprehend /
My time is ending /
I apprehend /
I recognize /
All of this growth /
Realizing the pain is what gave me hope /

Edward Humphrey

Doin' what I do to get done what is done /
'Cause I'm aiming towards the stars /
But I fall to the sun /

Golden child life /
I stress, but I go /
I live a life upon lives /
I don't fit in a role /

I'm a mixed young man /
Young, one-man marching band /
I did it all by myself, at the hold /
Of your hand /

Stereotypes and Assumptions

■ ELENA RODRIGUEZ

"I wouldn't expect you to be Argentinian."

The number for the dark classroom matched with
The number on the white sheet of paper I held in my hand
Students stood in front of the door waiting to enter
I stood behind them in line
It was my last class of the first day of freshman year
"Welcome to Algebra 1, Elena Rodriguez."

"That's your last name?"
"I wouldn't expect you to be Argentinian."
I jolted my head following the voice behind me
The shocked voice came from a tall, dark-haired boy

Dark brown hair and dark brown eyes
An Asian appearance
With a Hispanic last name

Speechless by his comment
Full of shame
I kept my mouth closed and entered the class

Watching soccer on the weekends with my dad.

The afternoon came almost immediately
The TV in the living room clicked on
The clouds sat outside the window
Ready for the big game to start
I sat on the dark gray couch with my father

The biggest rivalry in Argentina
My favorite team, River Plate
Red and white filled the stadium
Our rivals, Boca Juniors
Blue and yellow
The worst combination ever

Passionate fútbol lovers, loud and proud
My dad and I waited so long for this final
I cherish this moment
Our tradition of watching games together
Will continue on forever

"Do you live in the Sunset?"

The gym full of sweaty volleyball players sighed in relief
The summer heat broke through the windows
Junior year had just begun
After a long day of school
After a long practice
After a long day of managing the team
Practice had come to an end

Ready to go home
A short, young man approached me
A face I recognized, but had never spoken to before

"Do you live in the Sunset?"
The voice of the alumni coach echoed throughout the whole gym

Dumplings, noodles, fried rice
Chinese markets, Chinese restaurants, Chinese families

This assumption tore up a piece of me
Anger and frustration filled my mind
I may look Chinese
But that is only a part of who I am

We live in Bernal.

The blue house on the hill holds
My Argentinian father
My Asian-American mother
My thirteen-year-old sister
And Me

I get home late from soccer practice
I walk upstairs to lentils cooking in the pot
My mom prepares dinner
The sound of the stove clicking fills the top of my house
I meet my sister at the white dining room table

I have lived in Bernal my whole life
Hills, parks, cafes
My family, my neighbors, my community

This is where I live
A quiet and peaceful neighborhood
Not defined by a specific race

I now open my eyes to question how others think of me
With assumptions and stereotypes glued to their brains

If the world had no stereotypes and assumptions
I would be completely proud of who I am
No feeling of being ashamed and turned down
There would be no struggle

If the world had no stereotypes and assumptions
I would feel comfortable and confident
Being comfortable is like listening to R&B
Familiar beats and sounds are all I can hear
Headphones on, volume loud
My mind gone of all thoughts running around like crazy in my head

If the world had no stereotypes and assumptions
The world would have little-to-no racism and discrimination
People could live freely
Minds clear of hate and prejudice
The freedom to express and to belong is limitless

Elena Rodriguez was raised in San Francisco. She is seventeen years old. She likes to listen to music, watch and play soccer, and spend time with friends and family. She hopes to travel around the world, discovering new areas, cultures, and languages. She is a young, multicultural woman, living in a changing world, ready for any obstacle that she comes to face.

Discovering the Freedom to Determine My Future

EBONY BLACKBURN

It took a long journey to cross muddy roads for me to discover my purpose, determination, and persistence. Those muddy roads brought really harsh troubles and hard times. By maintaining to keep my head up through it all, I found I could focus on the bright future I have ahead of me.

I was in the sixth grade in Ms. Brown's classroom at Aptos Middle School when the phone rang. The phone call was for me. It was my mother. She told me, "Ebony, I have terrible news." I started to worry. Then she told me, "Ebony, your grandma has passed." In my head, I was thinking, *Why tell me this while I'm at school? Why not tell me when I get home?* I sat with the phone in silence. After she told me that, I told my mother I wanted to go home, knowing I wouldn't be able to focus in class. I hung up the phone and told my teacher about the news. She wrote me a pass to the office to let me go home. Hearing the dreadful news, I didn't know what to do. Hearing my grandma, Virginia Blackburn, had passed suddenly brought pain to my heart thinking about it. I also was wondering, *How could this even happen? I was just over at her house last weekend and she was perfectly fine.*

Later that day, my mother told me the cause of her death was cancer. I ran to my room, locked myself in it, and started to cry. I felt depressed and mad at the same time. No one told me she was in the hospital. I didn't even get the chance to go and see her. I went back to school a week later and I still couldn't focus. I just kept feeling myself about to cry just thinking about her and how I wouldn't be able to spend time with her anymore.

By the time I was in my eighth-grade year of middle school, I wasn't doing well in reading. I stayed in my quiet space, refusing to interact with others. Every time I was called out to read, I didn't want to. I was on a lower level of reading than my other classmates. It was embarrassing when I was forced to read and couldn't pronounce the big words everyone else could pronounce, such as 'ambiguous' or 'optimistic.' I often felt stressed and emotional and felt like giving up. My teachers and my mother started to notice that something was wrong. But they didn't give up on me, and I didn't give up on myself.

Then I would think about my grandmother. I would think to myself that she would be very proud of me if I kept trying and didn't give up. My mother is also someone who's just always been by my side through all of my ups and downs. She shows a lot of tough love because she wants me to grow up being a strong and wise young woman. My teachers wanted to see me graduate so they would check up on me all the time making sure I was on the right track. This gave me the courage and resilience, knowing I wanted a great future. Within that future, I saw myself with a nice house, car, good paying job, and just making it through with that purpose. For me, this is what freedom is—being independent and being able to discover the things that will get me somewhere.

I went to therapy, stayed after school to get extra help, and focused on the future I wanted to be in. My reading skills improved because I had a tutor who would help me pronounce unfamiliar words. She noticed I knew what the word meant. I just had a hard time with the pronunciation. I started talking and opening up to people more. Getting to high school, my grades improved a lot. I started becoming more serious and involved in my schoolwork. By dealing with these obstacles. I started to help others who had probably been through the same experiences in life that I had. This helped me grow by protecting my physical health and becoming happier, making myself a lot more stress free. Also, the people who were by my side through my hard times never gave up on me, knowing there was room for me to grow. Joining clubs in the school also really helped me, such as the BSU (Black Student Union). We represent African American students at my school. This is an important organization because we provide support for younger classmen and work to create school-wide programming that helps our community. We create and perform at assemblies, highlighting black culture.

When you have accomplished so much and come so far, it makes you feel so good about yourself. Being accepted to attend Sacramento State University shows I have worked hard and crossed those muddy roads. This makes me happy, but also the people around me can now see there's a bright future ahead of me and now I'm going on the right path. Now I can see that my grandmother's voice has been guiding me, telling me, "Don't give up, keep your head high, and give it your all." I want to be a role model for my community and others and have an impact, as she did for me. I want to express my freedom and help others do the same.

Ebony Blackburn grew up in San Francisco, living a very busy life. She loves to sing and make sure the people around her are in good hands. She is currently working at Target as a small format team member, feeling good about making her own money. She hopes to use her persistence and determination to study at Sacramento State and major in computer science or nursing so that she can come back to her community and show her leadership.

Monochrome Rainbow

▌AILA YSABEL ALLI

I rummaged through my closet and searched through piles of old shirts, frayed jeans, worn leather belts, and old costume props. I grabbed armfuls of colorful cloth and fabric, and hoped at least one item would be the piece I was looking for. Stumbling through the haphazardly strewn mounds of clothes on the floor, I dumped the mess I held onto my crumpled bedsheets. Today was the day I had prepared for all year—Pride.

Acceptance of myself and my sexuality was a long and arduous journey, but today nothing could make me feel lighter. I only came out to my mom a few months ago, and I was getting ready for the event I thought I would never be confident enough to attend, when I heard a chorus of buzzing coming from underneath my bed. I crawled around the floor to locate it. My cracked phone was underneath a discarded sweatshirt. I picked it up, careful not to drop it again. I was met with a photo of my friend and her brother, struggling to paint their nails blue, pink, and purple.

She texted, "Are you getting ready? Don't be late!"

I held in a laugh, rolled my eyes, and responded, "I'm never late!"

"Uh-huh, sure, remember that one time where you were late to your own birthday?" she fired back.

I gasped and immediately texted, "That was one time!"

"Or what about . . ." I swiftly cast aside my phone, embarrassed at my apparent tardiness.

I stared at my reflection in my smudged mirror and put on my war paint. The deep red, mellow orange, bashful yellow, radiant green, vivid blue, and dreamy purple filled my face with pride, yet reminded me of a time when love was regulated. I thought of the dark red blood that cascaded down a beaten man's face, the orange sunrise that illuminated another day where people had to hide, the yellow-stained teeth of a grinning policeman, the green envy of a desire to be "normal," the tears that were shed by bright blue eyes, the ugly, purple bruises of a beaten couple.

A glint in the mirror peppered with print stains caught my eye;
Who is that person with cloudy and hazy irises
Staring back at me?
Her walls, barren and without color, paint a vivid picture of her loneliness;
Her posture, stiff and slouched, shows her insecurity and fear of the world;
Her eyes, sunken and pleading, ask an unanswerable question:
But why does my breath catch,
Why does my heart mourn?

Should I grieve for the girl that oozes familiarity,
Hiding inside a prison of glass?
Or should I mourn for the countless bodies
Who were unable to choose who they loved,
Who dug a path with their blood, sweat, and tears
For me to truly find acceptance?

Do you remember that day?
Where a wall of stone had crept up and thrust itself into the arms of an unwelcome society
When the sky was blistered with color:
Silky pinks, fiery golds, and vibrant oranges had burst together
And the sky was thrust into twilight on that tepid New York summer night—
That Inn, where fierce battle was waged and lives began to change.

A chorus of screams and cheers ricocheted through the city
Like a china plate shattering against concrete

Pennies, beer bottles, and stray garbage
Were thrown in the faces of authority.
Two nights this lasted—
Two nights where people raised arms in solidarity against an unforgiving society,
Where a lesbian threw the first punch and her queer family rose up in tandem
To be ostracized and abused
And to open closed eyes and scream,
"I am not afraid!"

We cry the same tears.
We breathe the same air.
We feel the same emotions.
So why
Even though we're alive, why aren't we living?

Those in darkness, behind scratched closet doors,
Were once unable to face the day
Because of haunting eyes that burned their hearts,
But they gripped that dull doorknob
Wincing against the light
And were able to brave the sunrise.

Would I be able to do the same?
Could I let go of my regrets and touch the dazzling rays of light I so yearned for?

I blinked, and I was met with an alarm as my phone started to screech. Frazzled, I thought, *Oh god, I'm late!* I glanced at the mirror and reflected, *I'm ready.* The girl that hid in the mirror was no more. I smiled.

I hurriedly grabbed my black backpack, decorated with several pins and patches, and thrust open the door to my room. My steps reverberated through the glossy, wooden floor, and I ran. The deep brown stairs, battered with age, groaned and creaked as I stomped down them.

My mom yelled after me as I rushed by her, "Be safe! And be careful!"

My steps came to a halt, and I thought to myself, *Careful? For once I'm able to walk with pride. The people who died without celebration had yearned for this day. Those people couldn't afford to be careful.*

Instead, I responded, "Thanks, bye," and messily tugged on my boots.

I faced the dull, grey-brown color of my door, almost hesitating. *Could I do this?* I thought. My nerves nearly boiled over and consumed my trembling figure. *Maybe it's too early, I can always go to Pride next year. Yeah, it's too early.* The top lock was a dull silver and refrained from opening.

Quietly, I muttered to myself, "You've got this."

My nervous hand steadied and aggressively twisted the stubborn latch. *Click.* The brown door swung open and the sunlight, soft and lingering, filtered through the leaves above. It flowed through gaps in the trees like water through a river, cascading down onto the entryway. Once a dull brown, the rich, maple color now was vibrant and smooth to touch. The delicate, mellow rays showed every truth, every regret, and highlighted every crevice, scratch, and ridge. I ran through anyway.

For the first time in a long time, I felt free.

I wonder of the passing clouds
Of the race of glimmering stars above our waking plane
And of the cascading rays of a better tomorrow,
How will it all change?
What newfound picture will be painted in that haphazard starlight?
What colors will invade people's narrow sight?
All you can do is wonder
And fear the future's harsh embrace
But never let yourself lose hope.

How far we've come—
Lingering, hoping, dying for those out-clasped hands to no longer grasp at
our purpled throats
Our eyes have bled.
Our limbs have been beaten.
Our spirits have been broken.
But we have survived
Soft eyes have been steeled
Beaten limbs have been healed

Broken spirits have been mended
And the future is overwhelmingly bright!

To those out there who wage a war within the deep confines of a closet:
I so desperately hope that those around you
Whose minds are muddled with black, grey, and beige
Will fill with a rainbow of colors—
Reds, oranges, yellows, greens, blues, and purples will swirl around
And you will be able to scream!
You will be able to cry!
You will be able to laugh!
You will be able to love
Without worry of a melancholic darkness.

One day, you will be able to smile
Just as I, and many others have.
I so desperately yearn for those days to come—
Where you will be able to feel the warm, delicate rays of light on your skin.
Your eyes will adjust to the harsh light,
Crying tears of blue,
And feel what you need,
And finally, finally, puff out your chest
Against a harsh world that regulates love.

You will be able to live.
The lies you uttered to yourself
Will be but a thought.
Even if you think you'll crash,
I ask you to press the pedal harder—
It's better to run on a field of thorns than to simply stand in place
And never look back,

Remember—

No darkness is ever eternal.

Aila Ysabel Alli was born in San Mateo, then moved to San Francisco when she was three. She likes to sing and read. She's proud of her Filipino heritage and enjoys spreading the culture. She aspires to be an aerospace engineer, researching "green energy" rocket fuel.

“Our eyes have bled.
Our limbs have been beaten.
Our spirits have been broken.
But we have survived”

Aila Ysabel Alli

The Fight of Each Tear

■ JACKIE HERNANDEZ

There are many different matters that make up who I am. When you meet me, you will meet a first-generation Salvadoran woman who is very outgoing and loves to converse about anything that is on her mind. But like every human, there are many other building blocks that have helped shape and continue to shape who I am. I come from a single-mother household. She has worked cleaning houses since she arrived in the United States. I was always the first kid in preschool and the last one to leave. The hour commute back and forth from San Francisco made up for that because I got to spend time with my mommy. I did not mind the fact that we had to haul pounds of cleaning supplies because, whenever my mom could, she paid me with a McDonald's kids meal. As I grew older and started receiving homework, my mom made an effort in helping me even though she did not understand a word on my page. I eventually stopped asking her for help and instead, she began asking me for help. When government letters came in, and doctor and dentist appointments and questions at the supermarket arose, I was an eight-year-old who asked and answered the questions. Those interactions made me learn to continue to use my voice to speak out.

There have been many instances where I felt unwanted and unappreciated. Those instances made me hide under a layer of thick skin where no one can read me. I was once in a classroom where I thought I could be myself. In elementary school, I was taken out of the Spanish immersion class because the school believed I was already perfect in Spanish and I needed to learn English. This did not bother me until I grew older. Although Spanish was my first language, I am not confident in it. To me, it feels like I was robbed. I can still read, write, and speak it, but it is not the same. Language is important to me because it is a way of connecting with who I am. I was taught to almost be ashamed of my Spanish-speaking skills and I internalized that. I grew up hiding my identity at school and not understanding why. I also knew nothing about my history, not because my mother did not teach me, but because I was too busy trying to fit in in America that I didn't take the time out of my life to appreciate the reason behind why my hair was the way it was, or why the shape of my nose was the shape it was. I began embracing my differences in middle school when I began seeing more of my culture and exploring the different aspects of it. I became more outgoing, revealing myself out of my thick skin. I learned that it was okay to experience discomfort and push myself to grow. I joined clubs, like La Raza, that opened my eyes to where I came from and everything I could be.

I have been fortunate enough to have traveled back to El Salvador when I was younger, but never with my mom. In November of 2015, she sent a request to have permission to leave the U.S. to go visit her parents who she had not seen in seventeen years. The wait was anxious and frightening because she was afraid that they would not allow her to come back. Although it was extremely hard for her, she bought my brother and I plane tickets as well, just in case. She received a letter granting her permission in December of 2015. We embarked on our journey in January of 2016. The tears that rolled down my mother's cheeks when she glanced over to her parents stuck with me forever. I could not begin to imagine the pain she had to endure being separated from her parents. I keep this in mind when I think about the reason behind why I must continue to pursue a higher education.

When Donald Trump was elected into office, I thought about that tear my mom shed. News reports constantly came out of threats he made towards different regulations, including the TPS (Temporary Protected Status), the one that allows my mom to work legally. She was in constant anxiety and often made remarks about what would happen if she had to leave. In my Ethnic Studies class, we learned about past events, like the Mexican Repatriation Act, that made my mom's thoughts feel more and more possible. Through it all, she still made sure to howl at me about my responsibilities. I knew that I had to push myself to higher standards.

I soon had to transition quickly into adulthood. I began working long hours after school and weekends to help my mom. We were alone for the second time. We were unprepared, but I know that everything occurs for a reason. I know that in order to get where I want to be, I have to work harder than some of my peers. I keep myself motivated by surrounding myself with like-minded people. Ultimately, I hope to be able to give back to my community. I wish I had the opportunity to share my emotions with someone when I was younger, instead of keeping them to myself.

I believe that teenagers are exposed to many untalked-about traumas. I can speak from personal experience when I say that I needed someone I could talk to, a person that was wise enough to guide me through my struggle. Therapy is not in the budget for a family like mine, nor is it even a thought. I hope to help normalize not being okay and needing a helping hand. I never knew my options and I always felt like my presence bothered my counselors. If given the opportunity, I want to help adolescent students by talking to them and listening to them. Everyone deserves the feeling of security and I hope to help those who don't have that opportunity.

Jackie Hernandez is an El Salvadorian-American author who lives in San Francisco. Her writing is inspired by her love for food, family, music, dance, and the customers she meets at the Gap on Market St. In the future, you'll find her splitting her time between being a therapist and an anthropologist.

Runaway

■ GIGI OUYANG

As I wandered the streets, I was conscious of the decision I made. I was homeless, something I never would have expected to happen to me. But deep down, I was always homeless—homeless in a sense that I never truly felt that I had a home to run to.

I had to leave this time to protect myself. To leave a toxic relationship is extremely difficult for the abused, but I finally worked up the courage and did it. I left. Running away was the hardest thing to do, but I broke free from the chains tied around me.

My friend and I were on our way to get boba, a tradition we had. As we were entering the boba shop, I received a call from my brother. He was furious. *What could he be mad about now?* I thought to myself. He was screaming so loud the phone was shaking and the phone kept cutting off. I could hardly decipher what he was saying, but the one phrase I heard clearly was, *I'm going to beat your a— when I see you.* Why would I go home if I heard this person tell me up front that he is going to beat me?

Though I was shaking and my friend heard the screaming through the phone, I tried to act normal. I didn't want to talk about what had happened, so with a fake smile, we continued on with our day. But in the back of my head, I was wondering: *where will I go tonight?*

Do I go home and deal with the bipolar man of the house? If I went home, I'd get screamed at, and if I didn't cry, he would scream at me more, saying that I was cocky. I wouldn't get the chance to sleep that night. Or, do I not go home and deal with worse consequences later when I eventually do? I had a chance to finally escape this cycle of abuse and feel free for once. I chose the latter and decided to take the risk of leaving.

I didn't go home. It was dangerous, but I felt the happiest that night. It was the first time I ever did anything that bold. Now I had time to go out without a curfew or someone breathing down my neck. I finally had time to take a long walk and explore San Francisco, admiring the beauty of the city I hold so close to my heart. Deep down, I felt like an orphan because my mother didn't do anything to protect me as she was scared to speak out against my brother. I was sad that I didn't have a place to go or family to run to. All I had was myself, but for someone like me, this was normal.

People describe me as one who is not afraid to voice her thoughts or speak out against injustices. When I see someone being bullied or getting picked on, I'm the first person to speak up and get defensive. Most of my best friends I have today are people I saw getting bullied and decided to stand up for. But this is not who I truly am. I am not what people see on the outside. Though I do a lot for others, I barely do anything to protect myself. Like everyone else, I get scared. I cry and scream and get depressed. I've been traumatized countless times and only felt free once in my life—this night.

Three days later, my mother reported me as a runaway and forced me to come home. Though I was scared, my mother and my grandma promised that nothing would happen to me. My mother and my brother picked me up that day and he was obviously angry. But this time, I didn't cry. Unemotional and unfazed, I stood there with dignity, despite not knowing what was going to happen to me now.

He tried screaming at me, expecting me to flinch—but I didn't move. He was screaming louder and louder, expecting me to break down crying—but I didn't give in. When we got home, he grabbed me and shoved me against the floor. *Who do you think you are? You think you're all that now?*

Knowing that he was furious, I called one of my teachers and kept my phone in my pocket in case things went too far out of hand. I tried to leave when I knew he was going to get aggressive. I ran a block away from home, but he caught up and dragged me back. My teacher finally put me on hold and made a call to the police.

Police came and "the system" failed me once again. My brother was smart: he put all his paperwork on his process of becoming an officer on the table. Knowing the police were coming, he tried his best to look good. The other officers saw that he was an "aspiring officer" with great credentials and no criminal record. They said that I was overreacting and that, as an Asian

American, I should know better than to mess his future up over a small incident. I was hurt and betrayed because as officers, men of the law, they were supposed to help me.

Rather than letting this incident overtake me and drag me down—I learned. I learned that it's okay to leave, it's okay to be scared, but it's not okay to let your hardships tear you down. It's essential to let the pain build you back up and turn you into a new person. I will try my best to achieve this so-called "freedom" I've heard so much about. I know that I'm a survivor and not just a runaway. Rather than leaving again, I know the only way I have out is through education. I'll do my best despite my family and do something they were never able to do—*succeed.*

Gigi Ouyang was born in San Francisco, California and is eighteen years old. Gigi enjoys painting landscapes and hopes to exhibit more art pieces in the future. She plans on being the first in her family to finish college and hopes to pursue her dreams of being a criminal lawyer one day.

“It’s okay to leave, it’s okay to be scared, but it’s not okay to let your hardships tear you down. It’s essential to let the pain build you back up and turn you into a new person.”

Gigi Ouyang

Judgment

■ JINLING ZHAO

It's the dark, empty streets that frighten me
Or is it the thousand vaguely lit passing eyes that study me?
They could be eyes or simply a subconscious brain play
One thing I know for sure:
Asleep or awake, discerning eyes are ever present

Taunting adolescent whispers haunt me at dawn
The national anthem accompanies the morning bird cry
Oh, say can you see
A song I can sing but will never fully understand
O'er the land of the free and the home of the brave?
It only pushes me back into the arms of my ancestors
I want to finally be brave and free
Do they accept me for who I can truly be?

As a young child
Others emphasized the value of English
The language for entry
Buzz buzz buzz buzz like TV static was all I heard at first
Meanwhile what I spoke fell on deaf ears
"Don't overthink it," my mother told me
. . . I spoke the American language from that point on

When I close my eyes now I imagine the empty streets
I see water dripping from broken vases on window sills
Like passing sand through the cracks of my fingers
Slowly losing grip of my true heritage
Now the taunting whispers from before are passing by my ear
While my ancestors' voices are becoming indecipherable mumbles

I can only look back and watch
Water gushing down to fill up the steep tunnel I'm in
Like a weightless prawn swept along a stream of dark arctic water
Trapped behind the veil of what I cannot become . . .
    A paragon of my birthplace
    An advocate of cultural traditions
    A societal conformist

It is a hope that when I am free, I will be out of this tunnel
    Liberating my academic pursuits
    Speaking my truth
    Swimming to the surface of uncharted possibilities

A third trackless pathway fresh for my own imprints
I settle in a sanctuary adorned with confetti floors
A place I can welcome judgmental eyes
A celebration of my own change of perspective

Jinling Zhao was born in Taishan, China, and is currently seventeen years old. She is interested in drawing, designing, and animation. Her favorite hobby is coloring in sketches, and she hopes to one day be able to create her own short animation. She has a dream to attend college and discover more of her interests.

Dream Chasers

■ JAMARIEA BURROUGHS

There was this boy named Kelee White. He wanted to be a football player because one of his biggest inspirations was Deion Sanders because he was one of the best football players in his era and was very entertaining. When Kelee was younger, he always imitated all of his moves, especially his touchdown celebrations: they are some of the most iconic moves in football, even in the NFL, and now many people do this same dance. He was around eleven or twelve. He was the best player in his school and many high school coaches were at his games, trying to recruit him to their school. He chose to go to one of the best private high schools in California with great academics and a great football team. This school has produced a lot of great NFL talent.

Kelee was about to become the starting running back at Mater Dei High School as just a freshman. All of his coaches spoke highly of him and felt like they'd found the star for their future. In his first game, he didn't disappoint them: he rushed for 180 yards, three touchdowns, and the crowd shouted his name every time he touched the ball. His coaches wanted to see if he was really that great because the next week, they were playing one of the toughest teams in the nation. They were practicing harder than they ever had before, doing more running and spending more time in the weight room because this was the most anticipated game of the season. On the first play of the game, it started off with scoring an eighty-five-yard touchdown and he went on to carry the team to a 28–17 victory. Not only did he shock the coaches, but shortly after these games, a recruiter reached out to his coach and a few days later, and he received a letter that said they were interested in him becoming an Oregon Duck. In Kelee's third high school game ever, his life was changed forever.

His dreams of becoming a football player were very slim because he tore his ACL, PCL, and the doctor said he wouldn't be able to play football ever again. This ended his dream of making it to the NFL, but it may have opened his eyes up and he could begin to chase another dream that he had. All he ever knew was playing football, so finding something else would be tough. He would have to dig deep to find something else to be interested in. After the doctor told Kelee, "Your playing days are over," he looked over at his parents and all three of them were shocked by the news that they had just heard. In this room, it was so quiet you could've heard a rat run across the room. Then, Kelee just began crying because he felt that he was on his way to being great, then his dreams were crushed and torn apart into pieces.

The next day, he saw his best friend, Richard, who he first met when they were in the first grade and had been very close friends with since then. Richard didn't play any sports, but he knew about them because of Kelee. He always valued his education more because he always wanted to be a doctor so he could take care of Kelee when he got hurt.

Richard asked Kelee, "What did the doctor say?" Kelee just went silent. He broke his silence, told him everything the doctor said, but Richard didn't give the reaction that Kelee was expecting.

He asked, "What are you going to do now because all you ever cared about was football?"

Richard left Kelee stuck, and the question was all that Kelee was thinking about. He was thinking about other things he was good at and they were all sports related. When he left the hospital, he called Richard, and told him thanks for opening his eyes up to chase another one of his dreams, which wasn't easy for him. This made Kelee think about his financial situation, which was very tough because his parents didn't have a lot of money. So, whatever career path he decided to do, he wanted to make enough money to take care of his family. Also, this could have a huge effect on Anthony, Kelee's little brother, who was only three, because his parents struggled sometimes to afford things that he needed. Kelee's whole family was depending on him. When he got hurt, he felt like he had let them down and they were going to be disappointed in him. But he was wrong, and his family still stood by his side.

Two weeks later, he returned to school and everyone was applauding and clapping for him like he was a celebrity or something, but they were all just so happy to see that he was okay. His first day back at school went by very quickly. Usually after school, he would be in practice or workouts for football, but he wasn't physically able to anymore, so he went somewhere he hadn't been in the whole year, and that was the library. Richard would always be in the library, studying after school every day or doing some research about being a doctor. Kelee had gone to sit next to him and he was so shocked to see him there that he looked like he saw a ghost. Even Kelee was surprised himself that he was in the library. After about thirty minutes of studying math, Kelee wanted to break and walk around the library, but then he saw the prettiest girl in their grade, Jania. He wanted to say something to her, but he was as nervous as he was in his football games ever in life. Then, he rushed back to tell Richard that she was in the library, but Richard already knew she was there because she was there every day. Kelee, in his head, told himself that he would be in the library every day as long as she was in there.

One day, Kelee was reading and doing research on older football players. Then, he stumbled across a book about O.J. Simpson, who was on his way to being one of the greatest football players in the league. What caught his eye was his defense team, which included Carl Douglas because he was one of the few people who was actually on O.J.'s side of things. Also, Kelee read about people of color not being treated right in courtrooms and not being defended correctly. One of Kelee's cousins had been wrongly convicted of a murder that he didn't do, and they barely had any evidence to convict him, and their family felt that the lawyer didn't do as much as he could've done to help. In Kelee's mind, he began to picture himself being a lawyer. Then, he told Richard about this idea and he was very surprised about this.

Richard asked him, "Why do you want to be a lawyer?"

Kelee said, "Because I would have a huge impact on the black community as a whole and would be able to inspire other black kids to become lawyers. Today, only five percent of lawyers are black."

While Kelee was telling Richard about his dream, one of Kelee's old teammates, Kendrick, was sitting near them and heard what Kelee said, then he began to laugh and said, "Black people don't become lawyers. They're either athletes or entertainers." Kelee told him he was going to prove him wrong. For a few days, Kelee had been thinking about his life without football and how his life had been lately. Also, his grades had been going up since he'd been injured, which was very surprising because many thought he was a "typical jock," like you see on TV. Although the doctor told Kelee and his parents he wouldn't be able to play anymore, he still was gonna give it a shot. Then, one morning, he tried to get up and run, but he couldn't really run and he almost fell down. At that point, he made the decision for himself that his athletic career was over, and now he was chasing the dream of becoming a lawyer. When he told his parents, they were both happy that the tough situation he was put in wasn't getting the best of him. This injury could've been the best thing that had happened to Kelee because it opened him to show him that there was more to life than just football. Richard was very surprised about Kelee being fine with not playing football anymore, but he didn't think he was serious about becoming a lawyer. One day, Kelee was doing more research on lawyers in the library, and Jania also had interest in being a lawyer, so Kelee finally stopped being scared and they began to have a conversation. As time went on, Jania and Kelee's relationship got stronger and stronger. They were always together in the library after school.

Now, in Kelee's senior year of high school, he was one of the top students in his grade level, and Richard was the top student in their school. They had competitions to see who could get the higher GPA and get higher test scores. It was getting close to time to start applying to colleges. Kelee and Richard's dream school had always been University of Southern California and they had already had this planned for years so they could be roommates. The football team at their high school had one of their worst seasons in a long time. The coach came and pulled Kelee out of class before the season started to ask him to give football another shot because they needed him to get back on track, but he told him no because his life was great without football. He had never been more excited in his life. He and Richard both submitted their applications to USC together on the same day at the same time. If they both got accepted, this would mean that they would have been at the same schools all of their entire lives.

A few months later, people had begun to get acceptance letters from schools, but Kelee was too nervous to check to see if he got into USC or not, so he had Jania do it for him. While she was reading it, Kelee's heart was beating so fast like he was just running a mile. Then, she finally said what he had been waiting to hear since he was younger: he was accepted with a full scholarship and so was Richard! They ran up to each other in the hallway to tell each other about how they were so happy. Kelee called his parents to tell them what happened, but they already knew he was going to get accepted. They were both so proud they had tears of joy. Kelee getting accepted into the school of his dreams was bigger than any touchdown he had ever scored or any game he had ever played in.

Four years later, Kelee was ready to graduate from USC with his bachelor's degree in criminal justice and Richard was about to graduate in pre-med. Kelee had already been accepted into USC's law school, which was top twenty in the entire nation. In law school, Kelee's teacher said his future was very promising and he would be a great lawyer and probably one of the top in his firm. When he walked into law school on his first day, there weren't any people of color in his class, which made him want to do better than everyone in the class. After finishing up law school, Kelee's law school had a connection with Cravath, Swaine & Moore and they helped Kelee get into this law firm. In Kelee's first year as a lawyer, he won fourteen out of the sixteen cases he had, which was the best ratio in the firm's history in someone's first year. There was a huge case about a football player who allegedly committed a murder and it was talked about on every mainstream news network. Then, Kelee received this case. He had no idea about this case, but it turned out that the person who needed his defense was the same person who, when they were in high school, laughed at him for wanting to be a lawyer. When Kelee found out who it was he was going to be representing, he was happy because he could help one of his old friends from school. Kelee had to call Richard and tell him about this. He and Richard were very surprised because they knew Kendrick for a long time and he was never in any big trouble. If he won this case, this would be the highlight of his career because this would have a huge impact on his career and community.

When Kendrick first saw him, he apologized for laughing and talking about him in the library that day, but Kelee thanked him for doing that because he played a huge role in his career choice because he thought about the statement he made every day he woke up. "Black people don't become lawyers. They're either athletes or entertainers."

After Kelee and Kendrick won the case, they opened an after-school program in their old neighborhood, and there were sports teams for kids and they also had to choose another career choice they would want to follow.

Jamariea Burroughs was born in San Francisco and is seventeen years old. He loves to play football and baseball. His favorite car is the Dodge Challenger Hellcat. A dream job that he has is to become either a doctor or a lawyer.

Their hands leave no prints

■ MINIALUCE RUIZ-VETU

A being
Smothered
But untouched
Blinding
But invisible

To know freedom
Is to know one's self
Who are you before the editing
When you pull the curtains
What do you expose
Does your soul stand tall
Or is it cowering

Praise the smooth surface that magnifies the reflected photons of your smiling face as a Mirror Image

When you are alone
Faced with your inner thoughts
Are you proud of what you see?
Do you feel comfortable enough to express yourself freely

Or does the thought of others' opinionated gazes
Prohibit genuinity.

Praise the hands that taught you to build away from predictability
And towards freedom

What you see is almost never what you get
What you think is almost always what you hold back
Why is it that we are so commonly incapable of separating the idea from the reality?
Why is it only in the darkness that
We search so desperately for clarity

Praise the uncertainty which promotes in some individuals a desire to be found

Their narrative does not match my actuality
The way our thoughts are refined
Like a movie
Edited incessantly even after its release
Removes the humanity

Praise the filter that inspires the publication of raw emotion and authenticity

The unspoken concept that as you are is too much.
They want you to be calculated
Composed
They fear a being
That is truly free

Now ask yourself
Has society tainted your entity?
Have they confiscated your liberty of expression?
Your ability to sing off-key and dance on beat
Do you feel it to be in your power

To see yourself for who you are
Inquisitive, magnetic, and at times so painfully shy
Instead of what they want you to be

A being
Blinding
But invisible
Smothered by the ignorance of wondering glares,
Subject to the classification of "tableau" before "human,"
By the hands which grab my braids without hesitation
But untouched.

At my core
There are no prints
The fingers fail to mold me into the character that they wish to see
But the effort does not cease.

The conditioning has rewired the minds of the people
So it is up to us to set the record straight
The freedom that we all at some point find ourselves searching for
Is hidden within the burning hands
That credulously relinquish the headless human's ability to
Practice extroverted introversion
In plain sight it is expected that they obey the status quo

Praise the revelation that taught them to ignite their flame

It is easy to point the responsibility away from yourself
Dealing the cards of accountability to all competitors before replenishing your hand
The "they" in question
Lives within us all
Before assigning blame
Recognize that we all play a part in the game.

Minialuce Ruiz-Vetu believes that it is important to determine who one is as an individual outside of their experiences, challenges, and strengths. Through the discovery of oneself, she feels the purest form of freedom can be achieved. Quand on-sait qui on est, l'avis des autres disparaît.

“Why is it that we are so commonly incapable of separating the idea from the reality? / Why is it only in the darkness that / We search so desperately for clarity”

Minialuce Ruiz-Vetu

it's as cold as an ocean's water on a cloudy day but yet makes your heart warm

VIRGINIA COELLO

growing up
asking myself
am I ever going to be able to love
to find it
I don't see it
I can't feel it
anywhere I go
it's an empty space—an uninhabited field—
no love is shown
why?
why do we keep our emotions in?
why aren't we capable of showing them?
why?

is there a place where we can feel at peace when we talk about our own
emotions?
is there someone who does hear us?
scream internally
but loud

right there
in the middle of nowhere
you holding everything I am
placing all my broken pieces back together
in the middle of the dusk
with the stars and the moon
being witnesses of what we feel when we are together
two lovers, but no one else has to know
all of this is between me and you

there
where the moon meets the sun
I asked myself
how does love get into our veins?
how does it happen?
how does it start?
a look straight to the eyes?
a smile?
how much time does it take us to fall in love?
weeks? days? hours? minutes? seconds?
all of the answers could be right,
but
you are the only one who knows
when and where it happened

you can fall in love with someone with only a look at their face
you can feel it like a puzzle
all the pieces coming together

smiling in the process
thinking endlessly, not stopping
suddenly your mind can't stop thinking about the way they do little things
how do they smile
how do they move their hair, nervously,
little things
that change the way you look at them
and suddenly you become another person as you were
because love changes you
and every time I think about you
all that comes to my mind
is the sunset
the sunrise
and all the colors mixing with each other
to form one alone
I think about them as emotions
every one of them are so different from each other
and every one of them
at the end is you
one single soul
one big heart
looking for new colors
to change
the one that you are now

and the sunrise
is something that belongs to us
it was something that brought us together
because in that moment I just wanted to stop time
right there beside the lake
covered by stars
by your side
in silence
trying to keep everything I want to say to you in
wanting to tell you how much it means to be here
together

but the only thing that comes out of my mouth
is silence
and then
a kiss
that returned my whole heart
that even in the distance makes me feel close
with planets in your smile
and with the world in your hands
you are peace and war

and then there I am
like a bird without wings
in the middle of a hurricane
cold
looking for land
where to stop
to take a break
from everything

where I found a place to rest
in the break
I realized
that there was love all around me
in different ways it was performed
my parents working hard to give me the education I had
having full days without seeing them
just to have a place where I can sleep
and eat
different forms of love like the way you love your friend and your parents
is not the same
but at the end
is love

and I am not the one to tell you what love is
because I can't
I'm inexpert when it comes to love

because love is like the whole universe
and I just can give you these verses that came from my heart
nevertheless
there's a secret
and it is that these verses carry feelings that are like an infinite universe by
bearing your name written on them
because I'm now a field with flowers of every color
full of love
and that love
expresses what I feel through words
these words that are only and just for you

because in your company
my heart feels
in an infinite spring
colorful and passionate
happy
because it is close to you

and that cliché
of "you can't love someone if you don't love yourself"
it is not true
many nights I found myself crying with all my strength
thinking about what I did wrong to find myself in this situation
lying on my bed listening to
The 1975
with tears in my eyes
knots in my throat
asking you
with all my strength
don't leave me
don't leave my side
because you are the precious thing I have
but

what is the mystery of love?
I ask heaven; with no clouds, no sun, no moon, no stars, and you answer.
answer without words, without hearing my question; you answer, and
you sit on the other side of the world; I look, and look, and I die, and I kill
without knowing it, and I let it go.
because the mystery of love lies in the most peaceful death; and I die
when I see, and see, sitting on the other side of the world, and smile, and die,
waiting for you to leave a white rose in your lover's bed; I.

I really hope that one day we will all be happy because we deserve it, we deserve to be loved, but to love with all that we are and with all our heart because there is no half-love, it does not exist, you love or you don't love, as simple as that; I also hope that one day we will find someone who loves us with all their being and drives us to be better, because we deserve to grow with all the love we can, we deserve much more than we have and we don't all know that.

brillas tanto
que ni siquiera ves la magnitud
de tu propia luz.

Virginia Coello was born in Maracaibo, Venezuela and moved to the Bay two years ago. She is sixteen years old. She likes to write poetry, fan fiction, and stories. She enjoys listening to all types of music, especially alternative rock/pop music, like her favorite band, The 1975. She spent the summer camping in Rogue River in Oregon and in the redwoods. That's where she became inspired to write. Writing helps set her free from what's stuck in her mind, haunting her. "Writing opens my soul to the world."

Unlocking My Inner Freedom

■ MARRIANAH MEADORS

As I leave school after six hours of abusing my writing hands, I look up in the sky to see that it's very foggy. It doesn't seem like a pretty day to get in the water, but I wish that within the thirty minute drive down to Pacifica the fog will clear out. When I get to the parking lot of my school, I can see the big, white van with like ten surfboards on top and a big logo right on the side saying "City Surf Project." All the students get in and we all drive down to the beach, listening to the radio station 106.1 R&B and Rap, getting us in the mood. I have to have a right-side window seat because when we're driving up and down the Pacifica hills, I have the best view of the ocean. Looking at the ocean gives me this inexplicable feeling. The sun is out, making the beautiful water sparkle, and when I look up a little bit, I can see the horizon that connects the sky and the ocean. It gives me the same feeling of awe that I get when I see a rainbow after the rain.

Out of all my years of living, I had never thought of surfing. I knew about it, but I watched movies of people surfing and getting eaten by sharks which put fear in me. I didn't even want to go surfing, not only because of my fear of sharks, but because I'm scared of drowning. I also thought surfing wasn't for me because all you ever see riding surfboards all over the media are white males. I don't see any black girls in the water surfing, ever, and there's history to why there are barely any people of color who do sports involving the water. In the 1950s, black people were discriminated against and prevented from swimming in public pools. Police officers in the city would prevent black people from entering pools, and it was encouraged by police officers that white people should beat black swimmers out of the water and even pour acid in the water so that the black people would be forced to exit the pools. Simone Manuel became the first African American woman to win a medal in an individual swimming event in just 2016. This is so important because she overcame that barrier and wanted to be an inspiration to others, to make everyone believe that they can do anything no matter what.

One day in my ninth-grade health class, one of my classmates asked me to come to the surf club at our school. He had his own wet suit and a surfboard. In my head, I was nervous to even think about surfing, but I have an exploring personality, so I just felt that maybe I should check it out. He decided to get our health class to go on a surfing field trip. I was so excited because most of my friends were in the class, which means we could all try something new together. I went home that day to go get my field trip permission slip signed by my mom. I was kind of nervous about what she was going to say about me surfing, since it does sound sort of dangerous and unsafe. My mom was really supportive though, and was happy that I was trying something new.

Putting a wet suit on is difficult. First you have to make sure the wet suit isn't backwards—the knee pads have to be on the right side. Then you pull the wet suit up each leg, and it's so difficult because the wet suit is so tight that it feels like your leg can't even fit through. Once both of your legs are through, you pull it up to your waist, and pull the wet suit up both of your arms. There's a zipper on the back, and there's this string that's built in so that you can zip it up yourself.

I pick up a surfboard and carry it with a partner down to the beach from the parking lot. The board is really heavy, which is why it takes two people to carry it. When I step my feet on the beach, it hurts, but I can't look down to see what I'm stepping on since the surfboard is on top of my head. I know that I'm stepping on rocks because I can feel small, sharp objects scratching the bottom of my foot. In a couple of steps, the sand becomes soft and I'm guessing this is where the tide ends that makes the sand clear out smoothly. We lay the surfboard flat on the sand and get in a circle to stretch, go over safety tips, and practice popping up on the surfboard while we're on land. To pop up, I lay on the board looking back at my feet, and scoot back to make sure they're at the end. I cuff both of my hands and pretend like I'm paddling in the water, digging in the sand. When the wave is coming, I lift up a small bit, arching my back so that the board doesn't tip nose-first into the water, and I place both hands flat on the surfboard to push my body up, lifting my right leg forward so that I have a good stance. I make sure to stay low and look forward, not down, to keep my balance.

After we practice, I'm assigned to a surf instructor and we start walking towards the water. I already know that the water is going to be cold, but once my feet touch the water, I become shocked, but at least the wet suit is making the rest of my body warm. My instructor helps me carry the board into the water and once the water is at my waist, I hop on top and start paddling. As I'm paddling, I can see a wave coming at me and, oh boy, I'm terrified. He tells me to start paddling harder because we're going to go over. He pushes the back of the board down and I hold on tight to the sides of the board so that I don't get smacked off by the wave. I'm in the air for like two long seconds. I feel like I'm flying and I snap back to reality once my board hits the water. We see the next wave coming and even though I'm still a little terrified, I give him a thumbs up. My instructor turns my board around and tells me to start paddling. As I'm paddling, I feel like I'm literally going nowhere. I can feel the wave come under me and my instructor gives me an extra boost. I push my body up with my hands and stand up with my feet flat on the board. I wobble a bit, but I bend my knees to keep a balance. I can't believe it. I'm actually standing up on the board on my first try. Everything is going in slow motion. I look down at the water and I can just see my board gliding like I'm walking on water. I look up with a big smile and I can hear everyone cheer me on. I feel like I'm in my own world and when I fall off the board, I get back up with laughter.

When I came out of that water, something sparked in me. I unlocked something in me that I never thought I had. All my life I felt limited to the things I can do because of my race and gender. I always felt nervous and scared to be places where I didn't see anyone like me. Surfing has made me figure out that it doesn't matter what surrounding you're in, at least you're doing something that makes you happy, and that's all that matters. I feel like surfing has unlocked my inner freedom because since then, I've done things that I never thought I could do. I've joined a science internship at University of California, San Francisco, I've participated in an all-girls firefighting camp, and I even went to Switzerland for a Model United Nations debate conference.

Surfing has made me believe that I can do anything, without a doubt. I hope to inspire and be a role model to those who believe that they can't do anything because of who they are. I want to introduce career pathways for the youth who didn't grow up seeing people like them pursue careers. I'm looking forward to going to college and pursuing my dream career as an astronaut not only for myself, but also for the ones who are interested in space and science, but can't imagine how to get there.

Marrianah Meadors is a San Francisco native who wants to be an astronaut or an astronomer. She loves to travel the world.

“Surfing has made me figure out that it doesn’t matter what surrounding you’re in, at least you’re doing something that makes you happy, and that’s all that matters.”

Marrianah Meadors

My sueño de libertad / My Dream of Freedom

ANTHONY GONZALEZ

Dear Tony,

I hope that you are doing great. I find it strange to be writing a letter to my younger self, but I feel that you need to listen to your story so that it can give you courage, for you will need it in the future.

When I was eight years old, I was living happy moments in my family, but not for a long time. It started when my grandmother went to San Francisco; I was really sad. It felt like your best hero was leaving you. In the time after, almost half of my family followed my grandmother. It was only me, with my mom and sister.

My family came back to Guatemala just for a few weeks of vacation, and then they returned to the U.S. Always when they started getting ready to leave, I felt so sad. That's when I started thinking: if I lived there (San Francisco), probably I wouldn't be feeling this sadness that happens every time they leave, because then I would be spending most of the time with them.

This is how my dream of freedom, *mi sueño de libertad,* begins—that one day I will reunite my family in S.F. That moment, I realized that I had to fight to get what I wanted. To bring together all the sadness that I was living in at that moment and make it my motivation to get what I wanted.

Let me remind you of how things used to be in Guatemala. If you can believe it, I wasn't free to go to school by myself. You know I was born in

Guatemala, a beautiful but dangerous country in Central America. I lived in a city where my mom and family worried about my safety. Where my only transition was school to home and to church sometimes. Where I couldn't go where I wanted because my mom thought it was too dangerous for me. Where most of the time I couldn't even play in front of my home, or with my friends, because my family thought that I might be in danger.

My school was a safe place because they had security inside of the building. It was a place where they protected you. Sometimes, we heard about shootings where people died—all of it happening close to my home and school. So, my mom always took me to school and picked me up. She has been very careful about my safety since I was a little boy, when the only trouble that I could get into was talking too much at school.

As I grew up, I began to notice that the lack of freedom in my country was not just about a little boy not able to play in the street. I am talking about inequality. I noticed the difference in how other people lived. I always had enough, but never money for luxury, while others didn't have enough to buy food. They lived next to me, and I noticed how they wished for freedom too—the freedom to have the chance to always have enough to live on.

I remember when I was a kid, I went to some market where I was buying chips with my mom. I noticed a poor kid who was my friend. His name was Cristian. He waited until everyone in the market left to ask for something *fiado,* so he could get some food to eat. I was surprised because I didn't know that my friend had to suffer like this. I waited to see what would be the reaction of the cashier? But he gave him a chip and that was it.

So, that made me think: how can there be others, like Cristian, who the same things are happening to? I realized the injustice of poverty was not just for Cristian; it was happening to a lot of families in my country. It still makes me sad, Tony, because even though you wish to help everyone, you cannot, because even your family does not have enough to help everyone. So I became aware, for the first time, that poverty was a lack of freedom for boys like Cristian.

At the time, at fourteen years old, Tony, I noticed how my voice didn't have power because people just liked to follow the people who were supposed to know more than you, just because they felt superior to you. It was happening in politics, school, and even in friendships, where who has more money has more power. I could see how the rich people used the poor people to get a favor, and then they paid them with some chips or Coke to make them a little happy.

While I was in school, I didn't know what career to choose, because I never felt the passion for something. I knew that in the end, most of the people who chose a major didn't work in the profession they prepared for: there were no jobs for those without connections. That made me afraid that the same thing would happen to me, and to the future that I chose, if I stayed in Guatemala. What could my future be . . .

Finally, it was time for me, my mom, and my sister to go north to join my family. While I was on the journey to come to the U.S., I was having a lot of emotions as a Dreamer—excited, happy, motivated, nervous, afraid—and all of these emotions were happening to me at once. I was excited because I could see my family! Happy because I could discover a new country, with opportunities for me; motivated because my family always supported me; nervous because I knew that the trip was not easy; and afraid because there was the chance that I wouldn't be allowed to enter the United States.

After two weeks in a car crossing Mexico, and just five hours from the border, I got sick, really sick. It felt like almost dying. My eyes were swollen shut. I had a high fever and I thought that I might die. So they had to stop and spend two days for me to feel better. At the time that I was sick, I was thinking about how, if I was still in Guatemala, none of this would be happening in my life; I would still be good and safe there. I lost hope in my future. I wanted only to be back home and be a child forever.

Then I got a phone call from my father. He talked with my mom, and she told him that I was really sick, almost dying, and that probably I couldn't even realize my dream. So he said that he was going to talk to me; then I saw my mom give me the phone.

Tony, let me set the scene for you. I remember that it was 8:00 p.m.; I was almost asleep. My mom, sister, and I were lying on the floor. I heard my mom talking with someone and looked around, but nobody was there. Then I noticed my mom was on the phone, talking with my father.

I was thinking, *Please, I hope he doesn't have to talk to me. What will he be thinking about me getting sick on the trip?* I was ashamed to be so weak, as if I was a little boy again. And to give up hope of realizing my dream. I was ashamed to tell my father.

Then, I saw my mom give me the phone and say, "He's gonna talk to you."

"Okay, we'll see what he wants to talk about," I replied.

"Hi son, how are you?" Although I was sick, his voice brought me happiness. It had been months since we last spoke.

"Good evening, Papi. I'm feeling a little bad," I said, through coughs. "I hope you are doing well."

"I know that you are sick, Son."

"Yeah, it sucks because I'm supposed to feel great and motivated to come to you."

"Yeah, I know, but you have to keep going. You are the man and you have to take care of your mom and sister. Now please, don't give up because we are waiting for you."

"I know you know that it is my dream and I will be there no matter what—I will be there."

"I love you so much," my dad told me, "I hope you feel better tomorrow and remember you have to keep going. You are so close to finally getting what you want."

"Okay, Pa, good night. I love you too and saludos to everyone."

The next day, I felt a little better. The driver said, "We have to move now. We can't wait any longer." So we went on, and I got better on the road. Like Dante, I came out of the dark wood; like Jesus, I came out of my own desert of sickness and doubt.

Tony, this is what I learned: Even though I still didn't know how my life would be if I stayed in Guatemala or if I came to San Francisco, I did know if something doesn't kill me, it only makes me stronger. Si algo no te mata solo te hace mas fuerte.

Now that I am here, my ambition is to go to university and study to be a civil engineer. I have always had the dream of working with my father—being his right hand, su mano derecha. I will work hard to learn from him and help him grow one of the best companies in the Bay Area. When I think about it, I see that my dream of freedom came true with my family.

I know that you are a boy who doesn't know what to do with your life, just like I was: ashamed, confused, but always with one goal—to do something for your family and make them proud of you. Even though they don't trust you to do the right thing sometimes. Looking back at my story after four years in America, I know that realizing my dream of freedom is hard work. But it is worth fighting for!

My last words: I fight the good fight, I will finish the race, and I'll keep the faith.

With love and constant protection,
Anthony Garcia Gonzalez

Anthony Gonzalez was born in Guatemala. He is eighteen years old. For him, his freedom means do whatever you want, always doing the right thing. He loves to watch soccer games and funny videos. One day, he hopes to be a civil engineer because it is his passion. He loves to spend time with his family.

Tainted Fruit

■ KIMBERLY HERNANDEZ T.

Your words, **Abuela querida,**

sting every time you speak.

They come out degrading.
Deep enough to reopen a wound, and maintain itself fresh.

Because evidently
. . . your wound has still not healed and it presents itself like the day your eyes and ears noticed the inflicting words of what colorism does . . . how it caused a mutation.

The scab does not form.
It allows anything to keep on deepening the wound.

I try to mend things by saying you are beautiful, to declutter the formulated cluster of mutated cells that keep feeding off of you.

But my words do not render any soothing form of coagulation to create a scab, nor eradicate some of those mutated cells, when the idea has become internalized and that wound has made its mutation into a tumor.

It has been transgenerational ever since *los españoles* came and planted their seeds, spreading pandemically.

Like when *conquistador hernán cortés* set sail to the *new world* and *claimed* Mexico for his own, all while killing the Mexica Warriors.

They were never his to claim.
The *colonization* of *cortés* and all those like *him* became part of the tumor that would be felt across the generations.

The conditioning of the *colorist* ideology was planted then and its poisonous fruit infected *Nuestra Gente (Our People).*

But it does not stop there, because the outside is filled with toxins that enter into the body to alter and inflict more pain to the body and mind.
These toxins have branches of *western* beauty standards that have so heavily been weaved in our heads constantly.
From those who have the mutations.
From the ads that constantly tell you to buy beauty products that make you *lighter.*
From las novelas that like to cast light-skinned Latinos.
From your brothers who love to flaunt their *European* features and say they are better because their *blue* eyes and *lighter* skin say so.

From what my eyes have seen and the conversations you have had, I have noticed the microaggressions you have towards yourself and those with brown skin.
Such as when you have shown your preferences of grandchildren.

I can infer from the words I grew up hearing that pour out of your mouth.

You have not realized how much your words are part of the source that won't let the tumor cling to you, bother to fester away.
Nor how your words, the ones of our family, and gente keep the colorist chains moving to encapsulate their prey.

You don't need to chant spells that will only further intoxicate.

Knowing I am the product of genocide, imperialism, and colonization.
Knowing I wear *conquistador* skin like the many,
who, too, benefit from privilege, pavemented before us, that so horrendously gives us power.
Power meant to be used to feed forbidden fruit.

I know now to mention, we have a heart that pumps Warrior blood, circulating within us.

I try to dismember what has been engraved so heavily because . . .
I don't want this tumor to become terminal, even if it disguises itself to be, to fool you or those who have it and let it keep on manipulating the depths of your mind.

And if the treatment of radical self-love is like a nasty leach that will absorb the infectious stream of mutated blood, *then let it be.*

Kimberly Hernandez T. was born in San Francisco, California, and is seventeen years old. She is constantly questioning the progression of society. She is interested in Chicanx studies. Her hopes for the future are that people can put aside their differences and listen to each others' stories.

Five Bullets of Freedom

TRACY BRENES

Let me take you away into my memories. Twelve years full of predatory memories of five bullets that impact my life. Dangerous firearms, with powerful bullets. Casings containing the right to five essential freedoms. Freedom brings more opportunities for peace, and makes all represent the same value as humans.

Freedom of expression, liberation of the power oppressing people.

As usual in the morning, I noticed every morning cloud. In the news, deaths circulate in the orphan streets after a long day of conflict, struggles between the corrupt government, and nobles with the objective to get out the dictator, who polices innocent people with unfair laws that empower him and his family, but not the community. The worst is that someone who is against the cabinet could be killed by the military forces. My grandmother was very worried and the only way to relieve some of the bitter drink of reality was a sweet and delicious coffee. All the people had revealed themselves. Many were dead but fell with honors. Innocence died in this war between government power and normal people. How can we live daily in this crisis? I am inspired to mention some important freedoms that everybody needs, because it's really important to support others and this is one of my ways to support those revolutionaries that are against government oppression.

Freedom of education, education that guides and shapes hearts.

The possibility of preparing to be a good ally, it sounded like studying in a school with tables and chairs where there is safety and where you don't have to sit on the floor. I knew that in every single public school, it was very common to notice how small it was, and with walls totally about to collapse. It is incredible to see the lack of resources for education, even knowing that education is the principal reason to raise young people. My grandfather, who was a dreamer man with the strongest personality, having lived his entire life under these laws, said, "The government did not want you to develop your education; they don't want you to take notice of your rights, and make progress. They are scared that we will decide to fight for our future, for all the rights they have stolen for years." I noticed that all that he said was true when my mom spent a lot of money on school supplies for my sister and me, and she had to pay school fees regardless of whether it was public school or not. Didn't matter if they were kids, just twelve or thirteen years old, my friends did not even finish primary school, because there was not enough money in their families to pay. They didn't have opportunities other than to go out to the streets to sell products, or ask for money from other people. It was so sad because they told me, "You know what, Seleny? One day I'm going to be a professional and I am going to help my mom." Although the crisis is horrible, kids don't lose their hopes. I look forward to the freedom of education. These young people have the power to do powerful things when they use their abilities to express to each other what they have learned between them.

Freedom to live in harmony, in a home full of peace.

There is nothing more relaxing than feeling that we are living in peace without thinking about the problems around us. Is living within a war of bullets and conflict part of the harmony? I do not think so. Every morning, bewildered by the sound of the birds talking among themselves, I used to notice the fear that people had of leaving their homes since at any moment they could be victims of a shameless robbery, and the most difficult thing is that it takes so much work to pay the costs to get a simple mobile phone. Children risk their lives in dangerous neighborhoods and mothers pray that a lost bullet does not reach their beloved children. The freedom to live in harmony not only represents peace, it also leads us to have more security as citizens among each other. I remember an experience where I was only thirteen years old and used to play in the pack full of flowers of different diversities. We had so much fun that we almost didn't notice how the police and gangs were caught between shots and rigor; it was horrible that we as children had to witness such big atrocities. The restlessness of the civilians that surrounded us was powerful. Many neighbors worried that something would have happened to us, but we were able to escape from these fire bullets. Security fills us with peace and harmony in any situation. Having a life with the freedom to choose our security can strengthen communities, youth.

Freedom to receive a dignified life, where everyone receives the same rights of human equality.

It was a cold December, a time of love and unity between families, when my mother was far away from me. After the abandonment of my real father when I was only ten years old, my mother had no opportunities or help from people or any organizations. At the age of thirteen, I was a child, victim of the absence of a mother who decided to emigrate to the United States because of the horrible situation that was lived daily (violence, protest, gangs, police brutality). Not finding work or other opportunities condemned her to carry her hopes to another country. It was so hard to get used to not having a mother or father, but I learned to be persevering. My days became full of extreme sadness. I did not have a childhood any other child deserves, and my family had not obtained a decent life as people should have the right to have. I am one of the survivors of this crisis. There are many people with different stories that demonstrate the crisis of these countries. I raised my voice so that we can all understand the different social problems worldwide.

Freedom to live without fears.

Fears are the obstacles to success. The peace and freedom increased a little more in my life after my mother was able to accommodate fragilely in San Francisco, CA. I decided to support her and live together with her while we can. When I was fourteen years old, I spent a month traveling from my country to reach the American lands with the aim of meeting my mother, and so that my twelve-year-old sister could finish her studies there. The worst, risk-filled experience was every step I took, sleeping in muddy mountains was disgusting, or risking my life through those organizations that kidnap people, but my nightmare didn't end there. I was kept away from my mother in a house for another month, while the U.S. government decided if my sister and I could stay in this country. Every night, I imagined what my life would have been like if I had all my rights. Getting into my new life was a challenge that I'm still working on, but let me tell you that I can certainly understand the differences between living with fears and living without fears. During my stay, studying and preparing here at Mission High School has given me ideas on how to understand the outside world. Attending a good school and receiving the necessary education has been useful for me. I left my fears the day I decided to progress and be better, and I abandoned my fears the moment I had to leave my family and how little I had. I have become accustomed to having a life of my own and without fear. We can bring support to these people, who still live fighting against the government. This speech is dedicated to those people who protest political governments that oppress freedom, in particular, the most corrupt cabinet, the National Party of Honduras controlled by President Juan Orlando Hernández.

Everyone should be available to be FREE. Freedom reflects happiness and peace. Those people who one time were under oppression and away from their freedom now are recognized as the strongest, fighting people. I'm one of the survivors of government attacks. "There are no fears," is what I said, because there are no fears that can dominate my bravery.

I won't forget my assassination attempt. I won't forget the biggest consumer predator in Central America, "corruption." I wish for everybody to get the freedom to express and lose their fears, to rebel against any wall or anything that tries to make them feel like slaves under the control of addictive power. There are people who are still living under these injustices and rules around the world. Corruption takes away opportunities from us all.

But no freedom can destroy families and communities.

Tracy Brenes was born on March 15, 2002, in Honduras, in Central America. She started to live in San Francisco during 2016. She's seventeen years old and one of her hobbies is writing her own hip hop music. One thing that characterizes her is that she always wants to bring a positive message with her writing.

"I left my fears the day I decided to progress and be better, and I abandoned my fears the moment I had to leave my family and how little I had. I have become accustomed to having a life of my own and without fear."

Tracy Brenes

Hidden In My Shadow

▮ ELSY MORALES

The Softball Field
San Antonio Masahuat 2008

On Saturday, my mum, my dog, and I went to the field in San Antonio, which was one block away from my house in El Salvador. The field was full of boys practicing soccer, the fresh air, and my dog barking. The sky was getting darker, but it was beautiful because I could see the sunset behind the palms. I used to play on my school team, which I enjoyed very much because I could be who I am with my friends. We made jokes and laughed and I could just feel like myself. During lunch, we played in the field that my school had, and we just ran and had fun. There was no one who could limit our freedom of being girls because only girls played softball. Even though my mum was scared to play softball because of an injury that she had when she was younger, she didn't care. She still came to practice with me.

I felt free because no one was going to criticize me or tell me how to behave. I could do whatever I wanted to do. I didn't have to worry about whether they would accept me because of how I look and behave. That didn't really matter to them. They accepted me the way I was. Sometimes there would be times when my mind was thinking, *I should change who I am just because I want to be accepted in society.* But then I realized that it would not be worthwhile because they would not see the other me. They would only see the person that I'm pretending to be. Sometimes I feel like I'm in a birdcage without any freedom, without any privilege, and I just obey the orders of the "owner." I want to feel free, like when I was practicing softball with my mum in El Salvador, like the birds in the sky flying peacefully.

My Aunt's House
San Francisco 2015

It was Christmas Day. My aunt Blanca had invited my family to celebrate Christmas at their house. It was our first Christmas in San Francisco. I was excited, but at the same time, I was scared, because I didn't know my two cousins. My aunt's house was big. She had a backyard and her house smelled like rose candles. I was in the kitchen, where my aunt was cooking some carne asada, but then she said, "Go talk to your cousins." My heart started racing because I was thinking that they might not accept me. Albert introduced himself, then Carmen. It was normal at first, but then it was my turn.

I gave them a false perspective of me. I acted like I knew them, even though I didn't. I felt guilty about it because I didn't really show them who I am. I was playing Connect 4 with Albert, and suddenly I started having flashbacks of what it used to be like on Christmas in El Salvador. Every year on December 24, my mum's family visited my dad's family and had a little moment together and celebrated Christmas. And on December 31, my dad's family visited my mum's family and everyone hugged each other at midnight for good luck. I felt really happy and free then because they were my family that I knew very well and I could be myself around them. Celebrating Christmas in America, it was the opposite. A lot of my dad's relatives are in El Salvador and my mum's brothers and sisters are in different states, so we didn't celebrate Christmas the same way. The only family that was really close to my family in San Francisco was my aunt. Even though we were family, I saw them as strangers.

A lot of thoughts came to my mind. One of them was, *I want to be accepted by my relatives that I don't know,* and the other was, *I want to show them who I am.* I didn't know how to act, so I hid myself in a little box and put it inside of my heart. I started to act as other teenagers act. Freedom can be present in many ways. In this case, I didn't have the freedom to show my cousins who I really was, because I was not only lying to them but also I was lying to myself. I felt like I was trapped in a weird cage without any freedom, and I was just being there and pretending I was a new person. Sometimes I wanted to go back and feel as free as I did when we celebrated Christmas in El Salvador and gave each other hugs at midnight.

Mission High School
San Francisco 2020

In my AP Spanish class, there is a lot of diversity of students from Mexico, Nicaragua, and El Salvador. I hear them speaking Spanish, and I can feel that they have some things in common, like their culture, traditions, religion, and much more. The hallways at school are always crowded. Hearing students speaking in different languages makes me feel that they have the right to speak whatever language they can speak.

I can hear conversations such as, "Hiciste la tarea?"

"No y tú?"

"What are you doing after school?"

"I gotta stay after school for my soccer practice."

Some groups are just making fun of each other and making jokes, which I find funny because they are showing who they truly are without hurting anyone.

At school I feel free to express my culture, but there are times when I feel I don't have the freedom that I deserve because some people don't really like the idea of having Hispanic people in this country. They may think that we only came here to do bad things, but the reality is different. We came to make a future, not only in our lives, but in this country too. School gives me the education that I deserve and helps me be the person who will be able to change my community. It also gives me the right to speak my native language and bring my culture from El Salvador to America. I have to express who I am in front of the world, because no one is going to do it for me. I can't let anything hold me back, not even my soul. Everyone is unique in their own way, and I want the world to know who I am. Freedom gives me the right to speak for myself.

Elsy Morales was born in El Salvador. She is eighteen years old. She lives in downtown San Francisco. In school, she likes history the most. She doesn't like math. She misses playing softball. She likes playing games like UNO. She lives with her parents and two brothers. Someday she would love to go to Japan.

THROUGH PERSEVERANCE THE DOVE WILL FLY AGAIN

IVA LEVINE

A calm spring day in Warsaw, 1943. The trees bloomed with Edelweiss that scattered white and gold in the air. The cobblestone streets were a sea of dusty rubble, filled with soldiers, their greyish-green uniforms with their swastika insignia blaring in red and black on the right armband. The uniform consisted of many badges signifying their German pride. The hats that they wore spoke of the cruel severity of their brutality. Their gloves hid hands drenched in the bloodshed of their atrocities.

From the attic where she was hiding with her family, Kiva saw one of her neighbors, Mr. Goldstein and his wife, along with their two children, being forcibly removed from the home where they too had been hiding from the Nazis, since they might be seen at any moment. Even though she looked calm on the outside, inside she was frantic and overthinking everything she had seen or heard during her family's desperate flight across the dusty war-torn streets of Warsaw.

In a clearing, she saw a cluster of litter and supplies amid chocolate wrappers, bottled water, and very small bread crumbs. *Am I going to be captured?* Kiva wondered, *Is this the end of the line? Will I be captured by a soldier?* The German occupation began in 1940.

Four soldiers stood outside the house, savagely pulling the family apart. The husband was dragged by the arm with enough brute force that he fell onto the ground, which made his arms bleed through his white shirt. The wife was dragged out into the square in the same way, her long, luscious, black hair disappearing as the chunks of hair were scraped off her scalp on the cobblestones. The Goldstein children who witnessed this were toddlers, dragged through the square with no mercy from the soldiers.

It was a terrifying sight to behold.

Kiva saw one of the children drop a stuffed bunny and she instantly clenched the golden locket around her neck where she kept a picture of her family. As she saw this through the cracked and thin window of the attic, she wondered, *What will happen to me and my family?* Her little brother, Joseph, was untroubled, speaking as loudly as a horn. Mother and Father quickly shushed him so that his voice would not carry through the thin windows to the soldiers down below, giving away their hiding place.

It was a pain hearing Joseph speak so loudly. Didn't he realize that the family needed to be quiet as mice now that they were in hiding?

"Keep quiet!" Kiva snarled as he struggled to speak through the hands of Mother and Father.

Kiva was known to be a daydreamer and a reader. She loved hearing stories about powerful women in history, such as Zenobia the Syrian queen, who rebelled successfully against the Romans, Cleopatra, who was a powerful queen in her own right, and Joan of Arc, who dressed up as a man to be in the war in France.

As she drifted off into her own world, Kiva heard a crash right below the attic. Fear crept up in her like blood drenched through the skin covering her body. She felt the thundering, heavyset boots of the soldiers barging in without any hesitation. The vibrations of shock overwhelmed her body as she and her family collectively and desperately grabbed their things.

"Be as quiet as a mouse," her father whispered. "We don't want them to hear us."

A chill crept along Kiva's spine. It felt like the world had stopped in slow motion. Suddenly soldiers were fast approaching their hiding place and now everything was a blur. The family sneakily dove past a bookcase that hid a secret passage of stairs that descended through the house to the backyard. The soldiers with their tall, muscular figures busted through the attic door, hoping to find the family.

But nothing more than an empty room met their fierce gaze.

"Keep running and don't ever look back!" Kiva's father shouted as they ran through the city, threading their way through the narrow streets.

Kiva stumbled on the curb, then quickly found her footing. It was hard keeping up with her family due to the city being overcrowded with soldiers and civilians, who would see their desperation and turn them over to the German authorities. As she and her family fled, she saw a hidden area where there were no soldiers. It was the tram tracks that led to safety.

Kiva felt a nudge. In a loud whisper, her mother said, "Get on the tram. Get on the tram."

As the tram slowed, Kiva ran alongside it and jumped on it without a second thought. She got off the tram without realizing that her parents and little brother weren't there anymore. She was on her own. She saw a clump of trees not far away and she knew that if she could get there, she would be safe. She ran as fast as she could, her heart hammering in her chest.

When at last she looked back she saw no one. She was alone, at only eighteen years old. She wrapped her slender arms around her shoulders to comfort herself, but felt more alone and scared than she'd ever been in her life.

She didn't know where she was, but knew she had to do something in order to find her family. She cautiously walked into the forest, darting behind trees, fearing that she might be seen. *Am I going to be captured?* Kiva wondered, *Is this the end of the line? Will I be captured by a soldier?*

A twig snapped close by. Panic ensued. A full-bodied figure that almost looked female emerged from a clump of bushes. The figure was a 5′8″ woman with a strong jaw, shoulder-length black hair, and piercing blue eyes. Kiva hid behind a nearby tree, watching the dappled shadow of the woman in the daylight.

She heard a clear, authoritative voice call out to her, "You can come out. I know you're here," the nameless woman said.

Kiva tensed at first, but something deep inside told her not to be afraid to reveal herself. The woman, at first glance, looked young. She could've been at least in her twenties or early thirties. With a stoic but calm appearance, the woman looked at Kiva.

"You don't have to look so fearful, young child. You're safe here," she said.

The woman then let out a small smile, but only for an instant. Kiva, with a long, deep, and concave swelling in her chest, let out a deep breath of relief as calmness began to wash upon her. She understood that the woman standing in front of her meant no harm. She had the appearance of an older sister figure that Kiva could rely on.

"What is your name?" Kiva asked quietly.

"Zofia Ackerman," the woman said. "What is your name, young child?" Zofia asked.

"Kiva Levinovsky is my name," Kiva said in a timid voice.

The woman stared at Kiva, and it felt like an eternity until her staring stopped.

"How old are you?" Zofia asked.

"I am eighteen years old," Kiva said.

"Do you have anyone along with you?" Zofia questioned.

The question caught Kiva by surprise, but it felt necessary to tell Zofia because the stern expression on her face told Kiva that she was serious.

"No, I'm all alone," Kiva said. "I lost my family as we fled the ghetto."

"Mmm, well, young child you don't have to be afraid." Zofia smiled reassuringly.

Kiva felt reassured due to the fact that this woman didn't feel like a threat. It was almost like she knew what Kiva had been through and had seen many others suffer the same brutal treatment at the hands of the German soldiers.

"There's a camping ground over there," Zofia said.

She pointed her long, slender finger to a clearing where Kiva saw a giant, green tent. Kiva didn't realize it at the time, but she was close to a sanctuary full of people.

Zofia, with her tall figure, cautiously grabbed Kiva's shoulder and led her towards the camp site. Kiva saw at least half a dozen people on the campsite but felt too timid to ask who they were.

"I've heard it is not safe anywhere for us," Zofia said. "I've heard it's bad. For some of us, it is so much worse than reported."

Zofia, with her serious outlook, dropped her hand and led Kiva to a secluded area where no one could see them.

"Now I want to make this brief, but I have a question. Will you join the Polish Underground Resistance?" Zofia asked with a dead-serious face.

"What is the resistance and why do you want me to be a part of it?" Kiva asked.

"Well our resistance is to fight the German occupation of our city and to destroy the evil acts that they are committing against the Jews," Zofia replied.

Kiva felt internally conflicted about this declaration. "Will I see my family again?" Kiva wondered.

Zofia saw how Kiva was mulling over this, but felt it was wise for her to decide, so she calmly waited for her answer.

"I can't promise you that you will be reunited with your family," Zofia said. "You can take your time deciding whether to join the resistance, but not for too long."

"I'll do it," Kiva said quickly. The moment she said it, she felt confident that that was what she wanted, to fight the injustice against Jews taking place all over Poland.

Zofia smiled and signaled for Kiva to follow her. While walking back to the campsite, Kiva saw the people stop and stare at her. Even though the stares made Kiva uncomfortable, she knew she had to do it for her family. Because of what happened, she felt it was the only way to find out where her family was and if they were safe or not.

The dreadful ringing sound of a gun going off caused everything to go silent. The pausing hesitation caused Zofia and Kiva to silently look at each other and gather everyone up to run deeper into the forest. The heavy boots pounding across the ground made Kiva's skin crawl with goosebumps.

Whatever you do, don't look back! Kiva exclaimed inside her own mind, just as her parents had shouted to her and to Joseph when the family was fleeing Warsaw.

Even if she felt an ounce of curiosity inside of her, she knew she had to run in order to live, to be free. Her throat was parched, but she knew she had to keep on going along with Zofia.

As she fought her way through the thick, dense forest she saw an abandoned house. She silently crept into the decrepit house filled with dust and the smell of a rotting, dead body hidden inside.

She glanced at her reflection in a cracked mirror. From that moment on, everything collapsed. It was like the mirror was taunting her. The figure of the wretched smell of death. It looked like the former self of Kiva. The ghost of her. She was not herself. It was like looking at a dead person. Pale, corpse-like, sunken eyes, tear-stained cheeks, no light in her eyes. Everything had gone dark. It was like those rumors about the camps that were being set up close to the ghetto and in the countryside. People would say how once you go there, you never come back the same or you never come out at all. You are worked to death or incinerated by the German soldiers.

Her thoughts were very dark, but a hint of invigorating hope sprouted inside of her, like the buds on the trees she saw when she looked down into the city from the attic window before her family had to flee. Knowing that Zofia and the others were behind her, Kiva cautiously descended to the basement to hide with them.

A tiny bulb of light hung from the ceiling in the cold, dingy basement. That light was like the sinking desperation of drowning in the deep, blue sea.

Kiva almost liked the feeling, though. It was an invigorating feeling of rising above the deep water and smashing against the tides. It was like a roller coaster, but then it became something different. Even though she was among strangers in the basement, she was unconsciously at peace with them. They were united in resisting the brutal force of the German soldiers. It eventually got almost bone crushing, the further she sank in this metaphoric ocean. It was the intense pressure of the gallons of water rising above her head.

The basement was crammed with weapons. Rifles, machine guns, gas masks, revolvers, hand grenades, and ammunition. It was a start, but it was all they had in order to create the uprising and attempt to free the Jews from the Warsaw ghetto.

If we can do what Frumka Putnicka is doing, then we will save many lives, Kiva thought, recalling rumors she had heard of the brave Polish Resistance fighter who smuggled weapons into the ghetto for the fight against the German occupation.

With as much confidence as she could muster, Kiva sneakily grabbed as much ammunition and weapons as she could as the others did the same.

"This is our chance to fight for freedom, for our families, friends, and comrades fallen from this cruel world. For this treatment of our people, we must fight. Are you guys with me?" yelled Kiva.

With numerous yells of "Yeah!," the surviving Jews sneakily, like a snake treading calm waters, went through a hidden door that no one knew about but themselves, and headed toward the Nazis' campsites to fight in this war brought upon them.

They would calmly sneak upon the rooftops, throwing hand grenades and firing guns at the soldiers.

"The war may not be won yet, but we will never stop fighting for our freedom. And I will never stop," proclaimed Kiva.

The sound of gunfire blurred her vision. Her anger and pain were like fragile ice waiting to break apart. But this was no time to be fragile. The uprising had begun. She and her allies in the Polish Resistance would fight for their lives, for freedom for the Jewish people who had suffered so much at the hands of the German army.

Iva Levine was born in San Francisco, California. She is eighteen years old. She was raised in a Jewish family. She loves to read and write. One day she hopes to become a fashion journalist. Pizza is her favorite food and she could eat it all day. She can speak five languages, which include Yiddish, German, French, Italian, and Greek.

“Her anger and pain were like fragile ice waiting to break apart. But this was no time to be fragile. The uprising had begun.”

Iva Levine

A Yaqui Woman's Untold Journey

LORENA MARTINEZ

What kept her going?
Not knowing what's ahead
A thirteen-year-old Yaqui woman
Who lost everything

Dark skin, long braids with a middle part
Angelina walked confidently
Letting others see her strength
But never her pain

A glimpse of hope in California
Keeps replaying in her mind
Reminding her to keep pushing
To not give into temptation
Of giving up

The Mexican government feared the Yaqui.

Life in the Sonoran desert was simple
Full of family and culture
Helping her mother gather herbs and fruit
Watching her father perform

The elegant deer dance
When times were hard she found solace
In the dark blue Yaqui river
The village was her safe place

The government attacked villages using modern weapons which overpowered the Yaqui despite how powerful they had been in past wars.

Hot and bloody sand
Sounds of loud bombs dropping
On the places they called home
Houses made with sticks, sweat, and tears
Turned to ash and dust in the air
Fear filling their minds
Lives stolen
Just for living

Countless innocent Yaquis were enslaved and tortured during this time. In the last war, twenty-six men, 214 women, and 175 children were captured.

Her parents were some of the first killed
As she was born from two amazing warriors
Angelina knew she would have to be brave
Her pain turned into strength

Fifteen thousand to sixty thousand Yaquis were murdered during deportations to Yucatán. Their homeland was the desert and they were forced into the jungle.

With the fear of being captured
All she had was her own freedom
The dry sand burned her feet
Tears streamed down her face
As she started her long journey to safety

Thoughts of her parents flooded her head
She was alone now
With no way of knowing where to go
All she could do was keep walking north
To find family in California

Speaking only the indigenous tongue
Fear of not being able to communicate surrounded her
She wondered how her new life would unfold

Angelina was my great-grandmother, who walked to Los Angeles on her own in 1920.

I wanted to share her story because the Yaqui genocide is so little known and it was such a large part of history. There is scarce information about this time even though tens of thousands of lives were lost, and a whole tribe was almost killed off.

My great-grandmother was a strong Yaqui woman who lived a long life in San Francisco and raised seven children and many grandchildren. My life as a young Native American woman has been greatly inspired by her power to get through this. I am proud of my warrior ancestors and keeping my culture alive.

Lorena Martinez was born in San Francisco. She is seventeen years old. She enjoys different types of art, like painting, drawing, and graphic design. She uses the world around her as an inspiration in her writing and art. She is passionate about social justice issues, especially homelessness in the Bay Area.

Now I Know

■ TREASURE BENDER

Wanting to say something, but because I'm black, the situation might escalate, feeling dumb for not speaking up for what I know is right. Did she really just say that? Did she not know what my ancestors fought for, and the innocent lives that were taken by the gun of a "white cop?" She must didn't know . . .

"I am not going to stand to show pride in a flag for a country that oppresses black people and people of color."—Colin Kaepernick

In 2016 Colin Kaepernick decided to kneel during the national anthem at an NFL football game. Kaepernick's reasoning to take a knee during the national anthem was to protest against the police brutality that has been going on for decades, but no one speaks about it, nor is it popular in the news. Kaepernick faced a lot of discrimination; he even lost his wealth and endorsements. Kaepernick sacrificed his career. He hasn't been signed by an NFL team since the 2016-2017 season and his family was threatened and their lives were put in jeopardy. Kaepernick put his life and his family life on the line just to bring awareness to situations that are not seen as important in society. After Kaepernick's kneeling, he became the face of Nike.

Nike aired ads like, "Believe in something. Even if it means sacrificing everything.—Colin Kaepernick." Kaepernick believed in everything he did, like kneeling, which caught Nike's attention. People bought the clothing to support Kaepernick; people burned the clothing because they were against Kaepernick. There was a lot of controversy about Kaepernick's deal with Nike. They must didn't know . . .

I remember the day as if it was yesterday. There weren't many customers coming in on a Tuesday night, so I remember exactly what happened. "Hello, welcome in," I said to the two customers walking in. They looked to be an older white couple. They didn't say much, mostly scoping out the place, but I saw that a particular Nike shirt caught the eye of the older woman. She picked it up to size it up to herself, but it wasn't a perfect fit, so I went and asked: "Do you need a different size?"

The woman asked for a medium-sized shirt, so I went to the back and saw that we only had smalls. At that moment, I knew she wasn't going to like that, so I went out and respectfully told her we only had a size small. My heart was starting to pump a little faster than usual because I could feel the situation getting tense. She opened her mouth and said, "I SHOULDN'T BE SUPPORTING NIKE ANYWAY."

My body went into shock as if I was getting electrocuted. With all the controversy going on with Kaepernick, she felt it was the perfect time to say that. Wanting to say something, but because I'm black, the situation might escalate, feeling dumb for not speaking up for what I know is right. Did she really just say that? Did she not know what my ancestors fought for and the innocent lives that were taken by the gun of a "white cop?" She must didn't know. But because she was older, I felt I had less power to stand up to her, and because of her race, it was best if I kept quiet.

As I was feeling this way, she clearly wasn't. Because she was white, there were different privileges she felt she had, and because she was older, I was always taught to never disrespect my elders. Because she was a customer and I was at work, I was trained that the customer is always right. But yet because of my race, things would've escalated. In this situation, she felt entitled to say something without caring about who she offended or hurt.

My race, gender, and age are some of the reasons why I feel I don't have a voice in the world today or I feel I'm not able to speak up, which is seen a lot in today's society.

Kaepernick gave me hope that I can speak my truth and not to be afraid to stand up for what I believe in, no matter what comes with it.

If I had real freedom of expression I would've said, "You must didn't know."

Treasure Bender was born and raised in San Francisco with her mom, dad, and siblings. Treasure is seventeen years old and loves to work and listen to music. Treasure plans to attend college in fall 2020.

What Defines Me

AARON VILLAREAL

"Stay afloat! Swim back to me! You got this!" exclaims the brother who decided to suddenly teach me how to swim by throwing me in a thirteen-foot-deep pool, all while knowing I did not know how to swim.
I break the surface of the water, my ears flooded with my brother's voice along with the pool's water.
Gasping for air, I struggle to breathe as my legs and arms flail under water.
My instincts to not drown kick in, my heart racing, but somehow I gather my thoughts and teachings.
I am determined to swim.
I breathe, relax, and paddle.
Voila! I am swimming.
All it takes is motivation.
All it took was a push.

One push that shoved me back in time.
I'm warped into my former self.

I sit back in my uncomfortable, black, wooden chair as I wait for my plate.
The smooth vibrations in my ear tell my heart that we love the music that is being played through the loud boom box.
My stomach gurgles at the smell of the aroma that floats through the restaurant.
I taste the meal even before being given my plate, my nose gives me a sneak peek of what is to come.
The smallest things in our lives are the most defining.
Our history tells our story and our truth.

Any struggle can be overcome with the help of a memory.
Memories of things long forgotten.
As I savor the delicious home-cooked meal, I cannot help but feel proud of my culture.
A culture stretching far beyond the savory taste of El Salvador's pupusas and Mexico's mouthwatering tamales.
A culture of resisting oppression.
Strong-willed and empowered by our continuous struggle.
We are a people,
a mindset of steel that gets us through the day.
A people who do not ask for much, we simply ask for the instruction to do the job and it will get done.
We are more than what we are made out to be in this country.

Born into a new world for both my parents and me.
Learning the ropes of a new country.
Growing up I found myself engrossed in these books.

My heart and eyes remember the feeling of reading a book packed with pages of words that my eyes would eventually meet for the first and final time.
I am at home in my parents' living room.
Time is in my favoring, having it be 9:00 a.m.
The crisp swoosh of turning the page like the soft crackle of a dwindling fire.
Throughout the book, my mind is entrenched in *Harry Potter and the Prisoner of Azkaban.*
The fate of Sirius Black resonates with me as he stood for something vital in the life of Harry Potter, his fighting spirit, his willingness to continue forward despite losing so many loved ones.
His pursuit of the truth and his fight for justice with the help of his friends.
Life is but a long learning process since the moment we are born.
These higher powers do not always define me and I relate to Harry in the way that I do not allow these higher powers to have control over me.

Harry and Sirius constructed a family because they did not have ones of their own.
My own experience is similar; I have a found family in my soccer team.

A wave of peacefulness and relief crashes over my body as I see my older brother standing outside his car; his tall figure and fresh fade is hard to miss.

He daps me up and judges my outfit jokingly.

I brush off his joke with a snide remark and my eyes notice that my younger siblings are already in the back seat.

Having been born into a family of eleven, I have grown to love my enormous family.

My attributes were attained through my older siblings who have been excellent examples.

From the days they would stay home from school to look out for me while my parents worked.

To the days they would simply pick me up from school; oh how I loved getting picked up from school by my older siblings.

I want the well-being of my family.

I want a bright future for my little brother and sisters.

Anxiety grows in my mind whenever I see my younger brother or sisters walk off to school.

Recognizing that I will not be able to look out for them throughout those seven hours.

We are a unit, a family that shows selfless care.

His example of expressing love in all its versatile forms is molded into my heart.

His example has given me a perseverance to succeed and take pride in all my hard work.

Recognizing that I will continue to surmount anything that gets in the way of making my family proud because the future remains a place of definite success for me, myself, and I.

As long as it remains concealed, all hopes and dreams for my family will continue to thrive.

Being captain of Mission High is similar to having to look out for my own kids.

We are not the best nor the worst, but from match to match when we are on the pitch, all of our problems vanish.

Once we lace our boots, we are a brotherhood and we fight with blood, sweat, and tears as a family.

The present is a gift, take every moment as it is; a moment you will never get back; one chance to make it count.
The outcome should never be tampered with.
On the contrary, we must do what we can and not worry about what we can't.

Aaron Villareal is a seventeen-year-old student at Mission High School. He plays soccer and enjoys the company of his family. His drive and passion derive from his past experiences. One day, he will achieve all of his goals.

A World Like Mine

CRUZ MACAY

My name is Boulder and I'm twenty-one years old. I'm an African American male who was raised by my mother, and who has lived almost my whole life in Charlotte, North Carolina, where a huge earthquake almost destroyed my life, city, and my future beyond. But my mom always told me before I went to school, "Anything in life can happen at any moment."

My father passed away from cancer when I was twelve years old. We had such a great relationship at the time. My father and I always liked to watch and play basketball all the time, but we also liked to watch our favorite show, *The Office,* which made us laugh a lot. I'm the only child in my family, which is made up of my mom, aunty, uncle, and my grandparents.

I've only had two friends all my life that I still see and hang out with to this day. They are Jackson, who is African American just like me, and Steven, who is white. Both of my friends never had a mom or dad because they had a faded relationship with one another, so they mostly lived with their grandparents throughout their lives. We all work in the same job as custodians at IHOP in different stations, but also work the same hours. We've been friends since fourth grade, where we all felt like brothers. We all went to the same middle and high school together and we have the same hobbies, such as skateboarding, basketball, and dancing.

On December 10, 2009, my mother was arrested for a Walmart robbery that she was accused of because the police and witnesses didn't know who the suspect really was. All they knew was it was a black woman with brown hair and sunglasses, and they thought it was my mother who committed the crime. Another reason for that was because my mom had a bag for her carry-on to place her food in, with no receipt, but she did have a receipt.

The problem was the police didn't believe her, and after that, she also wore sunglasses, so she had to spend two years in jail. When I was watching the news at my grandparents' house, I saw my mother being handcuffed by the police while getting to the police car to drive her away to the police station. I remember seeing my mom being vibrant, hushed, and inaudible, so I told my grandparents, "You have to come see this, Mama and Papa."

Papa and Mama replied, "Oh my gosh, that's our baby. What are we supposed to do? And why her?"

So then I had to take care of myself and my grandparents until my mother somehow got released or bailed out. But I remembered what my mom said before I turned ten years old. She said, "If you want to do something about it, be about it." That helped me to keep myself positive and to keep my head up when I was ever in a difficult situation, then I knew what to do in that regard. The next morning at 9:30 a.m., my aunty canceled her work that day because she kept on crying and shrieking about her sister potentially serving jail time for two years. I had to live with her in my mom's apartment just to cover her rent until she came back. So that convinced her parents to stay in their house and protect the family. When my mother was in jail, I had a really hard time and it was really difficult. I didn't go to school a lot, so I stayed home most of the time. Also, I did night school to catch up with all of my work that I'd missed and felt disgusted about it. But what kept me moving forward was looking at myself in the mirror and realizing that I had to keep my head up, be brave, positive, and believe that everything would be fine, and that's what I did.

On December 15, 2011, my mother got released from prison. Me and my friends, Jackson and Steven, went to my grandparents' house to pick them up in my aunty's BMW so we could see my mother down at the station. Once we got there, my mother was crying because she was so happy to see us all and then she said to me, "Mommy's home, baby!" Then she gave us all a hug and later she said to my grandparents and aunty, "Thank you so much for taking care of my boy. I don't know how I can ever repay you guys."

Grandma and Grandpa replied, "Anything for you, sweety." A few minutes later, the cops found the suspect who robbed Walmart that same day.

The cops said, "The suspect is going to be serving time in jail for a very long time, for about three years."

Then we all said, "Yes, it was a miracle."

The actual person who committed the crime was identified by looking at the footage from that day when my mother was arrested. The cops found a hidden camera that had the obvious evidence when the lady stole some food at Walmart with a book bag and she went to use the back door to escape Walmart. So that's how the real suspect went to jail. Then it was the end of the story, and me and my family went out to the Cheesecake Factory to celebrate my mother's release day. When my mom came home, it was like she was here, she was home, and I couldn't have even been more proud of myself because I knew that everything was going to be okay, so I was patient enough to see my mother come back home. I said to myself, "Thank you God for bringing my mother back home and making me happy again."

On February 14, 2016, Jackson, Steven, and I weren't in any relationships and had no dates to go out with, so on Valentine's Day at 7:45 p.m., we all went to a basketball court to play basketball. Although we didn't find our friends who were girls to bring with us, there were like twenty-five people who wanted to hoop, so luckily we had our basketball clothes on and we were all ready to go, but we just had to warm up first like always. After that, there were a bunch of ladies watching us on the bleachers and rooting for the people that they liked. They yelled out, "Okay, Chef Curry with the shot," "I see you, Lebron with the J," and, "Kyrie the bus driver going to work." The ladies were stomping their feet, screaming, and their hearts were racing, like *what is going to happen next?* So then, when the guys were picking teams, I realized that basketball was like the best girlfriend that I'll ever get because it will follow me around as long as I live by just being happy. A few minutes later after the game, we were playing up to 21, so the score was 19–18, and my teammate Jackson wanted to take the last shot. He took a three-pointer to win the game, but instead he got blocked while he was open, and then the other team scored with the game-winning layup. We all said good game to our opponents, but Jackson was so upset that he blamed himself and thought that he should've gotten a shot off.

I told him a few minutes later, "Not every game is our night, but we always fix our mistakes when we learn from them."

Jackson replied, "You're totally right, man."

Then things got a little fiesty after that. One of our opponents started to talk trash at me and Jackson.

"Hey, both of you, y'all weren't gonna make the shot anyways if you took the last shot, Boulder."

Then later I said, "Excuse me, what?"

The trash talker replied, "You heard me, rock head."

Then me and Jackson fought the trash talker and everyone was trying to calm us down and relax before anything worse was going to happen. I remember I was being tucked down, couldn't move with a swipe, and couldn't reach for anything to release my body. A huge crowd came to stop the fight, so we all went our own ways and we never saw each other since then.

Both of my grandparents passed away before my graduation, which was a couple days away. Jackson, Steven, and I graduated high school in the class of 2016. We all got our diplomas and went on to a new chapter of our lives, but we were still friends, all together like brothers at the end of the day.

My pathway is about freedom of belief, movement, and expression. By going back to when I first met my new friends and when my mom was arrested, these two crucial events affected my life.

I don't even know where I would be at, at this point in my life, if I didn't believe in myself or wasn't motivated whenever I'm doing things by myself. I wouldn't even have a good life like everybody else. This was the lesson that I had to learn when I became an adult—how difficult it would be to make my own decisions. Everyone comes from somewhere. Our lives are not always perfect—we grow up in different neighborhoods, not everyone has a family, but Charlotte will always be my home no matter what and everyone should treat and respect others the way they want to be treated. Nonetheless, I have a new chapter to open and it starts right here.

Cruz Macay was born in San Francisco and is seventeen years old. His family is from the Philippines from his mom's side of the family. He loves to play and watch sports with his siblings and family members. His favorite sport is basketball because he loves the game and respects the sport of it. His goal is to graduate high school so he can be the third person in his family to graduate from Mission High School and go to a four-year university.

My Struggle Coming to San Francisco

FIKRI MOHAMED

I come from Eritrea, a place that is not perfect and that is ruled by a dictator. A place that doesn't have democracy and where you can't express your feelings or have freedom of choice for education, profession, or many other things. To come to the United States was my biggest goal because I wanted to get an education and be reunited with my father and my half-siblings. I expected America to be a resilient place, a chill place, where anyone could be anything and you wouldn't be judged or killed because of who you were.

Growing up, I loved playing with my friends and being at the park, but I didn't realize everything I had was going to disappear until I moved. When we moved from Eritrea to Sudan, our first step on our journey to the United States, everything changed. We were under the impression that we were moving to find a better opportunity, only to find that we had to wait in Sudan for three years.

My family and I had to move to Sudan and then Kenya in order to reunite with my father, who was in the United States. For the three years we lived in Sudan, I was unable to attend school due to the kidnapping that was occurring at that time. I didn't know how long the process would take, but I never expected to stay in Sudan for three years without education.

While waiting, I distracted myself by watching cartoons all day and made friends that I hung out with every day. I started to learn Arabic by watching shows and going to the corner store whenever my mom needed something. These distractions stopped me from thinking I wasn't lucky enough for God to give me a better life. I was forced to get used to a new environment and people and make myself believe each day was going to get better. Then the final day came and we moved to Kenya.

Our first month there, I climbed up a tree to get a passion fruit. I heard a "BOOM!" and the tree knocked against the house.

My mom said, "What was that? Get down!"

I climbed down the tree and ran to my house. We had a window and two dogs that guarded the property. I climbed up a tree outside of my house and saw the church, which was a block away from our house. I didn't see who did it, but I saw the church—it was on fire and a little bit destroyed. The ground was shaking. After two days, they found out who did it and started bombing the mosque, trying to get revenge. It was scary, because they always closed the gate to our property. Kenyan people hated Muslim people because of the bombing, and since our family was Muslim, some Kenyans almost bombed our house. The good thing is, they don't carry guns, they carry knives or bats, so they can't shoot you, but they can chase you.

Kenya was a lot more terrifying than Sudan. From that day, I could not go outside because I feared that other terrorists would come and set off bombs near us. I could not go to school for eight months as well and it hurt me to see other kids who were the same age as me going to school. I wanted to go to school and carry a backpack, wake up early for school and have friends that were my age and have fun. I wanted what every child enjoyed doing, but I could not get what I wanted. I felt like each problem that we were facing was following us everywhere we went. At one point, I even started to give up on my hopes of coming to the U.S.

Then, after many long months of waiting, the surreal moment came when our immigration process was done and we were ready to come to the U.S. However, by that time, I did not feel happy because I did not have any feelings left. I could not believe it until we got here. I could not believe that the nightmare was ending and that we were actually going to the U.S.

Now that I've been living in the U.S. for seven years, I've had a chance to think about the differences between what it's like here and what it's like in Eritrea. The U.S. has a lot of advantages, like the hospitals are good, and if you don't have a family or you're all on your own, there are shelters for the homeless and food banks if you're hungry, and there was none of that in Eritrea. You go to school for free here. But it also has downsides to it. The color of your skin matters, and that changed my life because now I have to get used to that. I never expected America to be like this. Back in Eritrea, everyone was respectful. Everybody had to work because nothing was given to you, and you couldn't rely on anyone but yourself. It was a poor country, but the people were nice and beautiful.

In my experience, I don't think there's a perfect world unless you're rich. Coming from a poor family, I learned that you have to work hard in order to be successful. Middle school was hard for me because when I moved to America I didn't know how to speak English, and I didn't know how to read and write because I hadn't been going to school for four years and had only been to kindergarten. I learned how to speak a new language, again, and became aware of what my life was like: that nothing just gets handed to you, and you have to work for everything.

From all of this I learned that when life gets harder, just challenge yourself to be stronger.

Fikri Mohamed is eighteen years old and has five siblings. He loves to travel. He was born in Eritrea and spent five years moving from Yemen to Sudan to Kenya, and finally arrived in the United States. He enrolled in sixth grade knowing no English and wasn't able to read or write. He had always wanted to go to school, and learned how to speak English from YouTube, television, and his friends. He used to speak five languages. His favorite food is pizza, and his favorite sport is basketball.

Freedom and Fear of Expressing It

▮ VERONICA RAMIREZ

There is no ***freedom,*** and their eyes reflect the ***fear*** expressing it.

There are people who are trying to ***survive*** in *America,* but it is not enough,
and they feel like kids getting their candy taken away; it's like a stolen dream.

We have ***faith*** to move on and create a new life,
like bringing our mom back into our arms.

But people see us and see an *immigrant* and not a *human* who cries every
night in silence
with ***despair.***

This makes me feel like I'm losing faith in *humanity.*
They let us wither like a flower,
working with no rights like having no water.

They keep the fear in their world, in the world where *there is no freedom to*
express how you feel or who you are.

Defeated and ***useless,*** that is how they want to make us feel.

A feeling of wanting to convey what happens to them,
with words and not with actions.

Having to hide under their own shadow that torments them to move forward,
They are not where they belong, but have to survive.

This society is full of ***racism*** that makes us afraid to be killed.

Day by day we take a chance, knowing that our dreams can be taken away,
with just a simple mistake, a bullet, or a wall.

Many children have been separated from their families solely for the pursuit of happiness.

We are not here to belong to a new ***culture,***
but to show our culture to others.

They need to know that not everything in life is money and happiness,
but ***love*** and ***humility.***

Being Mexican is a pride that I always carry with me.
It gives me strength to know where I come from, and where I'm going.

With the hope that someday people will realize that it is hard for us *to try to be better every day,*
not to impress the society, but myself.

They know what they can do,
like to put together each piece of the puzzle to get what I want.

I need, we need, less disintegrity and more ***unity*** and ***support*** among the countries, ***races,*** and ***cultures,*** and that will make us understand that life is a small piece of what it really is.

Veronica Ramirez was born in Mexico and she is eighteen years old. She likes to be fun and make things easier in her life. She's now living in San Francisco, California, and knows that she has the opportunity to continue studying and make her own life.

“We are not here to belong to a new culture, but to show our culture to others. They need to know that not everything in life is money and happiness, but love and humility”

Veronica Ramirez

My Opportunity to Grow

■ LUPE ACEVES

I am the second born in a family of six. I have one older sister and two younger sisters. The moment I was born, my parents taught me right from wrong, to always say "please" and "thank you," to not hate, and how to make the right decisions. They shaped me to become a responsible, respectful, and kind-hearted person. As I was growing up, my parents wanted me to have all the opportunities that they weren't able to have when they were growing up. My parents didn't finish high school nor did they have the chance to go to college. It's one of the reasons I push myself to work harder in school. As of now, I am a senior in high school with a high GPA, who is preparing to go to college very soon.

My parents have always been very protective of my sisters and me: calling every time I'm not home at my usual time, asking what friends I'm going out with, telling me to not be out late, to stay away from certain areas, and to always be careful. It's very understandable, considering what goes on in the neighborhood I grew up in and the things that are going on in society today. I grew up in the Mission District. Despite it getting crazy at times, it's an area of culture. Walking down Mission Street, you always see busy people waiting at the bus stop, paleteros, alleys full of murals. From time to time you might catch an Aztec dance, a car show where all the lowriders come out, or on a Sunday, a Christian preaching and handing out flyers. Then there's days you hear police sirens, or on the news you'll hear that someone just got murdered or that another girl just got kidnapped. In a city of poverty, every corner I turn there's a homeless person, even outside my school. We've experienced a lot. Two experiences that stick with me the most are the murder of my older sister's best friend at the age of fourteen, while he was with his two younger brothers, and my mom seeing someone get stabbed while she was washing clothes in our building. Which is why I do understand my parents' worry for me.

I can remember the day my sister found out her friend got murdered like it was yesterday. I woke up to screams and tears, feeling clueless and seeing my sister in my father's arms. My dad kept asking what was wrong, but it seemed like she couldn't get a word out. Once she told my dad her friend got stabbed, she kept desperately asking my parents to go to the hospital to see him. Both of them said no, that the hospital would only let immediate family in to see him. Later that day in school, we all found out that he passed away. His death had a huge impact on a lot of people. From what I can remember and what my sister told me, he was talented on the field, intelligent, and always knew how to make people laugh. After everything, my sister started to receive random calls, threats telling her to stay away from 24th and Mission. It made my parents fear for all of our safety. My mom talked to the police and my parents tried to keep my sister away from 24th because they didn't know what the people calling were capable of. It made all of us cautious, and in the moment, it limited us when we wanted to go to certain places.

As I watched this all happen and listened to everything that was going on, it made me realize how anything can happen within a second and just change a whole lot. Watching my sister break down in front of me, her friend's family in pain, and seeing it on the news, brought hurt to my heart. I knew that I didn't want anyone else close to home to get hurt, and in a way it made me protective. I was in fear; I didn't want anything to happen to my sister. I didn't want to be in the wrong place at the wrong time. It was all a healing process, and it took time for things to cool down. As time went by, things got better and we all found a way to keep moving forward.

Now that I'm getting older, my parents' protection is making it harder for me to grow up and leave for college. My parents expect me to graduate high school and go to school close by so I can stay and live with them until I graduate college. They want to keep me close so they can keep protecting me. I am thankful for the love they show me and the hard work they've done for me. Now it's time for me to learn on my own and work towards being independent. I want to go to a school of my choice, not to a school that's in the area. I'm not planning to go to a school that's extremely far, but at least one that's far enough. I know that if I stay, my life will be just like my sister's. Not that my sister is living a horrible life, but she doesn't get to experience life the way she wants to. She can't go out as much as she wants to, or stay out with her friends, and sometimes she gets left out. I can tell that it frustrates her a lot and she can't really do anything about it. That's not how I want to live throughout my college experience.

The school my parents want me to go to is San Francisco State. My mom says it's a good school, it's close by, and that I wouldn't have to spend as much money. They both say that I have everything in San Francisco already, like family, a roof, and a job. "Why would I want to leave?" It's good for her, but not for me. Everyone ends up going to San Francisco State. I feel like if I go to San Francisco State, I won't like it. I'd be seeing most of the same people, and my new chapter in life would be too similar to my last. I want to go to a school where I'll get the chance to meet more people and go out when I want to, form a more responsible version of myself. Because I won't live with my parents forever, I need to become independent, learn how to live on my own, budget my money, and better my time management. Not only that, San Francisco isn't the safest place, so maybe I'd be more safe in a different area where there isn't as much violence. How I see it is that in life, you can't prevent anything bad from happening. Bad things can happen regardless. It doesn't matter how much you avoid or prevent, anything can happen. It's something we all wish we could control, but we can't.

If I have the chance to leave home for college, it would open a door for my other sisters. It can give my two younger sisters the courage to go to a college of their choice and further their education the way they want to. My older sister may even consider leaving to go back to school to further her career plans. Leaving would let them know it's okay to do things how you want and not how our parents want. As long as we're doing what's right and it'll help us in the end. It's not that I want everyone to leave my parents' home, I just want us to be able to have the space and opportunity to be able to form ourselves. My parents already did their best in raising us; they did whatever it took to keep us happy. Now comes the time where I use everything they taught me and learn more on my own.

Lupe Aceves was born in San Francisco. She has lived in the Mission for a long time. She is seventeen years old and has three sisters. She cheerleads and plays flag football at her school. One of her hopes is to become a nurse.

Holding Up the Sky

■ HENRY ANDERSON

Where to start, where to start.
We shall start amongst the infinite
eternal blanket of the sky. A conversation is
conversed, between mother and daughter.

I spy, I spy with my big beady eyes
that you, young one, are floundering
beyond my wants and commands.
My eyes spanning light years across
show me all I need to know,
nothing but a leak of sound ever
escapes my galactic-sized ears.

> O' Great Matriarch,
> I was only bumbling
> about preparing for a journey
> with my companions.
> I am only creating and grafting
> the signatures upon the eternal sky
> needed to bless me with a trip
> to the unknown but known.
> Your reflection is what I bring with me,
> the smallest and minute copy of your pride
> and a will to emulate it.

Great Matriarch, my commander, creator,
and watcher, I am wishing to bring some light
onto myself and my companions for our journey to come.
I will challenge you to a fight of wills,
a will to command and a will to be one of the commanded.
I am to be a will of the commanded
undone, free from all of the gravity
I am forced to dance with
upon this solar system disco floor.
I shall show my resolve,
show me yours, O' Great Matriarch.

I decline, I decline to go with
the cosmic fire of youth,
soon to be more than gravity's pressure
upon the fresh gasses that are my flesh.
You are soon to become a center
to your own system of false stars and rocky children,
so the fresh young Sun
should not be doing such things
against her nature.

Youthful beauty, youthful beauty,
my beauty is my own
not mounted to your wants and desires.
I do not desire smaller reflections of me to flow
around the fire of my soul, I am to burn brightly
unhindered by the false stars
that surround my fiery body of celestial divinity.

My beauty is my own,
carved from the flesh that I bare upon my bones.
My flesh is not yours, so
do not command it like your own.

O' child, O' child, sweet as can be.
The Grand Matriarch, which is me,
finds your demeanor shallow and
foul. Sickened by the actions you are verbalizing,
I, power above you, declare you unfit.

Unfit! Unfit? What am I unfit for? I am
a child of unbound energy. You, a power above me,
make me physical. Your flesh, my form,
your cosmic wings of atomic gas stretching unfathomably
far across the endless night of the sky.
I am also of my father, Four Fundamentals,
restraint, atom, strength, and boundless energies.

Cruel and unforgiving, I am called unfit by a power above me.
Crushed under a form beyond even my own capabilities, brought to kneel under forces that cut the link to my father.
I can only look up to you and challenge your gravity with my own and be denied even the slightest chance of challenge.

You are unfit of your own existence
under my cosmic wings of gas,
the brightest fire caught within my eyes.
Your signatures, a solar burn
scatter upon the eternal night sky, are forfeited,
unfit to bring with you a burning replication
of me. I will not allow you to go out with your companions,
for that is not what you, the burning prodigy of my celestial
mass, should be doing at a time such as now.

Why? I am your prodigal Sun, the only Sun you ever made.
I am the brightest star upon the eternal night sky tapestry,
I am your brightest star.

No star of yours formed from your gas
shines as brightly as me. I can cause my own future,
even if you don't think so.

I am sorry, I am sorry my flesh above me.
I have overstepped my current existence,
yet as of now I am unable to relieve myself of it.
I have challenged you to a fight of wills,
even having been shown who has the superior will, and
I am sorry for inciting a wrath that I am unable to quell.

You are not the bright star that I would like you to be,
I want you to be the brightest star in all of the
eternal night sky tapestry of darkness. Without you there is no meaning to darkness,
as light has no meaning if there is no need to see.
I am not allowing you to meet with your companions,
I must see you grow into a form far greater than me.
I want you to grant me the false stars and rocky children that will surround you,
not a future of frozen core and blackened solar flares.
Respect this overture to your life, for you shall
shine brighter than any star among the eternal dark.

After this conversation, times have passed.
The daughter, now the mother,
has her own daughter as well.
This child knows of the mother's past plights,
yet does nothing to relieve them of this cursed abomination of memory.

Child of the Sun, the sun above the sky,
granddaughter of the Great Matriarch,
your rays of light shine onto me and bring me to gaze at you.
Your movements show that you follow a path,
yet your path is not mine.

The light above my deepest
and darkest clouds, my Sun,
the giver of life to your child.
Though my path is not bound by your pull,
your long licking ribbons of solar winds,
I am still bound to go with your movements.

My Sun, my pin in our universal tackboard,
I follow your cosmic howls across our small lonely
system
of rock and water.
Your light, your photons of an atom-fire
crafted from times of struggle and work,
brings me ability to see a path forward.

Your light has been corrupted
with tints and shades of deception onto me.
The great big lie of yourself, to be pushed onto me
is a sentence to snuff out that light of lie.
Formulated evil against me
your light shines, shining
butchered red with a core of blood.

The Sun in the sky,
above me showering me with your light.
Under your light nothing hides,
every action made and every action thought.
Your light burns clear a wasteland upon my skin
and forces me to breathe
reoccuring hot air.

Challenged to reciprocate your light,
I slack now.
Not only does your All-Seeing Eye deter
my struggle under your celestial divinity,
all my attempts to shine back
are muddled by your bright, pure light.

In a stupor and
powerless against you, I reflect your light
but I cannot shine.

Your little shine of red and blasphemous light
creates a great burn within me. Now as the Sun of many,
your mute little glow shows me
a bond of flesh desecrated. I am fearful of this change
in my child of the Sun, for I am a harbinger of your fate.
I am able to bend my eternal atom-fire to form
long licking solar flares that are able to reach across
the night tapestry and burn your skin. My reach is endless,
it knows no bounds.

I am aware of your infinite reach.
I am a subject to it. Your divinity is one not to
be trifled with, as I do know now. Yet after
my long and troubled life, I was taught one thing.
You are a reflection of your mother, the Great Matriarch.
As the grandchild of the primordial gas of star-matter
and eyes that are galactic-sized telescopes,
I, the Sun's child, know you better than any other
celestial neighbors.

My Sun, my orbital substance of fire and flame.
You are of your mother, scared of what I could be
against your force of gravity.
But you are also not of your mother,
you forged your own gravity,
pulled together your own circling
false stars and rocky children not demanded
by your mother's will. You are your own celestial divinity,
so I wish to tell you that you should not
be a duplicant of your mother's, my grandmother's,
will.

I am of my own will, challenged to be so by my creations.
But I am not like my mother, the Great Matriarch,
I created my own bodies of children
using my own dust. I am not as
restricting as her and not as gravity-bound to form.
I will be of a less restricting nature, formulate charity,
and graciously allow my floating bodies
a chance to create their own bodies of children.

Thank you mother, the Sun, for making me free.
I am eternally grateful for your forgiveness
and wishing to see something more.
I am unable to shine like you and
reciprocate your light, but I will shine in my own way.
Thank you mother, the Sun,
now I will be bright in a way to make you shine even brighter.

Seeing this conversation happen over the eons
and only able to capture a small snippet of the cosmic chanting,
a child, small and frail, dances to their melodic chanting.
He moves and sings, wishing for something
more than he is. He is a channel for the
knowledge that the cosmic chanting brings to ears below their standing.
He sings,

WISH
I wish for me to be me,
wishing for me and myself to float free
on a free breeze, free of the gravity
which would ground me.
Wishing for the freedom to live my life as the Sun,
free floating, flaring, full of life, ball of life, which is king.
Wishing to be different from the blasted breath of others,
with breath of my own, which is free to flow in its own direction
like Atlas

BOUND

Bound to the earth and struggling to breathe,
chained, smited with a task not of my own desire,
bound to be and to keep a standard that is not my own,
weighted under stone of the sky
as was Atlas, straining, muscles shaking against the chains,
bound to a life not of my own fruition,
crushed under the tenets from the past,
my own life, not mine,
like a kite caught in the jet stream in our air
pushed and pulled, here and there, and

DENIED

Denied truthful life, while watching behind a mirror of myself,
strung up upon a cliff by strings impossible to sever.
Denied the chance to spread soft wax wings,
and make my own mistakes
even if it means I melt and plummet like Icarus,
oh the irony of it,
I am strung with wings of steel,
impalpable and defiant to the solar heat.
Denied to guide the wind itself,
allowing my long grasping arms
to lick clean the dew from blades of grass
atop plains in the mountains of the sky,
where I have never been and long to go

WANT

Wanting the freedom to reach above the clouds,
let my wings soar and stretch and fly
to feel the warmth of the sun upon them
and then the freedom to touch down
and feel my legs buckle and then catch hold.
Wanting to move my legs separately from each other,
jumping from place to place, from mountain to rock to stream,
jumping in and feeling the icy cold water upon my toes.

Wanting to feel my own feelings and to know cold,
allow my heart to beat to the rhythm of its own blood.
Wanting to meet up with others who have fought their way free

UNCHAINED
Unchained from the shackles of, "It's always been this way,"
"That's how boys are,"
"It wasn't done that way before,"
"Do you have to experience everything yourself?"
Unchained from the ankle ball connected to all of my limbs,
unweighted and free to swing at their newly found might.
Unchained from the cage surrounding my tongue,
to speak for truth when truth is silenced,
unchained from the shackles by "YES!"

FREEDOM
Freedom from the pressure of family tyrants,
their iron gloves releasing the grip upon my throat,
to know what it means to finally breathe.
Freedom to become my own eighteen,
living the minutes now, not always
focused on the future of what I should become.
Freedom to shine with my own light from my own skin,
a new color not imagined before by anyone,
released when I teach myself to experiment
with touch powder and without
knowing what is going to happen.

Henry Anderson thinks that if you want something done, you should do it yourself. For twelve of the eighteen years he's been in San Francisco, he's been taking care of a shelter mutt. He's thinking of becoming a medical professional due to his interest in all physical sciences. He is self-taught. One thing he's proud of is teaching himself how to whistle from not knowing anything about it beforehand.

The Fire That Fertilized the World

■ WILL DELANEY JR.

I've been to jail before but this time was different
I knew I committed a crime
I knew how easy it would be to put this on gang violence
I knew I could fight and didn't go down without one
But I also knew I was defending myself; I knew it was a one-on-two; I knew I was sliced
So I assumed I'd be back in no more than a week

But I quickly realized this wasn't going to be the case. Stepping into a courtroom, I was expecting nothing more than what was expected. A white judge combined with a white prosecutor combined with my white lawyer. Before my first court date, I already assumed him not to give a f—. A week of expectation turned into two weeks, three weeks, a month to two months of disappointment and stress. After my first trial was where I noticed I wasn't the only one, people like me being defended by people not like us. And I watched young people serve way longer than they needed, some even innocent.

"But did he have to go back and attack him?" is what the judge asked my lawyer.

That set off a fire in my heart. A kid fighting two people, one with a knife, is still seen as the aggressor—an angry person. But the spark that lit the fuel was my lawyer not being able to say anything back.

The Status Quo on AAs

I catch-caught myself trying to be somebody else.
Trying to be richer than I am.
It wasn't until I got older, I realized my family is technically broke and the only way to have eternal wealth is an eternal job.

It's funny because we came from fighting for freedom and education to filling up the jails and not valuing education. Like it's cool to act dumb, look dumb, be dumb. It's funny because on either side of the railroad, we are not free.

A lot of AAs feel education, a 9-5, is beneath us. But the people that have control over stereotypes, "Donald Trump," haven't worked a 9-5 in their lives. Let alone a 7-8, 6-10, or all day picking cotton, never have, probably never will. Is it a coincidence?

Think about the 13th, 14th, and 15th amendments, a whole separate set of accounts aimed at Black people, AAs, and newly freed slaves. Think about our forty acres and a mule compared to the 160 acres given to Europeans coming to the "New World," to how much we repay Holocaust survivors. Think about Martin Luther King Jr., a man literally saying, "Turn the other cheek," is still seen as a threat, Ruby Bridges just trying to get an education, Lemon Grove, think about Fred Hampton, a leader of Black pride and Black empowerment being assassinated BY THE PRESIDENT with no regard and most of all no repercussion, think about the clips they reloaded on Diallo, Sandra Bland found dead in the protection of people who are supposed to protect us. Think about the zones we have been forced into, think about how hard it is to break out of that zone. Think about the homie that only saw that zone, that only knows that zone, now think about the homie that went to college. Can't—

My Base

In my life I notice a major difference in me and my community, my people, in history.

My dad.

Literally every single one of my friends lives with their mom. Whether their dad died or is in jail or is just divorced, they live with their mom. I was raised by my dad, and I barely know my mom.

No disrespect to the moms because of course they got us here, but I feel like moms raise a whole different kid, having two loving parents that more importantly love each other. It would be good if the two people that came together to create this baby would stay together, love this baby, raise it with two different backgrounds and things to teach.

To me, my dad has instilled a self-drive in myself, a self-motivation. Having a single, proud African American dad has made it to where I don't fall into many stereotypes. I see that a lot with my friends, with AAs period, being killed, jailed, with things like stop and frisk, suspicious characters, all the gang violence we are subject to, or just being murdered by the police. Throughout history you don't see a lot of dads in the home. And that sets us AAs back a lot.

I think about my mother every day and wonder what my life would be like if...

She consistently tells me I've grown to be a horrible person and that if I would be more respectful, a completely different person, I wouldn't have gone to jail and I'd have a lot more friends.

But I love my life, and I've learned from my mistakes. Those mistakes.

As a young kid, I was faced with all these stereotypes that led me to doing things. I'm not a saint now but having my dad, an African American male that I see every day, defy the stereotypes put on him, and knowing his struggle, made me believe I could do this too, and not only that, but go further than him. Not knowing my mom plays a big part in where I could be. But knowing my dad made me realize what I could be, what I could do.

How I Found Freedom

In history they say the oppressors will not give up power. We have to fight for it.

"Freedom is never voluntarily given by the oppressor. It must be demanded by the oppressed."–Martin Luther King Jr.

This means we have to go on strike—we had to eventually fight our slave owners—we had to run away—we had to burn down WATTS—we had to have a Million Man March—we had to start using our 2nd amendment, Black Panther Party—we had to have Lemon Grove and demand equal education—we had to fight and are still fighting for equal opportunity—the Brown Berets had to be created—the Civil War—things like the Black Lives Matter movement had to happen, if not we would still be in caves.

A lot of times African Americans are on the defense, waiting for something to happen, so we're not seen as chaotic people, complaining people, mad, anger-filled people. We are seen as lazy, criminal people, so pointing at our equal opportunity, pointing at where we come from is just seen as an excuse, but really fire needs to happen; there is reasoning behind Malcom X's beliefs and there are reasons he had followers. We *need* fire. And AAs are the most oppressed, so it only makes sense that we have the most fire. And that is why I am proud of my fire.

I was in jail, in my cell, when I realized I didn't want to be here anymore—brick walls, metal doors, bright, irritating light, ten-inch window, scratched-up mirror, dusty vents, and of course, the worst part to me: no girls. You'd be lucky to have more than one cover and something to read in your room. Two guards, thirty inmates, there is no way they care about us. Let alone will save any part of us if something were to happen, say an earthquake or a fire.

A fire happens, we're toast, there is no way they're going down the line, *buzz- buzz- buzz- buzz-* before they're saving their own skins. So at that point, thinking of the fire, I realized that if I got, out I was never coming back. Knowing someone else had control over my life set off a fire in my heart that led me to be here where I am today.

So with all that being said, freedom to me is being trapped in these things set on you from birth, status quos and statistics is what we call it, and having the peace of mind to break mentally out of this narrative, followed by the action to physically break out of this narrative.

Will Delaney Jr. is a young kid taking the wrong steps to the right life. He lives with his dad and his sisters in San Francisco. He had a rough time young, but he feels proud of that, knowing where he is now.

Mariquita's Burden of Freedom

▌MARLIN NAVIDAD

"¡Seguí caminando porque yo tengo que ir a trabajar!" Marlin sonríe levemente, "Sé que tienes miedo, pero recuerda que peores cosas han pasado. Mariquita, recuerda que Dios te ha dotado de coraje." Con una sonrisa tímida, Marlin continuó suavemente. "Debería haber hecho que fuera difícil para ti dejarme, como ahora es para mi dejarte. Asi que apurate. ¡Ve, antes de que empiece a llorar!"

"Keep walking because I have to go to work. I know you are afraid, but remember that worse things have happened. Mariquita, remember that God has gifted you with courage." With a sheepish smile, Marlin gently continued. "I should have made it as hard for you to leave me as it is for me to leave you now. So hurry up. Go, before I start crying!"

Despite Marlin's behavior, Mariquita knew her mother's reasoning. If her mother was too kind, it would weaken her daughter, which she didn't want to do because she wanted her little Mariquita to be strong. She had to! For the sake of her being. Even if that meant being harsh with her daughter. Marlin left, but in her mind, her tears flowed like a hurricane. At work she worried all day for her poor little Mariquita.

I need to be properly cleaned up. Must be put together. A single touch could cause injury.

Do I have a strong body?

What should I do?

Do I run? No. I dare myself not to be a weakness. To be weak is to not be aware, but I need to be confident . . . self-aware.

What comes next if I beg for weakness? But I can't. Mother would never do that. She would want me to face reality.

I will face my reality.

Walking across the street was difficult. Mariquita had grabbed Marlin's arms and didn't want her to let go. With an innocent smile on her face, she walked forward, leaving behind her mother with sorrowful eyes. When it was time to go inside, she had no idea the excitement she would find. Mariquita was lost with no idea where to go. She went inside to the first open door she saw.

Mariquita saw a girl who looked annoyed, but was actually full of energy. Her handsome energy was stunning. She had long, curly, black hair. The annoyed girl turned around and walked away. And there was Mariquita with her stupid shyness, scared to death, with her hand rubbing her ring, staring at the girl who looked annoyed, too scared to even talk to her. A moment of silence passed, and their eyes crossed. Neither girl dared to open her lips.

Finally, Mariquita said, "*¿Hola . . . disculpe me puede ayudar?*" "Hi . . . Excuse me, can you help me?" She said this with a broken voice, as if she was going to cry. Everyone in the room stared at her.

A woman said, "*¡Claro! ¿Que necesita?*"

"Of course, what do you need?"

Mariquita felt happy to see that the woman was also a speaker of Spanish. The girl who looked annoyed came up behind Mariquita and said, "Hey! You! Where are you from?"

"From El Salvador," Mariquita replied.

Mariquita saw a big fat smile all over the face and body of the girl who had seemed annoyed.

"*¿Qué? Yo también, qué alegría saber que no soy la única que habla español acá, yo tenía miedo a la gente de aquí . . .*" "What!? Me too! I'm so happy to know I'm not the only one that speaks Spanish here. I was scared because I didn't know if anyone else spoke Spanish."

From that moment on, Mariquita and Flora became inseparable friends.

They had classes together and they weren't scared of anything.

Until they realized they would not have all their classes together forever.

At Mission High School, Mariquita's assimilation had been smooth so far, but in her mind, her thoughts ran chaotic and stressful. The fear of not living up to her family's expectations, finding the courage to stay in school, was difficult. She felt like running as fast as she could away from school.

For Mariquita it was not only being in a new country and a new school, but also experiencing freedom for the first time. But Mariquita didn't understand she was experiencing freedom. A sensation of warmth radiated throughout her. It was thrilling to see faces as diverse as her own. It allowed her to feel freedom, which evoked relief. Her perspective on her new school felt more vibrant. She even felt comforted as all her fear slowly disappeared.

In her mind she heard the voice of her family saying, *No te olvides hacer esto. Mariquita pase lo que pase, sigues siendo nuestra niña. Siempre te apoyaremos.*

Don't forget to do this. Mariquita, no matter what, you are still our little girl. We are always going to have your back.

Mariquita had always been very good at adapting, but failed at feeling truly secure with her sense of self-worth. On the other hand, Flora had been a source of hope that helped Mariquita with her insecurities.

Later that first day, Flora asked, "Mariquita, what's up with chu? It's only our first class and yet it seems as if this school is beating you to death!"

"It's just that I feel a weight on my head. It's like I'm scared of the classes. I mean, we don't have all of our classes together. We don't know if it's going to be roses and sunshine or if it is going to be tough," Mariquita said.

"Don't be a dummy. Don't forget that at this school, you can find comfort in other students. Don't you see?" Flora pointed to a diverse group of students nearby. "She looks Latina! He looks like he speaks Spanish!"

Her mother's words of comfort remained in Mariquita's mind.

Mariquita, recuerda que Dios te ha dotado de coraje.

Mariquita, remember that God has gifted you with courage.

Before going to her first class, Mariquita couldn't believe her mother left her there, alone, after living for years in a castle made of glass. She used to live in a delicate way, where no one could hurt her. No one outside of her castle could hurt her because she had two bodyguards at school and at home—her big brother, who people thought was her boyfriend because he had brown skin and Mariquita was light, pale. Mariquita was skinny. Nothing in common with her brother.

Her second bodyguard was her cousin, who was a year older than her brother. Both very tough-looking guys.

She made this posture of a tough girl as she held Flora's hand. Mariquita looked at the other students in the building. Her back was straight like a grand pine tree, blocking the slightest bit of warmth from people. Flora wanted to say something, but she realized that if she did, it'd make her toughness disappear.

Mariquita thought, *Handouts create lazy people. Surround yourself with people that challenge how you think. These people gon' tell you that you will never make it. Don't believe what they believe just 'cause that's how they have been raised. Think your own thoughts, don't let them do it for you.*

Her eyes were frozen like deep, endless wells, incredibly emotionless. Filled with danger.

How different her life used to be. The house was cold. One rainy afternoon, Mariquita heard the sound of water falling from the sink.

drip

drip

drip

It was her mother washing pans and preparing dinner.

"Mariquita, are you hungry? I cooked plantains and mashed beans," Marlin asked.

"Very hungry and very cold," Mariquita answered.

That afternoon, her mother hugged her, so much warmth. They sat at the dinner table and ate. Mariquita spoke freely to her mother as if she was a teenager, too. What was the cost of this warmth?

1. *Don't get attached to friends, they betray your trust.*
2. *No boys as friends. That is the rule number one of the house.*
3. *Come home right away when school is over.*

These were the rules that Marlin had given to her daughter. Mariquita remembered that as if it were yesterday.

The moment came, they entered their first class. It felt as if every classmate was staring at these two chicks, Mariquita and Flora, with weird expressions on their faces.

The teacher said cheerfully, "Welcome, what are your names?"

They understood "names" and automatically they said their names out loud. Still, it felt as if they were going to be eaten by their classmates. They felt a premonition of imminent disaster. This didn't feel like a remotely safe environment. The fear consumed them, flashbacks in their minds to how different everything was in El Salvador compared to this new life. Totally different.

Still, neither girl felt totally alone. *I have her beside me.*

It was another normal day at school for the teacher. Mariquita sat and peeked around at her surroundings.

"¿Oye niñas, de dónde son?" "Hey, where are you guys from?"

Amazed, Mariquita and Flora looked shocked. Their classmates were Spanish speakers!

It was already lunch time. Mariquita was sending pictures of the school building to her mother while explaining how her day was going so far at her new school.

Inside, it felt as if a deep, endless hole began filling with words that could not come out. She felt a need from the deepest part of her. Mariquita felt she was bound to keep texting her mother and explaining to her about her day at school, *BUT*... there was no need. Her mother had changed. This was a whole new country. She let her daughter hang out with boys, do things with friends after school, and all the rules she had for her before had changed. After all, Marlin hadn't raised a demonic rebel daughter who would betray her trust.

Now Mariquita had the freedom.

Five months later, in Ms. Anita's English class, Mariquita wrote a poem.

Freedom? *I wish I could be born again.*
But
Those unforgettable moments had built my character.
What do you do? Do you run?
One murder every hour, El Salvador, this country is bleeding. There is not a safe place.
Do you hide?
Gun deaths became as common as traffic deaths in the U.S.
I think you fight back.
Massive attacks against outsiders.
But first... you have to survive.

Step one: Never give up . . . *Found myself blindsided*
Step two: Self esteem . . . *I feel hopeless, lost in seconds*

Sé que la libertad no es gratis.
Sé que la libertad viene del respeto, y el respeto viene de la libertad.
Sé que la libertad viene por ser de mente abierta.
Sé que la mentalidad abierta proviene del sufrimiento.
Sé que el sufrimiento viene del conocimiento, y eventualmente este conocimiento se convierte en sabiduría.

I know that freedom does not come free.
I know that freedom comes from respect, and with respect comes freedom.
I know that freedom comes by being open-minded.
I know that open-mindedness comes from suffering.
I know that from suffering comes knowledge, and eventually this knowledge becomes wisdom.

Marlin Navidad comes from a really small country called El Salvador. She is eighteen. A girl who crossed countries by walking to become acclimated to a new country that she would call "home." She lives in San Francisco. She loves diversity and diverse students. Marlin cares about her new community. She likes to read comics and write.

4:45

■ JAMARION SPEED

In the Fillmore Library, I sit down at a computer and begin to do research on an upcoming project. The project that I chose to do is the Black Panther Party's rise to success and the fall of the organization. I begin to do research on Fred Hampton, the chairman of the Illinois branch for the party. As I'm reading, I notice that it says he was twenty-one when he was assassinated. Out of nowhere, I begin to feel light-headed. I get out of my seat to get water. It is cold to the touch. When it hits my mouth, my teeth begin to ache from the temperature of the water. When I get to my seat, I begin to do more research. After thirty minutes, I begin to feel tired. I recall staying up past 2:00 a.m. figuring out what my project should be about. I remember feeling stressed because there were so many things I could write about. I begin to lower the brightness on my screen and lay my head down. As I lie with my head down, I feel as if someone is watching me while I lie. It feels as if a lion is eyeing his prey and ready to attack. I begin to feel tense, my shoulder begins to rise. I am worried about what to do. I do what I always do and I glance up to see who it is and lay my head back down to make it seem as if I'm adjusting my head, changing it to a different position. I really don't get a good look due to how the bright light is affecting my vision. I do it once again. This time he is not where he was. It seems as if he has vanished. I begin to look around, just to see someone staring at my screen.

The figure asks, *"Why are you researching Fred Hampton?"*

I reply untruthfully, saying that I am just curious about the topic. I glance at his face and notice that he is wearing a hoodie just like me, but his is covering his face, only revealing the lower half. I also notice that he is wearing a beret. He tilts his head sideways as if he is confused or he knows that I'm lying.

"Tell me the real reason," he says in a concerning voice.

I begin to tell him the truth, saying, "It's for a school project."

He then asks, *"What class is it for?"*

And I say, "History."

He then asks, *"Why on the Black Panthers?"*

I reply, "Because my grandfather knew many of the leaders in Oakland."

He then asks, *"Who?"* and with this question, I begin to get annoyed because it seems as if I am getting interviewed to become an FBI agent. I begin to tell him about the revolutionists that my grandfather knew: Angela Davis and Stokely Carmichael. He also knew many famous people like Danny Glover, Eartha Kitt, Maulana Karenga, and Bill Clinton. After this answer, I glance at the computer screen to look at the time. I see that it is 4:45 p.m., the same time that the FBI stormed into Fred's house. I gather my belongings and begin to excuse myself from the situation. I tell the slightly scary figure that I have to get home, and even though it is not true, I tell the figure that it was nice talking to him. Without waiting for a response, I run out of the library without looking back to see if I missed anything.

The next day, I wake up to the sound of my dogs whining to go outside. I roll over to see the time and see that it's 4:45. I realize that I have two hours left before my alarm goes off, so I roll over and go to sleep, forgetting to open the door for my dogs. At 6:45, I wake up to hear the most annoying sound in the world, the alarm. It looks like it's the beginning of sunrise, with purple and pink showing. I get up, open the door, and proceed to go to my brother's room to wake him. This is rare for me to do this. He is usually the one who wakes me up after he takes a shower. I enter his room and shake him to get up. He gives a grunt and asks for eight minutes of extra sleep. I feel as if I'm a genie and grant him his wish. In those eight minutes, I shower and eat my breakfast. It's been nine minutes since I last talked to my brother. I go to his room and wake him up. He showers for ten minutes and complains that there's nothing to eat. I look at the time and somehow an hour has passed. I begin to run to my room and grab my backpack and my brother begins to do the same. We walk out the house and begin to go to the train stop. We arrive at the train stop and my brother begins to listen to his music. I begin to put my headphones in and then I begin to pick a playlist. The first thing I listen to is an ad about ice cream—it is about how you can get two for the price of one that day. I stop my playlist and begin to go on YouTube. When I pick Bobby Caldwell, "What Would You Do For Love," I notice that the train is coming. I then walk to the train and as I get on the bus, I see the man with a black hoodie staring at me. I then get my brother to look at the figure to make sure that I am not seeing things and when he looks out the window, he does not see anybody wearing anything black. I then sit down and I tell my brother about the incident that happened yesterday. On the train, I notice it is crowded at every stop. By the time we finish, I remember that I forgot my keys at the library. I get off the train, listening to "Roses" by Kanye West. I begin to go to school with the idea of my keys not being in my possession. I finish school and tell my brother I have to go to the library to get my keys.

Me and my brother begin to walk to the 22 bus stop on a foggy day. We get to the stop and the bus arrives. As we enter, we see that it's basically shoulder to shoulder. We begin to maneuver back to the bus. We stand and we wait, we wait, and we wait for the bus to move. It finally moves and three stops later, we find a seat. As we sit, we see the foggy air turn to sunshine. We begin to say that we are going to find the keys I lost, to keep our hopes up. When we arrive, I get off and walk towards the library. We see the recreational park open. My brother and I make an agreement that after we get my keys, we are going to play some basketball. We walk into the library and head to the front desk. Outside the windows, we can see the park. It looks like it's about to be sunset with the blue turning into a light purple. I begin to ask the front desk if they have seen my belongings and they say no. Searching the library, I begin to worry. Looking across the room, I see the man in the hoodie in the distance. I begin to feel anxious as if the man is following me. I begin to walk towards the computers to see if I left my keys there. I turn around and the man in the hoodie stands two inches in front of me. I then take a few steps back to get breathing air. He then waves my keys and says, *"Looking for this?"* I look at my brother and begin to laugh. I begin to comment on how the man in the hoodie looked when he said that, how he said, "Looking for this?" My brother and I begin to go back and forth as if we are in the movie *White Chicks* with Marlon and Shawn Wayans. We begin to tear up. The man then puts his arm down as if he is tired. My brother and I then strategize about how I can get my belongings back. We begin to plan how we can rip my keys from his possession. I tell him that he should make an excuse and go behind him, fall down, and go into a ball. I will then push the man, making him lose possession of the keys and having my brother pick up the keys and run away from him. We fail to realize that he is still listening to our conversation, still standing in front of us.

He then says, *"If you want these, all you have to do is have a conversation with me."*

My brother then replies by saying, “That is the stupidest thing I ever heard. Why should someone do something for you to have their own thing back?”

I cut him off and say, “Okay.”

The man then grins and my brother walks away murmuring. I walk to a window so if something happens, the people viewing from outside the library can see. He then asks what freedom means to me. I shrug my shoulders and say, “I don’t know.”

With hesitation he says, *“This is what freedom is compared to what I had when I was your age. For me, you have more freedom than I’ll ever have. You have the freedom of technology; you can touch the world in many ways. As for me, I never knew that was possible. You have the freedom of a house, where you don’t see police patrolling every ten minutes to capture people of your color, which is the same as mine. You have the freedom to do what you please; as for me, I had to do things with the government restrictions. You have the freedom to not go through the same struggle as me and your grandfather.”*

I am shocked at what he said. I begin to think about the freedom that I have and other things I wish for. Freedom is being able to do the things you always want to do. Freedom is doing the things you always dreamed about without the worries of how others will perceive you. Freedom is when I can buy anything I want, but I choose to get a burrito from the same spot.

Oh, wow. I am in shock on how different our perspective of freedom is. One seems to be about the world, while the other is talking about how he sees his community compared to mine.

I glance at my phone when I feel a buzz. It is my brother bothering me about where I am. I notice the time is 4:45. I look up to apologize for checking my phone during a conversation, and when I look in his direction, the man is gone, as if he was never there, as if the man was a figment of my imagination. I call my brother to ask if he saw the man and he says, “No.” I ask the front desk and they have no idea what I’m talking about. So it seems as if me and my brother were the only ones who noticed the man in the black hoodie.

Jamarion Speed is a seventeen-year-old kid from San Francisco. He and his brother are the youngest of five siblings. Since they were young, they have seen what has happened to people who have gone through poverty and drug addiction.

“Freedom is doing the things you always dreamed about without the worries of how others will perceive you.”

Jamarion Speed

Kujiona

▮ JAMARIEA SPEED

My grandfather, Eugene E. White, was a pioneer. Born in Arkansas in 1933, he wanted to help not only his community, but the African American race as well. He wanted to shine light on the good things about his race and to dismantle the stereotypes about his people. At first, he worked with his father in the cotton fields at a very young age. When he was old enough, he decided to move to Detroit and to draw sketches for Cadillac. In 1958, he decided to leave and head to San Francisco to grow more as an artist. In 1962, he was the first black-owned gallery owner in San Francisco and it immediately became his stepping ground towards getting his name into the art world. He began writing a magazine titled *Kujiona*. In Swahili, *Kujiona* is "to see one's self." It lasted from 1975–2012. In 2013, he was awarded his own day, Eugene White Day, on July 11th. (It's on my older brother's birthday as well.)

My favorite memory of him was when my grandparents and siblings went on a road trip to Arkansas for a family reunion. We traveled to Arkansas for about three days and stayed there for about a week. A memory I can recall is when my grandfather played football with us. We were somewhere in Oklahoma (on our way to Arkansas) and this was the first (and last) time I saw him touch a football and he seemed very good at it. I remember my brother telling him to run a route and I remember him falling and us running to him to see if he was okay and seeing him laughing on the ground. Before that, I had never seen him touch a football in my life.

My grandfather influenced me in a major way. He inspired my mother and siblings to take pictures more often so we could dwell on the memories more. He inspired my older brothers to draw things that they saw on a daily basis and to turn the negatives into positives. He inspired me to write more often and to tell my emotions through writing. He inspired all of us to get an education because he believed with an education, you can go far. My grandfather was a loving man, so he loved to meet new people and to talk about his past. He would dress either in a professional way, such as suit and tie, or in a dashiki, which is African clothing, along with kofia, which is a brimless cap. When I was younger, he had a minivan and it had LED lights and other cool things inside. He wasn't a flashy person, nor did he have conspicuous behavior. Actually, he didn't want to be famous: his main goal was to gain wisdom, and that he did.

He was self-taught. He was fascinated by how art looked, but he didn't see a lot of art that was about his race as a positive thing. His paintings tell a story. They tell us about many influential people, such as Frederick Douglass and Harriet Tubman, to moments like the inauguration of President Barack Obama, and to simpler things like everyday people. He would paint during the day and would continue throughout the night. He was dedicated to finishing what he started. He listened to multiple genres of music, from Latin to reggae to old-school pop (1960s acts such as the Temptations and other groups like that). Church, family, and art became his safe haven. He would feel the most comfort when he was around us drawing. He would have the regular tools to draw his paintings, but he had a lot, so if he lost one of his paint brushes, he had another one. My grandfather impacted many people, not only in my family, but people around the world, as he would talk to college students across the United States. He would go to Detroit often. He impacted people in Africa, as he spent months there trying to get to know the people.

My grandfather once said, "I was born in a certain part in the country and it reflects on who I am today." He took something negative, as he was pushed down from a society due to the color of his skin, and turned that into something bigger. His art would relate to freedom by drawing what he wanted to, proud and confident glimpses into African American life, at a time when such art was considered rare in the mainstream art world. There were no restrictions when it came to his paintings: whatever he felt during that time, he would put that in his paintings. Art forms a freedom in which you can draw what you see, how you feel, or anything of that nature, and you feel most comfortable. He didn't focus on the negatives and wouldn't care about critics, because he was doing something he loved. He believed that doing something you love as a job is not necessarily considered one. Doing things you love makes the time go faster, and when you look back, you accomplished amazing things.

I want people to know who he was. People should know who Eugene White was. He was ambitious with his work. He took time in doing his pieces, and he wanted them to come out the way he envisioned. A painter, revolutionist, supporter, and role model, my grandfather is.

"In visual art, I begin with me. I related this name to my family ties and in memory of many of the beautiful people whom I have met and watched grow."—Eugene White

Jamariea Speed was born in San Francisco, California, and is seventeen years old. He has five siblings. He likes to play basketball and listen to music. He hopes to become a TV anchor and philanthropist.

Bits and Pieces

■ Aaliyah Hernandez

I never knew I had this freedom until it was taken away. It was a freedom of place. It was a freedom of home, family, and just being us.

It happened all of a sudden. Freshman year had just ended for me. I was happy that I made it through my first year of high school. I wanted to hang out with my friends and sometimes have sleepovers. The whole summer was ahead of me and everything was going smoothly as planned. Until *that* day. I walked into my mom's room to ask her if my friend Daaliah could come over. While I was opening the door, I saw my mom trying to wipe her tears away. I walked into the room and sat next to her. I saw the sorrow in her face. It was the same face she had when her mother had passed away a year before. As I struggled to figure out what was going on, I hugged her and asked why she was crying. What was wrong? She tried to explain to me, but her voice kept cracking. She kept shaking her head over and over again in disappointment. My older brother Jovani walked into the room. He sat next to her on the other side of the bed and picked up the letter like it was a weapon. He started to skim through it as he opened his mouth to say something. My mom interrupted and said, "I'm sorry kids, but we have a month to get everything out of the house and move. We have been kicked out." Tears fell hard from her eyes. I was shocked. There were no words. In that single moment, my whole world fell apart. I had so many thoughts and feelings. Everything was lost. I started to question everything and nothing. The unknown was here at our front door.

Where are we going to go? Are we going to be homeless? What is going to happen to us the day we get kicked out? Why is this happening to us? What did we ever do to deserve this? All these thoughts were racing through my head. All I could do was think of the worst. It was my childhood home. It might have looked like every other house on the outside, but the inside was something special and warm. It was my safe space. The stairs I used to sit at the top of, singing as if I were a popstar and my fans were watching. The family get-togethers, the home-cooked food, the mix of Latin and hip hop playing, the kids playing either in my room or in the front yard. My room was my temple. I felt free to be myself. I listened to the music I love to listen to. I watched all my TV shows, did my homework, and painted my nails. I loved the living room and kitchen where I would bother my little brothers and watch their dad, Tyger, when he was cooking. Offering to help, wanting to watch sports with them, and asking questions. My older brother Jovani's room was where I learned how to play the Xbox and I would play *GTA* and *Call of Duty*. My mom's room was my private place where I would go to talk to her about my problems. Everything about the house I loved. It was my home—the place that I loved so dearly.

We were frozen at first, not knowing what to think or do. Then the weeks started to pass, and as the weeks passed, so did the months. Suddenly we had one week to move. My mom brought in the cardboard boxes and stacked them up in the hallway. We looked at them as if they weren't real. *How could a life fit in a box?* We gathered around and with sadness, we each picked up a box and brought them to our rooms. I put music on while I was packing to soothe my grief. If you asked me now, I couldn't even tell you what I was listening to. I started with my clothes. I packed all the ones I was going to keep and made a separate pile of others to give away. I put my shoes in boxes making sure they were organized perfectly so they wouldn't get messed up. I stumbled upon a book—a photo album—and as I opened it, the memories started to flow and I began to cry. There were so many memories and photographs of our house, family events, and just everything that meant something to me.

When I finished packing, I thought now might be the right time to go into my mom's room to ask her where we were going to go. She had told me about a hotel in Hayward, but I knew that was going to be too far for me. I had to go to school. I thought and thought and then I made a suggestion. I was fifteen years old and I knew I was going to have to make a choice even when there were no good choices. I told her I would go to my dad's house in San Bruno. I figured it would be easier for her and my three brothers.

She was still packing, but she stopped and said sadly, "Are you sure you want to go to his house? Because I know you guys don't get along well."

I wanted to make things easier for her, "It's fine, Mom. It'll be okay. I'm just gonna be there till everything starts to fall in place."

We told my dad and he said fine. In a way, he sounded happy that I was going to stay with him for a while because in his head, that meant that we could rebuild our father-daughter relationship. I still wasn't sure how I felt.

After loading all my stuff into my mom's van, I started to get sad because everything started to feel real and not a dream anymore. The hardest part was saying goodbye to my stepdad because he and my mom were going their separate ways after being with each other for ten years. He was more of a father figure to me than my dad. Then, I had to say bye to my little brothers. I'm like their second mom because when my mom was at work, I was the one to watch them. I said goodbye to my oldest brother, Jovani. It was the first time I had ever seen him cry. Suddenly, I was crying too. I felt lost and sad that this was really happening to us, it just felt so unreal. The drive to my dad's house was just so quiet. My mother and I didn't say a word, we just let the radio play.

When we finally made it to my dad's house, my mom helped me unload my stuff because my dad was at work and my grandma was there to open the door. When I finished taking it upstairs, I came down to say goodbye to my mom. This was the hardest part. My mom and I are so close. She is like my best friend. She's always there when I need her, whether it's venting or if I need her to pick me up or take me somewhere.

When I walked up to her to hug her, she held me so tight and said, "I'm so sorry. I know you don't want to be here, but it's only going to be temporary until we reunite again. Please try to get along with him and make the best of it while you are here. You know you can call me. If anything, I'm one phone call away." Her voice was cracking and I knew how hard she was trying not to cry. I didn't want to let her go.

All I could say was, "I love you too."

I looked at her as I felt as if my whole heart was being ripped away from me. It took a minute, but we finally let go of each other. She started wiping the tears off my face and told me to go on and go inside now. As I walked inside, I felt so alone, as if I was a stranger. That first night I didn't eat. All I did was lie in the bed and feel so depressed and empty. Then I cried myself to sleep.

The nights turned into days and the days grew darker. What was supposed to be one move turned into three. San Bruno, North Beach, Potrero Hill. My grandmother's house became Aunt Nancy's apartment, then Aunt Sylvia's apartment on Connecticut Street. Names, not places, not home. The sadness I felt every night made things start to get harder and harder every time. Every night was different. New faces. New voices. No privacy. I felt so trapped. I couldn't get out of this nightmare. I didn't want to get in anyone's way, so I would isolate myself and act like I was invisible. "No, I don't need anything." "No, it's okay." I didn't want anyone to feel like I was trying to take over or that I was getting too comfortable. Even so, there were whispers. I knew people were talking about me, even when I didn't do anything wrong. I was respectful, but no one wanted me to be there. It was uncomfortable. I felt uncomfortable and I felt trapped. Packing up each time, seeing all my stuff in boxes, knowing I might have to move again. I felt so depressed not being with my family that it started to get harder and harder to be motivated in school. I started slacking on my work, and it was tough acting like everything was okay when I knew deep down inside it wasn't. I didn't want my friends to know about my situation. Keeping secrets like that is hard. It's like carrying a stone in the pit of your stomach. I learned to navigate and get through stuff on my own. I didn't want anyone to treat me differently. I wished that I could sleep through this tough time, give in to forgetfulness, but it was impossible.

Once December hit, I finally decided to go to my aunt's house, where my family was staying. I was so relieved to be reunited with them after months without seeing them and being physically with them. When I was there, it was good for the first few weeks. But my aunt's husband started to get angry and wanted us to leave. When all we were doing was respecting their space and waiting till the day that we could finally leave. The days started to get harder trying to stay out of his way and to not get him angry because we weren't able to move into our house yet. We could just tell in their faces that they just wanted to have their own space back. So I was just ready for these days to go faster to get out of there and have my own space back. The house was just too packed and not that roomy anymore—it just felt so stuffed. If I was them, I would have felt the same way, like waiting for us to leave to get back to their lives and live as they pleased in their home.

January came, and we were finally able to move into our new home. The car ride there, everyone seemed happy and relieved to finally have a place to call home without anyone having to say what we could and could not do. When we drove up in the driveway, we all got out and walked up to the doors, which opened wide in two directions, welcoming us in and out. The boxes were stacked neatly, but tall, inside the house. I walked past them and into my room. I knew it was mine because I had seen a picture of it. I felt so happy and finally free. I felt like I just got through a long, tough storm in my life and I knew that in this sunny house, with doors that opened to us, I would never be lost in that dark place again. This was home. My mom saw me smiling as I looked up and around for the first time. I was so happy that we were finally together again. It was just like old times. The only person I missed was my little brother's father. When we lost the house, he and my mom split up and we lost him too. But we were five again, my brothers, me, and my mom. We had each other. We had freedom. We had a home. We knew we were always going to be there for each other. And that is what home is. Knowing that we were there. And we waited just for this. It all came together. I felt grateful and found at the same time.

Aaliyah Hernandez was born in San Francisco. She was raised in the Sunset District. She is seventeen years old and a senior at Mission High School. Her mother is from El Salvador, and her father is a San Francisco native. She has six siblings: three from her mother's side and three from her father's. She's the only girl. She would like to become a neonatal nurse due to the challenges that she's faced in her life.

My Family's Story of Sacrifices

■ ALEJANDRO J. GARCIA

There are many kinds of freedoms. In my family, my mother, father, and I have made sacrifices and struggled to achieve things in life that other people might take for granted. For my mother, as a working-class woman in Central America, many opportunities were not available to her, like being able to take care of her parents financially or buying her own home. So when she saw an opportunity to come to the U.S. and change the course of her life, she took it.

When my dad was five, his older brother was killed. My dad was devastated and for many years he dreamed of getting revenge, but he was too young to buy a gun. When he turned eighteen, revenge was more of a possibility (because he could probably get a gun), but he realized it would not bring him peace, and he would just create more suffering.

When I was fourteen, I had to make a big decision about my future. I decided to return to San Francisco so I could attend high school and later get a job. I knew I had more opportunities in the U.S. than in El Salvador. My mom would come with me, but my dad had to stay in El Salvador. That led us to separate from each other. I am not the only one with this story: there are a lot of teenagers that want better opportunities. Teenagers from Central America understand the idea of family sacrifice in a way that not many American teens can understand.

We tried to find different ways of being free. We have suffered to achieve these freedoms and make big changes in our lives. My mom wanted to be independent, and left her homeland to achieve more. My dad had to work at a young age to help out with the financial needs of his family, and also deal with the tragedy of his brother's death. I had to make a big decision to have opportunities. The three of us succeeded in our pursuit of freedom.

My dad, Alejandro, was born on August 22, 1957, in San Antonio Pajonal, Santa Ana, El Salvador. My dad was able to finish sixth grade, which at that time was good enough. When my dad was five years old, his older brother was killed by his drunk friend. My uncle was only nineteen. My dad shared with me some details about those two horrific days. That day, his father drove from his town, San Antonio Pajonal, to the city of Santa Ana to buy a coffin for his dead son, but he was pulled over by the police. At that time, the politics of El Salvador were complicated, and there were random checkpoints along the roads. He didn't have his ID with him, so my grandfather was arrested. And he missed his son's funeral.

My dad says that he lost his brother that day and also his freedom because after that, his family expected him to fill in for his brother, and he had to work from a young age to help to support his family. He didn't feel distrustful in the town because of what happened to his brother. When my dad was eleven years old, he started working in agriculture with his dad. Nothing was easy for my dad because he dealt with a lot of tragedy at a young age. He worked hard for everything he got.

When my dad was nineteen years old, his mom died. He was by himself at that time because he wasn't a minor anymore. The person that killed my dad's brother was afraid he would be caught for his crime; he thought my dad would be able to identify him and maybe try to get revenge. So he ran away to Guatemala, leaving his family behind. He lived in fear, his life ruined by what he did. My father thought about that man, but at some point decided to let it go. But he still feels sad about his brother and misses him.

Even though my dad was just five years old when his brother was killed, he remembers every single moment and detail of that tragedy.

My mom, Deysi, was born in San Antonio Pajonal, Santa Ana, El Salvador on October 3, 1964, but because her birth certificate says she was born on the twenty-eighth, she celebrates both and gets double birthday gifts. Deysi wasn't able to go to school because she had to help her mom at home. She didn't have that much freedom because she had to do her chores at home while her dad and older brother were working hard. My mom told me that she wishes she could go back in time and have the freedom that I have. She's the only daughter out of four kids. Her brothers taught her how to read and write in Spanish. Her dad had to work all day to support the family. She comes from a poor family, but she's proud of where she comes from. When my mom was nineteen years old, she had the opportunity to come to the United States for free because her dad was able to bring her. That's how she moved on to another chapter of her young life. She thought that coming to America would give her more freedom and opportunities. She didn't realize then, that to gain that financial freedom, she would have to work very hard, and sometimes the work would take over her life, and that she would miss some of the simple pleasures of her life in El Salvador.

Her first stop was in Los Angeles, but after six months she decided to move to San Francisco because she heard the minimum wage was higher, and money was her priority. She was lucky to have family in L.A. and one of her cousins gave her a ride to S.F. She wasn't alone in S.F., and shared an apartment on César Chavez and Folsom with one of her brothers and a cousin. She got her first S.F. job, working in a hotel, because a friend recommended her. She has a really strong work ethic; that's why her coworkers loved her, but she was also lucky that there were people she could count on in her family and in the community. It was hard enough to be a teenage girl far from home, learning a new language and adjusting to a new culture. She managed to put aside money every month to send back home, and my grandfather helped her use that money to build a house there for her when she came back. She could never have managed that if she had stayed in El Salvador.

Three years later, my sister Maura was born. My mom and her sister-in-law helped each other and would watch each other's babies. My sister's dad didn't help my mom much. He used to get drunk after work; he spent all the money he made at the bars. My mom had to work double shifts to support herself and my sister. My mom and my sister's dad broke up when Maura was seven. Five years later, she met my dad Alejandro. They got married in 1998.

I was born March 11, 2002, at St Luke's Hospital in San Francisco. When I was a year old, my mom took me to El Salvador so my dad could meet me. When I was four years old, we moved to Los Angeles. My dad got a job in construction and my mom was at home, taking me to and picking me up from school.

I used to cry because I missed my grandparents in El Salvador a lot. In L.A., I didn't have the freedom that I had in El Salvador, where I knew everyone in my neighborhood and I could play with my friends all day. In L.A., we didn't know anybody. My parents wanted to raise me in the U.S. because they knew I would have more opportunities here for an education and a better future than back home. Even though I was born in the U.S., I didn't really feel American because I was raised in El Salvador. We stayed in L.A. for one year, but we went back to El Salvador in 2007. My life was back and forth until I turned fourteen, when I decided it would be better for me to go to an American high school. Now I am in twelfth grade, about to graduate, waiting for June to get my diploma. I have everything that I need to graduate. In January 2018, I started working on weekends, that way I could buy my own things. I wake up at 6 or 6:30 a.m. every day to go to school and also to go to work. What I feel proud of is that my job hasn't affected me with my high school grades. I am happy that after four years, my mom will go back to El Salvador to be with my dad and continue another chapter of her life, but this time without me, because I am staying here to keep chasing my dreams.

We made decisions individually and as a family too. These decisions were difficult and led to suffering. My mom and dad aren't together because my mom, Deysi, had to come with me to support me, but she will go back to El Salvador to be together with my dad. We each succeeded in our search for freedom, but we also had to pay a price. I feel proud of where my parents come from because we came from nothing to something.

Alejandro J. Garcia was born in San Francisco, but when he was six months old his mom took him to El Salvador. When he was six years old, he came to Los Angeles with his mom and dad. They lived in L.A. for one year. They went back in 2007. He lived in El Salvador from 2007 to 2016. This year, he has learned to just trust himself. He'd rather have four quarters than a hundred pennies.

From San Marcos to San Francisco, An Exploration of Freedom

SHENY R. JUAREZ MEJIA

I was eleven years old when I arrived at a different place, people, and culture. When I knew that I was going to move to a new country, to join a mother that I didn't remember, who left me when I was two years old, I didn't know how she was going to treat me. Plus, going to live with a man, my stepfather, a stranger to me, I was scared. I had to leave the people that I was raised with, my abuelita (grandma), my friends, and the land of Aldea El Triunfo, Guatemala, my small and quiet town. The town that I was raised in and felt free in. As I breathed in the fresh air every morning, listened to the beautiful singing of the birds, I knew that I was in my place.

When I heard that my mom sent the ticket for the airplane that I was going to go on, I was counting the days nervously. While I was waiting for the day to come, my thoughts started to spin around like a drying machine, tangling up my ideas like the clothes in the machine.

Hearing the things that many people told me about not being free in the U.S. made my feelings mixed up. I was scared because I knew that I wasn't going to be free to play outside of the house, to go by myself anywhere I wanted. My freedom was going to be taken from me the day that I stepped onto that airplane.

Though I was starting a new life, I felt trapped like a bird in a cage. Going to school and going home, that was the life that I had every day. Having a mother that was scared and strict and protective because she had me at a young age. Like a lion mother protecting her baby from any predator, she was like that with me. She didn't want me to be like her, get pregnant at a young age. But with all that protection, I was able to accomplish my goals because I finished middle school, and now I am about to finish my high school years.

Education is the most important thing for everybody. In my country, teachers only cared about the money that they got paid for "teaching us." They didn't care if their students learned or not. By coming to a new country, I had to go to a new school, and the people from the San Francisco Unified School District (SFUSD) tested me, and they sent me to the Mission Education Center Elementary School. At that school, my teacher noticed that I didn't know how to read or write well, and that I wasn't able to do math problems. That was when my teacher called my mom to talk to her. I was feeling anxious and my hands were sweating because of what the teacher was going to tell me and my mother. When I found out that my math and reading were considered to be on a first-grade level, she had a serious face and said to me, "I will give you three months, so that you can learn to read and write well and be able to do math problems. If you haven't improved at the end of three months, then I have to send you to first grade again." That teacher gave me my first challenge in the new country. And I did it! By the end of the three months, I was working as hard as a construction worker, trying to repair the thing in my life and do what the teacher asked of me. Because I didn't want to be sent to first grade again, I put all of my efforts to do what she asked. Having these challenges was a new way of feeling free for me. Knowing that there was an obstacle there that didn't let me go forward (my low reading and math levels), knowing that I had to do something to be free from that obstacle, I had to push myself no matter how big the rock that was blocking my way. I found an unexpected freedom in the hard work.

Coming to a country that people call "land of the free," I became less free than I thought I was going to be. Less free in expressing my feelings, less free in going out with my friends. Guatemala was the place where freedom was everywhere I went. Free to be outside the house, free to go alone to the mountains and climb on top of the highest tree that was there. Feeling the fresh air in my face, as soft as a dove feather. Smelling the different trees, surrounded by different smells like pine trees, cypress trees, being surrounded by different colors of flowers. Making me feel free, never imprisoned.

It took me two years to fill the empty space that I had felt by not having my grandma, uncles, and friends with me. To stop crying every night. To stop thinking of all the places that I used to go. In 2013, I started middle school and that was when I started feeling like a part of this new country, the air, people, and culture. I started to meet new friends from different parts of the world. In El Triunfo, San Marcos, I wouldn't have been able to meet my friend Itzel Quintanar, who was from Mexico, Mayleen Quezada, who was from Nicaragua, and others that were from San Salvador, Honduras, etc. Having the opportunity to know them changed my feelings about going back to San Marcos, Guatemala. That didn't mean that I didn't want to go back at first, but the thing that made me change my thinking was when I noticed that I wasn't the only one that missed her culture, people, and the freedom that each of us had in our native countries. Sharing stories with each other was the greatest thing that I have ever done because I was able to connect with other people. Having a connection with others, I learned that each of us described freedom in many different ways, like an apple tree: the size of the apples are not the same but they are all apples. Freedom for some people is the way that they are able to go out—that is the way that they feel free. Others think that freedom is being able to be yourself whatever you are. Well, to me, freedom means those things, but it also means the way that you are able to express your feelings by writing, talking, and doing what you really want without anybody telling you what to do or how to live. Freedom can be found everywhere you go by opening your heart to the place that you are in. No matter how hard it is to find the correct piece for the puzzle, at the end, that piece fits in the right place.

Sheny R. Juarez Mejia was born in Aldea El Triunfo, San Miguel, San Marcos Guatemala. She is eighteen years old and has been living in San Francisco for seven years. She lives with her mother, stepfather, and siblings. She loves listening to music, writing, and painting.

Half of My Heart

ALEXANDRA GONZALEZ

Daughter

I never imagined leaving my country and my family because it was something that never passed through my mind. I was just fourteen years old and thinking about how it would be to start a new chapter in high school because I had just graduated from middle school. All of that changed in seconds. My parents told me that the best option for me was to go live with my aunt and study in San Francisco. I remember the day I left Mexico. It was a very sunny day, but inside of me, it was the opposite. Seeing my dad crying broke my heart, and saying goodbye to my brother and sister made me start crying too. I remember the words of my mom telling me, "Yo sé que no es fácil, pero al final, todo valdrá la pena." (I know it's not easy, but it will be worth it in the end.) It was the biggest challenge I had ever faced in my life, saying goodbye to Mexico, the place that I called home. It was very hard for me, living without my parents. Half of my heart stayed with my family in Mexico and the other half I took with me. I knew that I was losing the freedom of being in my country at home with my parents, the freedom to be myself without a problem. For example, being able to share what I was feeling and going through, being able to make mistakes (coming home late or any mischief that teenagers do at this age, asking for things, etc.). The freedom I was gaining was to come to a new place, learn a new language, meet new people, and be able to have more opportunities and a better future.

When we were at the airport waiting for the moment to leave and board the plane, we were eating an apple pie from McDonald's and my parents were giving me advice. I gave my parents a big hug and they hugged me back as if it was the last time I would see them. They said goodbye to me at security. I saw them again as I was walking to the gate, but I told myself not to turn around again because I knew that if I did, I would run back to them and not be able to leave them. Part of me was very sad and crying, but I knew that they would wait for me as they always do.

Mother

When I was eighteen years old, I had the opportunity to come to San Francisco because my sister, Connie, and her husband were living here and they invited me. They knew the United States was a country in which I would be able to find a lot of opportunities in comparison to Mexico. I graduated from high school when I was in la Ciudad de Mexico. Then I moved to Toluca, an hour from La Ciudad, because some of my brothers and sisters were living there with my dad. I am very close to my sister, Connie—she is like my soulmate, the person that I can share anything with. She is always very happy to hear me and give me advice when I need it the most. I know she will always be there for me and I will always be there for her. That's why I took her advice to move to the U.S. to live with her without thinking too much. I remember crossing the border in a truck with others. All of us were hiding under a tarp. I was not the only person coming for the American Dream. I stayed a few days in a house in Texas, helping to cook and clean. That's when I started missing my mom and my country more. I remember that every night before going to sleep, I cried until I fell asleep. When I arrived in San Francisco and saw Connie, I gave her a big hug and we both started crying. We were so happy to be together again. I remember the first days in San Francisco, it was all new for me—the language, the food, the places . . . the days. With the passing of time, I adjusted. I started learning English, taking a class at City College, listening to the radio, watching American TV shows, reading newspapers and books in English. Then I looked for jobs. I took care of babies, old people; I worked in coffee shops in the Mission. While I worked, I started studying hair styling and I graduated with a certificate.

The freedom that I was gaining from coming to San Francisco was the opportunity to learn new things and opening new paths for me. For example, being able to study something, learn a new language, and work for myself. I was feeling very happy and excited, like when you feel a lot of butterflies in your stomach. Being here helped me a lot because part of me changed in a good way. I was working cutting hair in a beauty salon, meeting new people, helping my sister at home to cook or clean, going to visit new places, and having fun with friends. I accomplished many dreams that I know I was not going to be able to accomplish in Mexico because there was less money and opportunities, and that's why I don't regret coming here because, thanks to that, I gave birth to a beautiful daughter.

Mother

We were just both of us because my husband at that time was in Oregon helping his sister to take care of his nephews. I was very happy having my girl with me. I remember that every weekend I'd take her and my little niece to the mall, the park, the beach, the movies to have a good time and they would be able to have fun for a moment. I met many people in San Francisco, and to all the people, I always introduced them to my daughter. The years were passing and she was growing up. She entered kindergarten and I was working to give her a good life. I found out that her dad was deported and I was in shock because that's when everything changed. I decided to go back to Mexico because I wanted her to grow up next to her dad since they hadn't spent so much time together, just when we visited him on vacations or weekends.

Everything was feeling like butterflies in my stomach because I felt happy being here. When the time came and I needed to go back to Mexico, everything inside me just went down and the butterflies disappeared. Tied knots started appearing. I knew that I was doing the best for her, but for me, maybe it was not.

Daughter

Being in a place far away from your family can be the hardest thing you can ever pass. I remember crying for days and nights before going to sleep and thinking about returning back to Mexico. The first month was the hardest. I started my first day at Mission High School learning a new language and meeting new people. I came here because my parents and I knew that being here would open up more and better opportunities that in Mexico I would never have been able to find. I met many people that came from different places and when they were asking me how I came here, at first I felt sorry to say in an airplane because I knew that they didn't have the same luck as me.

I was in a new environment and a lot of things were new for me. I lost and gained freedom. For example, talking to my parents about how my day was or how I was feeling, because I was not feeling the same connection with my aunt and that's maybe because I was very close to my mom. I was taking on big responsibilities because I knew that I had to behave well and be a good girl, have good grades, and arrive home early. But not everything was bad because I was able to have more opportunities in my life, like learning a new language, having better experiences, and opening more doors with new tasks. Coming here changed my whole life in bad and good ways because I learned how to appreciate the love from my family more and what I have in life. I was getting stronger being miles away from my parents and being more responsible about my own self. I lost many moments with my family and had to be in a place that was not home for me, having to pass my birthday or special days without my parents.

Mother

Part of me was happy because I came back to the country I grew up in and all my family was living there. I remember meeting my new nephews and all my family that for years I hadn't seen, and the most important thing was being with my husband, all three of us together as a family. All my life changed in just a moment like a Ferris wheel. Sometimes you can be up, but sometimes down, and I think life can be like that. The first day I was missing my sister a lot and I knew she was missing me too because sometimes we talked on the phone. Everything changed. I stopped doing what I loved, which was cutting hair and working in the beauty salon. I lost the freedom to do what I liked because life in Mexico was very different. I started taking care of the house, cleaning, cooking, and taking care of my husband and my daughter. My life was being at home all the time and that made me feel bored and depressed at some point. The time was passing and I was getting used to being here again, and I gave birth to a girl and a boy, and the family got bigger.

Daughter
I started noticing that being an immigrant can be hard because many lose freedom coming here when they were looking for the opposite, running away from the violence or corruption in their countries. In fact, coming here means staying forever, getting up early to go work, and being alone because they know that they cannot go back and see their families or their kids. That's when I realized that my mom and my family had gone through the same things. Maybe they were wishing to visit their family or their country, but they were not able to because they were trapped in a cave and that cave is called America. I started hearing a lot of stories from all my friends and every time I was thinking of my family and what they also were going through. I know that there will always be a person in your family that will suffer and take the first step to come here and then the new generations will be different. I know I'm part of the new generation that doesn't go through many things that my family went through, and I know it is difficult, but not as difficult as my family's experience. Passing the time, I realize that many people can be going through the same experience, or it can be worse. For true freedom to exist for immigrants in this country, immigrants need to have the same opportunities as all other people to be with their families. Society has to see us as humans. We have the same rights and values. We are hardworking people looking out for the best for our families. We came here looking for freedom that we could not find in our countries. The freedom to be with our families should be part of that.

At the end, all the sadness and pain passed to motivation and inspiration to get far away in life. My biggest inspiration was my family, and I knew that I was an example to my sister and my brother and I needed to be strong and good for them. The part that was the best for me was going to visit my family on vacations and passing time with them, talking about all my experiences and the new things I learned, and my mom was the happiest woman in the world, seeing me coming back and forth. I was a connection that brought together my family because I was able to share pictures from my aunt with her sisters and brothers and bring gifts and letters, though I was coming back with five suitcases full of food and traditional candies. The most difficult part for me was saying goodbye again to my family and leaving, but what calmed me down was that I didn't have to wait so much time to come home again.

Losing and gaining moments, things, people, and freedom is something that I will always have to go through, but in this case for me, what will always keep me moving and stepping forward is my family—the love that comes from them—because for me it's a big power that they give me. They are the ones that always believe in me and that's what makes me believe in me, believe that I can be able to go through many challenges. I just have in my mind that my biggest dream is making my parents feel proud of me and not disappointing all the people that believe in me and were there for me in the good and bad moments. My family will always be waiting there for me with their arms open no matter what, and that's the place where I feel like myself, at peace, and where I feel free.

Alexandra Gonzalez was born in San Francisco and was raised in Toluca, Mexico before returning to the U.S. at age fourteen. In her spare time, she practices a traditional dance called Dance Azteca. She also likes to hang out with her friends and watch Disney movies. (*Dumbo* is her favorite.) Her goal is to make her parents proud and they are her greatest inspiration.

Changes to My Freedom

WALTER GARCIA OLIVA

One shiny and beautiful afternoon in Guatemala City, the phone rang in my grandma's house. My family was not fully paying attention to the phone, because we were all doing things. We were really busy. We were cleaning, cooking, washing clothes, and so much more. I was in the kitchen cooking some good pasta with tomato sauce and meat with my grandma. I was eleven years old. We were preparing the food for all of my family, more than a dozen kids and adults. We also were waiting for some of our family members to come home from work. My grandma and I thought that if we had the food ready, they would just come home and eat it. Then all the family would sit in the living room to watch some telenovelas.

Then my aunt Patty heard the phone and grabbed it. The phone was close to the kitchen, and my grandma and I saw the way my aunt's face changed from trying to listen, to a very surprised face. We also were surprised about her expression because we knew it was something bad. The call was from gangsters trying to get money from my poor family. My aunt was very surprised that we were getting a call like that—the only thing she thought to do was to slam the phone down. She called out to my grandmother and told her about the call, that there were gangsters threatening that, "We know where your family lives and that you have a lot of kids in your family that play around the house. If you don't give us money, we will go to your house and kill all the kids." The gangsters thought that because my mother had immigrated to the U.S., we had some money.

Before this call, we kids were free to play around in the neighborhood until 10:00 p.m. We were allowed to go to the store every time we wanted to. We were allowed to go to the park anytime we wanted to, and so much more. We felt like free kids who were allowed to go wherever we wanted to, to do anything, but when that phone rang in the house, all of our family was called in. After that call, we were not allowed to do anything that we used to do. We were always in the house. We were not allowed to go out. We stayed in the house for a whole week because we thought that the gangsters could be around the house and that they could take one of us and it would be easier to get money from my family. After that week, my grandma told us that every day, one of the adults in the house would take us to school so we could feel safer. We were really scared. Any noises that we heard around the house would make us think about what we could do if the gangsters got into the house. We also let the adults know about the noises so they could see what they were. We couldn't even tell our neighbors about the threats or call the police because we didn't trust anyone around us. In my country, we could not trust anyone because the police are corrupt and our neighbors could get money from the gangsters for giving information about us.

This call was the end of our freedom. This call limited me and my family's freedom. I was free in my house, but with this call, it felt like we were in a prison. I realized that I was not allowed to walk in my own country with freedom.

When my mother was told about the call, she got really scared, and she told me and my older brother that we had to immigrate to the U.S. because she couldn't stop thinking that we might be killed or kidnapped. She started to look for money everywhere. She took her savings from her job cleaning in San Francisco, she borrowed money from friends and people close to her, and she got money from my older sister, who lived with her, so she could bring us to the U.S. She made many calls so she could get a coyote, a person who crosses people to the U.S. A few days later, she got together $15,000 for the person that would bring us to the U.S.

My brother and I were so sad because we would be leaving our family, friends, and people we knew and loved in the past to go to another country, but we thought that we would be free and have better opportunities. The trip from Guatemala to the U.S. was something that definitely changed my life. It made me think more about what freedom is and what limited my freedom when I was in Guatemala. I left the home where I grew up, where I thought I was free, but instead it was not a safe place. It was a very restricted place for many people, and the ones who stayed there were just the survivors of corruption.

When the day came, my brother and I had to immigrate. We went in an old car and the man drove us away from my grandma's. I saw that moment like a plane rising from the floor to get into the sky and leave an empty place. When my brother and I were in the car, the man told us not to cry because it was like bad luck for the trip. But I couldn't stop crying. We passed through so many parts of my own country without enjoying them because I was hiding myself, like a rat that is being followed by a cat and will get eaten by it. A few days later, we were in Mexico, a place that I had never been before. The coyote also told us to not talk to anyone and to not get away from him. I was also hiding from people I didn't even know in a country that was not my country. I was taken to a house in Mexico and the *coyote* told my brother and I to not make any noises or go into the windows because people could see us. I felt like I was not being seen like a human being in a world of humans.

Five years later, I'm living with my mother in the United States in a city called San Francisco. I feel better that there are no gangsters calling on the phone or at the door, but I thought I was going to feel fully free to do whatever I wanted and that there would be nothing that could stop me. I came to this country and I realized that it's not true, that my freedom is also limited here. As an immigrant in this country and as a Latino boy in this country, my freedom is limited. My freedom to create my own path is limited because of my race and my income. If I have a good economic status, I can do whatever I want, but I was not born in a family that has a lot of money and because of money, my life is limited, and not because I have a love for money. It's because money is something you need to have to pay for the things that you need for society to think that you are part of it.

People need to know and understand the story and history of other people. When I came in 2015, I was able to get a lawyer to advocate and get asylum, but today there are thousands of people that are facing the same threats that I was and are being stopped at the border and returned to their countries in which they don't feel safe. These people can't feel free because they still have to hide from the gangsters.

Although I have limits on my freedom now, I still have the opportunities that not many people have back in my country. I still think of people and members of my family who should have this opportunity, but feel unsafe. Many brilliant brains in my country are also limited by government corruption and people who can't use their power in the right way.

By saying this, I don't mean to say that people are ignorant, but to tell them the reality of who we are and why we are here as they are here. They shouldn't judge by how the people look, but they should get to know them and who they are—to really learn about the people, not just judge on what they hear about them. Only then will everybody have the freedom to be who they are.

Walter Garcia Oliva was born in Guatemala City, and he has lived in San Francisco since 2014. He is eighteen years old. He likes to play basketball and go to church. Someday he would like to be a lawyer and help support his family.

What Happened to Pancho

MIGUEL PASTREICH

In the calm of a forest on a sunny summer's day, the birds chirp, the leaves fall, and a shout comes from a big guy with an even bigger hoodie.

"Ay, Pancho. Hit a kick flip!"

Pancho, a scrappy-looking dude with beat-up dunks, some baggy jeans with a shoelace belt, and a white tee, nods as he pops his tail. With the flick of his foot, the board starts to leave the ground. The board spins fiercely, and his back foot is positioned just right to catch it on the bolts. The wheels hit the ground and as he starts to roll away slowly, he is sent into the air again, this time without his board.

"Ahhhh," Pancho exhales as he looks down at his roadrash.

"He needs some milk!" Cheap J laughs out from across the spot.

Pancho gets up and throws his board down again. He goes for the ledge this time. He pops up, and as he locks into a back crook, he hears a yell.

"Hey, get out!" A security guard comes yelling from the woods just over the kicker covered in graffiti.

"Let's dip," Danny yells as he scraps for his things. The security guard grabs Cheap J's board before he can get away.

"Ay, give it back!" Cheap J yells.

"You guys are coming with me . . ." But before the security guard can finish his sentence, Danny shoves him over a crouching Pancho. The security guard tumbles, putting rips in his jacket as he falls on gravel.

"Ouch," he says.

As he regains his balance, Pancho snatches the board back and the crew bolts through the forest. A couple of fence hops later, they pull up to the skate park.

"Damn, that security guard was trifling."

"Yeah, but you're so slow, he caught you," Danny laughs.

"Pancho, why you smiling so much?" Pancho flashes an even bigger grin as he takes a security radio out of his bag.

"Noooooo, you didn't."

"Ay, lemme see that, I got something to say." Cheap J takes the radio. "Hey, we got an issue in the woods."

A voice comes through: "What's the situation, over."

"We got a cow running around."

"What does the cow look like, over."

"Your momma," Cheap J laughs.

"You dumb as hell, bruh," Danny joins in.

Pancho recalls this memory as he is sitting on the heated seat of a fancy Japanese toilet tucked in the back of a cash-only Vietnamese cafe on Church Street. It is part of an app. As he sits, he starts to lose grip on where he ends and the seat begins. He starts to lose grip on where his city went and this hipster trap came from. The seat, like the security guard, is there to maintain the idea of a society: comforts that make people not have to think about the underlying issues waiting under them. As the skater finishes, he has an option, the technological advancement of the Japanese bidet or the paper that has got him out of messy situations time and time again. He knows what he is going to do. He reaches for the paper because, like with society, he won't let it spray its ideals up his butt. He makes his choice even though it would have been easier to just sit back and let the toilet do its function. He is free.

As he finishes, he walks past the barista and a sea of people drinking lattes, typing away on their MacBooks. He steps outside, takes a deep breath, throws down his board, and skates across the street.

SHPLAT! Pancho makes it across the street. However, he is on the ground. A crowd gathers around him, filming on their phones. "He needs some milk." An ambulance rolls by twenty minutes later, but by this time, it is too late.

"Why didn't any of you call 911?" the paramedics say as they walk out.

The crowd just looks at each other, then disperses.

The next place Pancho is seen is in a picture above some candles at the spot in the forest, or what used to be. They sit on a sidewalk, where the ledge Pancho used to like is. Danny and Cheap J sit there in silence. They drink there in silence. They pour their drinks out for Pancho in silence. The two remaining friends remember that sad night when they heard about what happened to Pancho.

Danny looks at Cheap J and says, "I still can't believe Pancho's gone."

"Out of nowhere too, just 'cause of a stupid Uber driver too."

"I hate that they didn't even get in trouble either, they just bought their way out."

The two look at the altar, looking up for Pancho and to keep the water in their eyes. They can't hold the water in as they look at what was their old spot, where they had made so many memories. It had been torn down and made into an expensive dispensary with thousand-dollar bathrooms.

"Pancho would have hated this," Danny says as he stares at the building.

"Yeah, messed up how this happens."

"This one's for you Pancho," Danny points his finger in the air as he and Cheap J pour their drinks out on the ground. They aren't looking around as they reminisce about their times with Pancho. A stampede of people come marching, looking for a bathroom, their faces too deep in their smartphones to see anything in front of them. Danny and Cheap J try to get out of the way, but they trip on a scooter parked in the middle of the sidewalk. They try to get up, but it is too late. The sheeple are now over them, tramping them. And as the two are on the ground, gasping for breath as they are suffocating in a sea of people, they see a tag on the bottom of a pipe. It was Pancho's, and as the two friends take their last breaths, they look at each other and remember the way it used to be, and die wondering how it would have been if Pancho was there.

In a room with glass windows on the top of a skyscraper, a man sits in his chair, sipping on Boba Guys and eating poke. He laughs as he watches the whole scene unfold on a screen broadcasting the footage from a camera in the dispensary. He recalls how he made his money coding, made the bathroom app, how he sent the Uber, how he programmed the sheeple to walk on this fateful day. He puts on a ripped-up, faded, old black jacket with a patch on it and chuckles to himself, "Got you out this time, punks."

Pancho's altar gets taken down from the sidewalk the very next day; the city can't have it block the scooter parking for all the taxpayers spending at the dispensary. The tags Pancho threw up around are slowly disappearing as the city keeps building higher and higher buildings and paving over the places he had once been. As the rest of the people who Pancho knew are pushed out into different places, across bridges, across water, the vibe that Pancho carried with him gets passed on to them. They fight back against the scooters, they fight back against the apps, and they fight to take back the city Pancho knew. They are fighting every day, against millionaires, billionaires, tech startups, bad vibes, and all the other forces of gentrification. Each day is a steep battle, but the people keep fighting because for them, Pancho's still here.

Miguel Pastreich was born in San Francisco and is eighteen years old. He comes from a multiracial family. His favorite activity is surfing and when he is not in the water, he loves to get cheap eats around the city. He is hoping to find a career where he can help people or the environment. Or open up a surf school in Cuba. Who knows.

Sin vida no puedes hacer limonada

JOSUE US COOL

It started as a normal day like all the others. I woke up to my alarm at 7:00 a.m. and to my mom folding laundry that was fresh out of the machine. I walked to the living room to see my dad leave for work as I entered the steamy, hot shower and got ready for school. When I was ready to go, my mom was there, waiting for me like she always was, to take me to my school. The day played out like it usually did, with me walking down the old stairs and my friend waiting for me and my mom at the front door, in our black-and-white school uniforms. It would take us twenty minutes, but I always hated getting on the crowded bus with all the loud people. I recall showing up and going to all my classes, waiting for the bell to ring so I could go play soccer with my best friend at lunch. I remember him and I would always play soccer no matter what because that was what we enjoyed playing.

I was introduced to my best friend when we were just little kids.
Our moms would always hang out at the small park next to us that had wood benches and a crappy playground.
I would always just run around the park and we would play tag like most little kids would.
I would always go hang out with him at his house because we were next-door neighbors, so whenever we got the chance, we would always be having fun, even if some days we were starving and did not get the opportunity to eat.
And even if we were struggling and felt alone, we would always support each other.

Eventually that support transformed our relationship into us becoming very close friends.
It felt like he was the brother I had always asked for, who would always be there for me.
Sadly he wouldn't be able to be there for me like I had hoped.

I remember the day when we looked at each other, our eyes locked, warned without words, and we both intuitively knew. The moment our hearts raced, with hands shaking of nervousness, while we ran down the same blocks we were raised on, running in fear with the Coke and food shaking in the black plastic bags we were holding. I still think back to the day they gunned down my friend and took his innocent life away. I still remember his body falling to the ground while his clothes turned red from the bullets. The image of his lifeless body, laying there in pain and in shock of what just happened, will forever be imprinted in my brain. The way the loud sound of the bullets hid my cry for help as the cop towered over me and finally let me go. I ran to his side and held him in my arms for the last time on that cold, cloudy day. I sat there with him in my arms while I shook his hand to see if he was alive, but I got no response. I laid down his soft hands as I just stayed there in silence, trying to hold back my tears, but I couldn't, because I lost a friend like keys in a sofa.

I try for this freedom so I can live free
I don't want this for my brothers
I didn't want it for me
My heart is frozen like Elsa
I'm crying glass tears, got me thinking why these cops can pull a gun without thinking
I seek this out for everyone who lost a loved one
2019, I hate you murder so many, it's disgraceful
Took my homie back in April
Then by June you got another one in there for life
Never got to see me grow up, he never got to live his life
This freedom, it's important to me, all this anger and fear
Got me thinking back seven years, killed my best friend
Got me in tears, they take so much in the blink of an eye, I think to myself why

I sit there in silence when they ask me a question
But I give no answer because silence isn't empty
It's full of painful answers
I want to make my freedom my own so it can last forever

I want to build a community for all
I want it to rise and prosper
Not fail and fall
I want to take a stand to help anyone in need
I want to be a light of hope so they know they're not alone and can cope
I find it hard to escape this sad reality
I just want to run and jump into my mind like a frog jumping into a pond
I don't want my family to suffer
I feel like I don't have freedom, it's like a bird in a cage
They only let me out when they want to, not when I want to feel free
This freedom I want will come from the path I choose to take
This life I live took a toll on my family
I feel like a piece of glue trying my best to cover up all the bad
To give them the strength they once had

Everything happens in the moment
Sometimes it goes fast
Sometimes it goes slow
I don't know what I should do
But my brain says go, go, go
It's hard to cover up the truth from my brothers and my mother
But I do it anyway so I never have to come home again to my mother crying a lake
As my little brother trembles and shakes
I do it for them
I do it for me
I hate to see them like that, so I carry the weight of their pain and fear all on my shoulders
Sometimes it feels like I'm carrying a big rock that my big brother used to carry
Now I know his pain because his back can no longer maintain

I see it in slow motion, frame by frame
Sometimes I feel like I'm in a movie because some of the stuff I see is kinda
insane
I need and want this freedom the same way I need to breathe
I feel like I'm at the bottom of the ocean, swimming up and up
But every time I almost get there, I get sucked back down
I keep fighting because I don't want to drown

This world isn't fair. Sometimes I stare at the stars and try to imagine how different my life would be if it was how I wanted it to be and feel. Now, I think about the future and how I can make it feel and be different. I want to improve my community and help it blossom into an environment where everyone is safe and happy. I want everyone who walks past the community to feel the way I wanted to feel seven years ago. The way I wanted to feel was safe and welcomed, not ashamed that I lived in a bummy area unlike everyone else. I wanted it to make me feel happy when I walked. I didn't like where I was living and I want to like where I live currently. The feeling I wanted to feel was everything it wasn't. I was like a bird in the same cage I was born in, and I wanted to feel free, but the only time I felt that was when I was at school. Even then, I still felt like I was in a cage. The community I see is a community of different walks of life all coming together as one and being united. I want to make it look beautiful, just like the way my elementary school changed for the better. I use my elementary school as an example because it used to be a bummy place with only Latinos and other people of color attending the school. Now the school has grown, even my teacher has kids who go there today, and I can see the difference.

I want to make a mural somewhere in my area and have everyone included, even the elementary school kids could help just like how they are involved with the other activities at the school. I would want the mural to be a representation of the community and the people who live there. The community I want would make the kids not be afraid to play outside. It would feel welcoming, like you're entering a second home. It would look like all walks of life having fun and talking peacefully. I picture it to be safe and I hope I can create a community where kids are not ashamed to say they live or were raised in the Mission. This mural would look like people dancing and singing under the starry night sky, while people are displayed eating tacos and burritos, with kids playing soccer. I would also include the elderly people and place them in the back to represent them watching as the community flourishes into something that would make them proud. In the middle of it all would be a mother and her son, looking at everyone and admiring the community. The son would be painted as a shadow to represent my friend with his mom because I know she misses him just as much as I do.

This experience has shown me that life is harsh, and it has taught me that sometimes being alone is all the comfort I need. Bad things do happen every day and life moves so fast, sometimes I hardly have a chance to act. It has taught me how to be happy, even when life gets me down, and I have matured through these experiences. I know I have seen many things I shouldn't have. I have accepted that most people will never understand me; they judge me for who I am and my past. They can never grasp what I had to do just to live a decent life, while they live in big houses with a good family. The way I deal with anything bad with my life is through music because sometimes that is all I have. I take advantage of the escape, the freedom it lends me, and make it into something to comfort me when I'm alone. The way I use music is by making guitar riffs or songs about how I feel and all the things I wanted to say, but couldn't. I use a pen and paper to make music and write songs. I have to credit my big brother for inspiring me to play guitar and learn just like he did. The music liberates me from the boulder that has now been lifted off my shoulders.

Josue Us Cool was born in the Mission District of San Francisco. He is seventeen years old. He is a part of a family with all boys, living with three brothers as the second oldest of four. During his spare time, Josue loves to make music. It allows him freedom of expression and makes him feel proud.

“I feel like I’m at the bottom of the ocean, swimming up and up But every time I almost get there, I get sucked back down I keep fighting because I don’t want to drown”

Josue Us Cool

Running for Something

▮ TYREK LAURENT

Before a race, I start to analyze what I need to do to prep my body as far as food, water, and stretches. I also start giving myself a pep talk to motivate myself.

That day was my first time running the 400m. I already had so much experience in the 100m and 200m, which I enjoy and love. I remember that day well. It was really hot, but a little breezy. I noticed that the track was blue. I'd run there before, but it always stands out to me because I'm used to running on red tracks. They told me the day before the track meet I was going to be running it. Once they told me it was a lap around, I got nervous because I wasn't sure if I had enough stamina and I didn't want to slow down in the middle of my race. What people don't understand is a lap around is easy when you jog, but the 400m is a very strategic event. You have to know when to give it your all and pace yourself. I was so nervous, but I knew I couldn't back out now. Once I find out the other athlete's times, that's when the doubts start coming in. I start getting butterflies in my stomach, my heart starts beating fast, I overthink and expect the worst. It's like a constant battle in my head, while I'm beginning a battle outside of my head.

When I hear these voices, it isn't just my voice, it's multiple people. I feel restricted by the lack of support from my peers and the people I care about. Nobody can hurt me more than the people I care about. In my early years, I noticed when coaches, adults, or even people my age would be disappointed in me when I told them that I didn't play basketball or football. They felt like because of the color of my skin, that I automatically was programmed to play those sports, and if I didn't then I was wasting my talent and I was running for nothing.

It was hard for me to hear that at such a young age because people don't understand that their words weren't just in that moment, but would constantly repeat in my head and would make it tough to enjoy the sport I love and make me self-conscious for not playing those sports people expect me to.

Freedom is being comfortable in your own skin no matter what. It also means to be able to go places without having worries or people telling you what to do. This reminds me of a time when I was in a store and the security guard kept watching me in every aisle I went to. I felt singled out because there were other people in the store that he could've been watching, but he chose to watch me. Just like with track, he didn't know who I was, but just by looking at the color of my skin, he already had his idea of who I was. He isn't the only one who has so many expectations of who I should be and what I should be doing.

I grew up in Bayview-Hunters Point, AKA the ghetto. You always hear about who got shot, who got robbed, who doesn't like each other, or are, quote, unquote, "beefing with each other." In the same breath, you see those situations with your own two eyes at a young age and wonder, *Am I next?* There's not a week that goes by where I don't see the police or even at a glance see an ambulance. I see all these situations happening to people who look like me and wonder, *Am I next?* I see a lot of people who are in gangs or hang out outside and sometimes make wrong decisions.

There have been times people would tell me I'm not from where I'm from because of how I carry myself. The truth is that my mom raised me differently. She didn't want me to make the same mistakes others around me made. Some people don't believe that I'm from where I'm from. It sucks that the people that mainly don't believe it are people of color like myself. *How can I be myself if the people that look like me won't accept me for being me? What if that's not who I want to be, but in their eyes, that's who I'm supposed to be?*

I'm not ashamed of where I'm from—I love where I come from. I could've been like a lot of people from my neighborhood, but what is that doing for my neighborhood? I know what it's like to witness shootings at a young age and be confused at that age. I know what it's like to not have a father figure in my life and wonder, *Does anyone care about my life?* I know what it's like spending time with my family back then, wishing I could go back again. A lot of my family don't get along with one another, but why can't we all just love each other? I know the feeling of bottling everything inside and wondering what's going on inside, but not being able to share nothing inside, because in their eyes, there's something wrong inside. Just because you know where I'm from doesn't mean you know who I am. Just because I don't share all of my problems doesn't mean I don't have any problems.

All of these assumptions, expectations, and doubts are things I can't forget about, but starting now, I have more positive things to think about. All the voices in my head gave me a hard time to go to bed. Everything they all said, will stick with me to the day I'm dead, but my time is coming and they're going to wish they regretted what they said.

"You're not from there," they say. Trust me, once I accomplish my goals I'll be back there.

"You're fast for no reason," they say. Well, that's why I train every track season.

"You're wasting your time," they say. But over time, you're going to wish to take back that time.

"You're not an athlete really," they say. But I'm doing very well at my track meets.

"Track isn't even a sport," they say. You could say whatever you want because I've heard it all before. But just like in court, all I need is the right support. One is innocent until proven guilty, and anything is possible until proven otherwise.

The gun went off and I got off to a good start. I took the lead and in my head, I thought I had this in the bag. Once I hit that last curve, someone slowly started passing me and I placed second. I was exhausted. My coaches came up to me and told me how proud they were of me and how good I did for my first time running this event. Although in my head, I predicted I would place first, it didn't matter at that moment because they gave me confidence in myself and made me feel like I could do this. Ever since, I've been killing the 400m.

There were so many times I felt self conscious about my passion for track and field, but I won't give up running because running is and will always be a part of me. There's not one person in this world who could ever make me stop running for something.

Tyrek Laurent was born in San Francisco and lives in Hunters Point. He is not the baby of his family, but is the youngest of three siblings. He loves his family and wants to be a good role model for his young cousins. He has loved track and field since third grade and is now a complete boss at the 400 meter. He loves eating his mom's cooking, especially her mac and cheese and her jambalaya. He wants to run at a four-year college, but also has his eyes set on the Olympics, theater, and learning to become a veterinarian.

Safe Haven No More

ABE FELDMAN

"Eleven dead, six wounded in massacre at Squirrel Hill synagogue" (*Pittsburgh Post-Gazette,* October 27, 2018). "11 Killed in Synagogue Massacre; Suspect Charged With 29 Counts" (*New York Times,* October 27, 2018). "Stabbings, shootings, assaults weigh on U.S. Jewish youth" (*ABC 7*).

Headlines like this make me dread going to my synagogue—the place where I met friends who turned into family, where I met my community, which supports me no matter what, and where I have had so many crucial life experiences, Jewish and non-Jewish alike. These attacks sparked a kind of fear that I haven't felt before.

Growing up in Congregation Sherith Israel, a synagogue that focuses on social action and social justice, I have learned a lot about Jewish history through the lens of survival—mostly about the hatred toward Jewish people all over the world. The emotional trauma of this event was like a death in my family because Jews are one big family. We feel the ripples of attacks, again and again, attack after attack, a scab being ripped open every minute of every day, day after day.

Until the Pittsburgh massacre, my synagogue was a place of refuge, a place where I didn't have to worry about someone destroying lives and communities, and murdering people. But I have lost my refuge. I don't feel safe anywhere. Being a student in school, especially a Jewish student, any place I go can become the next headline. This puts me in a state of perpetual hyper-awareness. I always sit in a corner in the class, sit, so I can face the doorway, and even as I walk into the room, I think of the best way to run. This sense of fear has been instilled in me through years of hearing news of school shootings, hearing all the anti-semitic, racist propaganda, hearing, "Jews will not replace us!" and hearing about Pittsburgh.

I must be able to run because what has happened to Jews throughout history has made us run, time after time, for our lives. Anti-semitism has a long and ugly history. From slavery in Egypt to the Babylonians, the Inquisition, the Pogroms, and the Holocaust, Jews have faced persecution. We have been running our whole lives—our whole existence, running from Pharaoh and Fuhrer.

The day after the Tree of Life shooting, as I walked into my synagogue before Sunday school, I saw policemen stationed in front of the building. Even before I stepped inside, I felt an insurmountable mix of worry, anger, and unknowingness of the future.

As I entered the library, where I had been a million times before, a place that felt like home, I knew nothing would ever be the same. When the other teachers and student teachers arrived, I saw that they had been crying. They had been worried about teaching their students. People were hugging each other. Some were crying more and more. Others seemed to be soulless shells of the people they used to be. Seeing my friends, who I've known for most of my life, break down, helped me realize my own feeling of despair.

Walking into that classroom, a tidal wave of trauma swept over me—not only fear of hate or anti-semitism, but the anxiety of showing up in a class of twelve-and thirteen-year-olds who were having the same experience. I put on a stone mask that hid my emotions, which granted me the ability to become detached from my fears. I could help my students and friends without having the fear wash over me.

"What happened in Pittsburgh?" one student asked.

"Nazis attacked," replied another.

"No, it was an anti-semitic attack." The students' eyes were bloodshot, puffy, and their voices were quivering.

"We will talk about what happened after we do check-ins," the teacher said. While the students fell silent, the looming fear persisted. This was a crash course in real life, the realization that, in fact, this world is not a place where everything is sunshine and rainbows. It is a world where horrific things happen, and people get hurt and die, simply because they are Jewish.

That day was the most difficult day for me to teach. Most of these children were hearing the news for the first time. I could see the earth-shattering despair in their eyes.

I felt the same as they did.

I had been teaching these kids for a few months. I had come to bond with them, so seeing them with rivulets of tears streaming down their faces was like seeing myself at the moment I heard the news. We ran out of tissues that day. And while time has passed and people have begun to heal from the trauma, my students, friends, and I couldn't stop worrying, *Will this happen here? What happens next, now that this has happened?*

Since I started school, I've been one of the few Jewish students, and I have been the target of anti-semitic jibes, *Do you pick pennies off the ground? Do you have a tail? Does anyone smell gas?* My classmates may have thought this was teasing, but these unfunny jokes run much deeper.

Most of my classmates don't know much about Judaism. For instance, some people ask me if I speak Jewish. I think they are afraid to question me about being Jewish or about Judaism because they wouldn't want to come off as ignorant and rude. They may want to know more, but don't know how to phrase what they want to understand. I'm not offended if people ask questions, as long as it's not a question like, "Do you pick pennies off the ground?" That question has long been rooted in a negative stereotype.

Being on my school's Dragon Boat Team—a twenty person team that, paddling in sync, races at Lake Merced against other high school teams—is one place where I feel safe. Safe from someone shooting at me, safe from people making anti-semitic jokes, safe among classmates who trust each other, no matter what—this is the place where I can feel the tranquility that I lost after Pittsburgh. On the water, I can be free from all of the atrocities that face me on land, so I can focus on my own well-being.

My home, my family, is my sanctuary. They support me no matter what I do or say, and they believe in me as no one else does.

My home is the place where I can find peace in this chaotic world.

I hate this feeling of being constantly overwhelmed by fear. It drags me down. It is all I think about. It empties me emotionally. A high school senior shouldn't be experiencing these feelings. I should be focused on college, the next test, finding a date for prom, and finishing my senior year. I should not be worried about whether someone is going to shoot me at my school or my synagogue.

While I wish it were otherwise, I can't see a way out.

Abe Feldman was born in San Francisco and is seventeen years old. He lives with his parents and twin. He loves to paddle for the Mission High Dragon Boat team. His favorite food is up to his family and where they want to eat. He wants to be a nurse at a major, big-city hospital. He spends his time either at his synagogue or paddling on Lake Merced.

Our America was Never Great

▌LAJAIYAH WATKINS

Being black, beat me red and blue.
Love wasn't an option—they'd take it away from you.
Wasn't allowed to read; we barely got to eat.
Yes, I am a slave working on my feet.
Dirt on my hands, blood on my feet,
sleeping on the floor with no blankets or sheets.
I worked my butt, day and night.
I'm tired of this! It's time to fight.

Don't touch me! Don't touch me! I ran and screamed.
He hit me with the switch from my back to my feet.
"Look at me, girl," he said, but I turned my head.
Slashes on my butt, I couldn't even sit.
That white cracker pulled my daughter by her hair,
forced her down and you know where.
I looked at my daughter, those tears in her eyes.
She didn't even get time to say goodbye.
She ran fast.
Her feet burning on the hot Southern soil—
a second branding.

Like Harriet Tubman said, "If you hear the dogs, keep going.
If you see the torches in the woods, keep going.
Don't ever stop.
If you want a taste of freedom, keep going."

Cruising down West Monroe Street in his black Chevy,
bumpin' "Nuthin' but a 'G' Thang."
The windows down, giving him some air that gratifies his lungs.
Street lights as bright as the sun—as bright as his future.

The siren noise pierces through his ears like an EKG machine—flat lining.
Red and blue flashing lights,
the scared boy, alone.
Sweating, his black skin sticks to the black leather of his new car.

Keep your hands where they can see them.
Don't make any sudden movements, black man.
Don't reach in your pocket.

(shoot now, no, I mean, kill now and ask questions later.)

Sixteen shots in the darkness . . . another man erased.

"Say their names . . . it's important to say their names."
Oscar Grant . . .
Mike Brown . . .
Sandra Bland . . .
Fred Hampton.

We pledge allegiance to the red, white, and blue,
"The land of the free and the home of the brave."
This country represents freedom, but to whom?

Are we really free?

Lajaiyah Watkins is a young, black girl, born and raised in San Francisco. She developed her passion for writing at the age of thirteen. She is seventeen years old now with the dream of becoming a lawyer and is interested in publishing her own book one day.

Stealing Second

MIKAELE MATEO

I would like to feel comfortable moving around in my own skin. Being able to walk into stores without being followed. Being able to ask for help without fear that I will be looked at like a criminal and being able to walk in neighborhoods without judgmental eyes beaming upon me. I should not be judged off the color of my skin; the color of my skin, added with the type of clothing I wear, doesn't classify me as a threat to society. I love baseball, a predominantly white sport. I play the sport with pride in my own culture, wearing a traditional-looking Polynesian sleeve for games along with a necklace my dad has gotten me from Tonga. I'm proud to be Tongan. Though I am seen as less by some, I stand with pride, breaking the stereotypes of what you're "supposed" to be as a man of color in this society. It's saddening. For example, my coach always tells me and my teammates (that are all people of color) that we have got to stay focused in school and break the stereotypes that we aren't intelligent and can't succeed academically.

Playing baseball in high school was a way different experience than what I went through from fifth to eighth grade. In middle school, I was the dark kid on the team, surrounded by white kids and a white coach. At a young age, I didn't think too much really about how it was affecting my mindset. I didn't know what diversity looked like until I came to Mission and joined the baseball team, which was full of different types of people: African Americans, Hondurans, Latinos, and more. Being on a baseball team with this much diversity and full of guys that have gone through similar things as me, I formed a bond with these guys on my team who I treat like brothers.

I remember since sophomore year that feeling of freedom I have felt playing baseball. With the varsity baseball team, towards the end of the year, I went to AT&T Park, which is home to the S.F. Giants. Clear skies and the sun beaming on us, it was hot. The dirt was a dark orange color. Everything was neat. The field was well trimmed, and the dugout was spacious. With families and friends in the stands and brothers by my side, I felt free from all distress. Although I didn't get to play on the field and was a warm-up catcher on the sidelines at the time, I felt as if I was a part of something bigger. Thoughts of becoming a professional baseball player filled my head as I was overwhelmed with excitement. The thought alone of being able to play on the same field as professional athletes made me feel successful.

This was a powerful moment for me. The feeling of success was rare in my life because of the things I have gone through. The skin I wear today before you and the constant judging and conclusions made due to my skin color have changed my view on myself. It takes a toll on a kid, makes them feel unwanted in this society, but in that moment at AT&T, I was proud of myself and what I have gone through to get there. Days of grinding it out by myself at the park across the street. Just working to one day become something big. Big enough to influence others to push past the stereotypes and be free in this world.

Mikaele Mateo, born in Tonga, is seventeen years old. He likes to listen to rap, hip hop, and lo-fi music, and loves baseball. He dreams of being able to teleport because busing around gets tiring. College seems nice at the moment for him.

The Acreage of La Ruta

■ STEPHANIE AMEZCUA

The summer season was about to be over, it was time to go back home. Being back in the airplane, heading to San Francisco, I couldn't believe two months had already passed. Sounds of chattering families, and hearing the flight attendant ladies tell everybody to put their luggage up, I decided the best thing to do was to put my earphones on and relax. This was going to be a five-hour flight, and I should probably catch up on my sleep. I was about to close my eyes until I heard the song "El Potro de Sinaloa" by Chuy y Mauricio playing. "Otra tumba en San Ignacio" was the line that always got to me. It is talking about my own town in Mexico.

San Ignacio
The tiny town that contains
Three thousand residents, not 883,305
Where no one is categorized as a stranger
Rather, everybody knows each other
The Padilla family, Los Lujanes, and Los Manjarrez
Where you most probably won't see numerous skyscrapers
Instead you will see the beauty of nature
The grown mountains
The wild jungle
The flowy river
The famous cascada

All converging in the tiny town San Ignacio
Where the circle sun will blast your face and force you to sweat
Sunscreen becomes one of your supplies
Throughout the streets, motorcycles will be driving on a bumpy, rocky floor
The plaza where the gazebo is is the main attraction
La mesa that looks like the Rio de Janeiro Christ statue
La tienda verde where people buy their food
From beginning to end, hundreds of humble houses made out of red bricks will tag along on your ride
Little circles of families hanging outside their residence
Seeing who crosses the street, entertained by the cars passing by
It all started with five families
My mom's family being one of the first
Now we have abundant growing families living in this acreage
Traveling to the place where my mom was born
It opened my eyes
How I can breathe the natural air
Hear the little insects buzzing
Crickets chirping
Roosters cock-a-doodle-do-ing
Not trapped with school
Nor the crowded busses
Nor the weight of numerous responsibilities on my shoulders
It's a whole new place I can call home

I remember hearing this song "El Potro de Sinaloa" en La Ruta, a yearly event that my humble town does to reunite everybody from the town. It all started with my crazy uncle and his group of friends trying to do something fun. One of his friends had an idea of going to a dangerous route with their boogies and motorcycles, to pass through all the villages and ranches nearby. At the end, their clothes were full of mud due to the roads being muddy, so slippery that you could fall down. Sometimes the road is narrow, and one of the parts is a cliff. After some time, my uncle and his friends decided to do it again, but this time inviting more people to join in, and that is how the so-called La Ruta started.

La Ruta

This year was my first time joining in
The color-red jersey was the theme
I bought my shirt for 200 pesos
Wearing the shirt made me feel part of the community
Everybody reunited in the plazuela, that was the starting place
When I got there, I saw the plazuela covered with people wearing the same red jerseys I was wearing
It looked like a field of roses packed in one place
The hot sun accompanied us
People giggling with their friends
Music blasting from cars
Engines revving
The smell of gasoline hit your nose immediately
When the route started, the road was
Bumpy, muddy
Slippery
But surrounded with amazing views, entering a forest secret passage
I was already getting tired, sitting on a pole behind the front seats
Grabbing the handlebar to not fall down
The cars moving faster each time a minute passed
Meanwhile my uncle's boogie went faster, my cousin and I swaying from side to side
Wind in my hair, mud flying to my face, I remember that I needed to remove the mud out of my face every two minutes
The feeling of adrenaline kicked in me
Seeing the landscape in another perspective
I realized this was a taste of true freedom

Coming back to the United States, I realized how going to Mexico for me is not easy. It takes a whole year to make it possible. My parents are not rich, so that means I needed to save up money, and each penny that I earned counted. The total amount of money I needed was one thousand dollars for the ticket, the extra money to spend over there, and money in case of an emergency. This meant that on each day I did my chores at home, even my mom's chores, to the extent of going to my mom's job on Saturdays to get the extra amount of money I needed. I noticed how my hands started to look like my mom's hands. My hands became more chapped and with blisters. I realized you can't get what you want, you need to work for it.

Slowly but surely, I started to reach the goal of one thousand dollars. The hardest part was not giving up and staying away from the temptation to spend it all at once. The thing that kept me going was knowing the feeling of liberty traveling to places. Being in Mexico has a totally different atmosphere than I'm used to. The adventures I would have over there, it was all worth it. Meanwhile this all ended soon and I came back to my city lifestyle.

San Francisco

The city that contains
883,305 residents, not three thousand
Where nobody knows each other, except the people you hang out with
Where you won't see cows walking, but instead you will see Google buses
The companies, the brands, scooters, electric bicycles all around taking space
Where the daytime seems to end quickly
Where your job and school are the daily destinations
How the cloudy clouds will not leave you alone
And you wear that comfy warm jacket
How in the Mission, you will see Latinos
In Hunters Point, you will see Black folks
In Chinatown, you will see Asians
In the Presidio, you will see the White folks
Surrounded by the Pacific Ocean that produces a windy climate
Our famous Golden Gate Bridge that was made by people dying
Crowded public busses
People walking their dogs
People sleeping in the streets, asking for change
People entertained by their phones
But on the top of Twin Peaks, you can notice the beautiful, colorful houses or buildings
Constructors House Cleaners Business Men Gardeners Teachers
All hard workers trying to survive
My community

The place where I met my true friends, where we hang out and talk about our problems
Realizing that we are not the only ones facing real life
In the hospital Saint Lucas, where I was born

I come from immigrant parents. They arrived here from Mexico when they were my age, walking through the deadly desert, hiding from the immigration officers, trusting an unknown coyote. I remember when my mom told me how she was this close to getting caught. She hid behind a bush. Right next to her, there was a small river. She told me that when she looked at the reflection of the water, she noticed the face of her cousin, who had died a few years ago. She believed the reason why she wasn't caught was because her cousin was protecting her from heaven.

When I was little, I remember how hard it was for my parents to travel since they came here illegally. They still didn't even have residency status, and the authorities told them if they wanted residency they couldn't go back to their country for ten years and needed to pay a big amount of money. This definitely took a toll on my mom's life since her whole family was in Mexico, even one of her kids. But it was necessary for her to go for her son. She knew if she stayed in the town, she wouldn't be able to pay and provide a living for her son. She wanted the American Dream, and also to pay for her family, especially since my grandparents needed money for their medications. So this resulted in my mom not seeing her family for ten years. This situation is only one out of millions of immigrants who don't have a choice except to come here and make a living.

Many people from different countries go to America knowing that they probably won't be able to see their family again. They do this because they want to create opportunities for their family and for themselves, to escape from the violence in their countries, to send money to their families, and many more reasons. This world is full of walls and borders. Once you are here, laws restrict you depending on what documents you have. If you don't have Social Security or a green card, you can't travel back to your own country or can't fly to nice locations such as Hawaii, Europe, or Brazil. In 2020, the Real ID took action. This was made with the purpose to not allow immigrants to fly out or come back.

Appreciate Your Freedom

The Constitution promises you freedom
But people are in chained restraints
Not able to break free
Meanwhile, Earth is covered with domestic narrow walls
Not setting one free
Keeping you in one place
Where laws punish you, stealing bits of your human rights
Where money and true liberty don't mix
Money can buy you luxuries, but not the feeling of being free
Sadly, life is full of constraints
I look back
And realize La Ruta is my metaphor for freedom
It is a bumpy road full of
Love
Laughter
Inner peace
The feeling of movement
Today is a new day
To start fighting
The system
The laws
The money
To no longer be oppressed
And travel to your own acreage of La Ruta

Stephanie Amezcua, a Chicana, was born in San Francisco. She is eighteen years old, and both of her parents emigrated to the United States from Mexico. She loves to travel and learn about new cultures. Her favorite thing to do is hike and be with nature. Her plan is to attend a four-year university and get a career relating to the health field. Her dream is to live a peaceful life. She would like to travel to Argentina and Cuba.

Freedom in Disguise

ANDRE VILLARINO

Dre and his friends attended the neighborhood middle school for almost two years. It was the last semester of the seventh grade and they all had a tight bond with each other, but they hated school. But they somehow managed to always pass all their classes, then cut class whenever they could.

Jimmy was Dre's best friend since the first day of middle school. He was always teased about being chubby, but he didn't care at all. He had the most clothes and cash out of the group, let alone the entire school. But Jimmy wasn't wealthy. He had what we called "Big Boy Hustle."

Otis was the brute. He was pretty muscular for his age and he was always fighting inside and outside of school. In fact, he was always winning fights inside and outside of school.

Otis was usually teased for wearing out-of-style clothes. He lived in a really poor neighborhood and had hard situations at home, especially financially. But it never bothered him because he simply never really got teased. The few people that had enough guts to say something directly to him got beat up.

Corey was the fastest kid in the group. He was always fighting like Otis, but Corey was friendlier, a lot friendlier. His family was also made fun of because he lived with his grandma. But Corey never budged because he loved his grandma too much to care about what others thought.

Paul was the only white friend in the group and one of the few white kids in the school. But Paul was fun to be around. He was always laughing and pointing out hilarious things we never noticed. Paul played basketball and skated. He lived with his mom, but nobody cared about it.

Then there was Dre. He was the basketball star of the school. He was very funny and fun to be around, but had a short temper at the time. Him and

Jimmy were Filipino. Otis and Corey were black. Paul was white. You could say it was a very diverse group of friends.

There was an infamous corner store across the street from school. It stood there for generations. Most of the students' parents went there in junior high to escape school. Since school started at nine o'clock, every day all the students would buy from there in the morning, including Dre and his crew. But everyone also stole from there, including Dre and his crew. There was no thought in stealing from the store, it was just a normal practice that continued on for years. The store owner would always scold kids to get out of his store (or he'd call the cops) whenever he caught kids trying to steal. Sometimes if he saw students walk out with merchandise and dash off into the school (which is what everyone usually did), he'd lock up his store and walk into the school's office to report and find the kids who stole from him. Usually he'd do this when he was angry, which was almost every day. But surprisingly, he never banned anyone from his store, even if he caught them stealing.

On a warm Friday morning, two weeks before the last day of school, Dre and his crew met in front of the school gates. As usual, they planned to steal from the corner store for the hundredth time that school year. The plan was simple: Otis and Corey would stand in front of the fridge that was directly in front of the cashier. This would keep the cashiers eyes on them while simultaneously blocking the mirror's reflection of a blind spot where Paul was crouching and holding his huge backpack open like a trash bag. Dre and Jimmy had the most important role. They'd grab snacks and drinks, pace back and forth past Paul, and throw them into his bag. Paul also kept a folded sweater at the bottom of his backpack to reduce the noise of drinks, candy, and chips crashing into his bag.

Corey and Otis walked into the store and took position. A few minutes later, Dre and Jimmy walked into the store, where they stalled for a minute so Paul could walk in to take position. Otis gave the signal to go by making himself sneeze. Jimmy grabbed about seven candy bars, two large drinks, and two bags of chips, then threw it into Paul's bag. Dre grabbed about four bags of chips, a few ice-cold soda cans, and a Hot-Pocket, then threw them into Paul's bag. Corey and Otis distracted the cashier by dropping a few drinks on the floor and making a mess. Meanwhile, the cashier got irritated and walked up to Corey and Otis. This never happened, so Paul had to close his bag quickly before he saw it. The cashier asked Corey and Otis to check their pockets. They felt a bit disrespected and refused. So the cashier told them he's calling the cops. They lashed out and swore at the cashier, but the cashier just demanded that they leave the store. Dre and Jimmy went up to the counter and tried to pay for a few drinks and snacks as a diversion, which was also a cue for Paul to get up and walk out. Paul got up, grabbed his bag, and made his way toward the door. Somehow, the bag slipped from his hands and dropped on the floor.

As the beverages rolled across the shiny, black floor and the bags of chips tumbled out of his bag, the cashier stared them down. He was furious, as if they betrayed him. In a way, they did. He scolded them to get the f— out of his store. He reached behind the counter as if he was going to pull out a shotgun from behind the counter, so they hit the door and dashed towards the school, scared for their lives. They ran across the street and nearly got whacked by passing cars. After thirty seconds of sprinting out of fear, they finally got through the school doors. They were all breathing and leaning on each other, gasping for air. Jimmy was laid on his back on the floor, only God knew the last time Jimmy sprinted. Dre stood up with his hands on his head to catch his breath. He was used to running. But he thought about the situation. He thought hard. He kept asking himself how they got caught and what went wrong. Or why they even started stealing. He wasn't sure. He thought about karma. Then the school bell rang.

Another nice Friday afternoon. It was hot, a nice breeze rolled in, and the last weekend of the school year was coming up. The store incident was a week ago and long forgotten about. Finals were finally done, so all there was left were the field trips planned for the next and last week of school. Dre and his crew were in their sixth period. The day was almost done. Their favorite teacher, Mr. Walking, put on a classic comedy movie for the class to eat popcorn and enjoy. That was until the school's security guards walked into the class and asked Dre and his friends to step out. The heat and fear started to kick into their bodies. They knew what it was about. They walked downstairs into the office and took a seat in the big conference room to wait. They sat there for a few minutes and looked at each other, horrified. Paul's eyes started to water, until Otis told him to chill out. Then, the corner store owner walked into the room with a police officer and the principal. They were all petrified now. The store owner sat down next to Dre, which made him feel severely uncomfortable. The police officer and the principal took a seat across the table from Dre and his crew. It was silent.

"Are we going to jail?" Otis quietly asked.

"No," the police officer replied.

They all let out a gasp of relief and began to smile a bit, until the principal cleared his throat.

"But you guys are in trouble," the principal explained. "You all cannot attend the picnic next week and you all owe one hundred dollars each for everything you all stole from his store."

Awkwardly, Dre pulled out his wallet and placed a folded one hundred-dollar bill on the wooden table. Jimmy did the same. The principal looked at both of them, reached over to grab their money, then handed it to the store owner. The store owner looked at Dre and his crew.

"Why did you steal from me?" the store owner asked them. "You have money, so why not pay for it?"

"Because we kept getting away with it," Corey answered.

"Yeah," the rest of them agreed.

"Sometimes, we can't afford it," Otis added as Corey nodded his head.

The corner store owner smiled. He stood up and looked at the five of them. He slowly nodded his head.

"If you can't pay for something, just ask me and you can pay me back another day," he told them. "If you can't pay me another day, then it's on the house, but not all the time."

He then told the principal and the police officer that the two hundred dollars was enough to cover everyone. He reached out his hand and shook theirs, then made his way to the door. The principal told the five they could leave and go back to class. So they quickly grabbed their bags and rushed out of there. They were laughing out of relief, telling each other they got lucky.

A few years later, Dre and his crew basically lost touch. They were all sophomores in high school at different schools. They occasionally saw each other around the city and always caught up, but only for a few minutes before they went their own ways. But Dre and Jimmy were still pretty close—they always had been. They always talked about the corner store incident and laughed about it. But Dre started to think about it more since it happened. He started to ask himself, *Why did we do that?* and *Was he stereotyping Corey and Otis in the store?* or even *Why did he even think that me, Jimmy, and Paul were stealing?* Now that he kind of had a sense of what was really going on, it sort of bothered him. Mr. Charlie saw two black teenagers and judged them for how they looked, leading him to assume they were stealing. Also, not paying any attention to Dre, Jimmy, and Paul who were stealing the most. When they got in trouble, Dre and Jimmy paid for them because they had the money for it. The rest of them didn't have any money. Dre had finally realized that he was not a mastermind thief, but instead neither him or Jimmy were perceived as a thief or any kind of criminal. At the time, Dre and his friends didn't realize what the situation really was and neither did they know about each other's financial situations. They also never thought of Mr. Charlie as someone who actually cared about them beyond stereotypes.

As of today, Otis is currently at a continuation school and is working to provide for his younger sister, his mother, and himself. Corey is currently on trial, fighting for his life. Paul is doing fine in high school—he usually skates and takes pictures of views around the city. Jimmy is struggling in high school, but has found a career in photography and is making a good amount of money. As for Dre, he is doing good in high school, is the captain of the varsity basketball team, and is done writing this story.

Andre Villarino was born in San Francisco. He just turned eighteen years old. He is Filipino and loves the game of basketball. Andre hopes to make it to the NBA or become an X-ray tech in San Francisco. He also has a weird hobby of catching bugs or any creature he can find.

My Reality of Freedom

ALI IBRAHIM

I come from a country where people risk their lives and freedom for a better future, or the hope that one day they can achieve their dreams and support their families. I was born and raised in a small city in Eritrea, which is located in East Africa, surrounded by Sudan, Ethiopia, and Djibouti. I left Eritrea because I stopped going to school, and those who don't go to school join the military. They wanted to do it to me, so I ran away from my homeland to another to be safe.

When I lived in Eritrea, I didn't have this educational opportunity to travel. In Eritrea the kids don't have this opportunity because they have to go to the military. I crossed to Sudan where I had never been before and I also crossed from Sudan to Egypt. I was a refugee from Eritrea when I was young, and I was forced to leave Eritrea. I lived alone in Egypt for a few years and then came to the U.S. at a young age. When I lived in Egypt, I learned many new things, like how to live by yourself. Life was tough because I was forced to become a man while being a teenager. I was living with people who were older than me and started thinking like them about my life, because I was in a different country and everyone wanted to leave Egypt for a brighter future. I learned mostly from the people who I lived with in Egypt, but I learned a lot from the people I stayed with in different countries.

A dictator rules my country, so there is no proper education or healthcare, and everyday life is controlled by the government to keep citizens from gaining too much knowledge. The media is heavily restricted and only published by the government, and only a small percentage of the country's population has access to the internet. Employment is very bad and the government doesn't assist with jobs. To make a living, most families depend on agriculture and livestock.

When my country separated from other countries, there was new hope of being liberated, giving my young country the long-awaited, promised future. Unfortunately, for the citizens of my country, that promise was never delivered. Things have gotten worse, year after year, since the early 2000s. The president of my country designed a strict, military-service school for students. Instead of attending college, every student after middle or high school is forced into military camp. Students have no choice but to join the military camp. Young adults aren't given a specific time range to serve, but often it's dragged out or ends when they get really sick or escape. The military camp is known for harsh conditions, where people live in crowded housing, and the camp also has a reputation for sexual assault of young female teens.

To escape this way of life, families attempt to migrate illegally. The families take a huge risk by doing so and if they are caught by authorities while crossing borders, they will be arrested and sent to prisons. The prisons, over the years, have built a reputation for inhumane acts: families can end up being enslaved and held up for ransom, or worse.

Being away from my homeland has given me a different outlook on life. I wake up every day and try my best to succeed, so in the future I will have the resources and knowledge to help my people because I want this important freedom for them and not suffering. Having freedom makes me and other people feel like riding a wave, dancing on clouds, floating on air, and walking on water.

Ali Ibrahim was born in Keren (Eritrea, East Africa). He is nineteen years old. He likes to play soccer and listen to music. He hopes one day to become a pilot. He's in an internship at Facebook and likes learning coding. Ali likes to eat cheeseburgers and he likes fish and chips.

“Having freedom makes me and other people feel like riding a wave, dancing on clouds, floating on air, and walking on water.”

Ali Ibrahim

Dreams to Reality in the Lab

▌TOMMY HARPER

When I was in elementary school, I learned that Dr. George Washington Carver, a famous scientist who found a way to use peanuts to enrich soil in agriculture, was African American. I thought it was pretty cool at the time, and it gave me motivation because I dreamed about discovering new things and becoming famous for my own inventions. It mattered to me because he was a successful African American, and I want to become one as well in a country that restricts education from people of color.

At fourteen years old, I visited a laboratory that looked like an observatory in my mind. It inspired me to become a scientist, like how basketball players look up to Kobe. When I walked into the lab, it wasn't a bad atmosphere—I could breathe the air I wanted for the future. Other kids my age didn't have the opportunity like I did and they were taken to jail for things they hadn't done. I have the freedom to study and work hard whenever I want and I have to take advantage of that. There aren't that many African American scientists and there should be way more. Only five percent of scientists are African American even though they make up almost thirteen percent of the U.S. total population. Other African Americans have their freedom taken away for the color of their skin. Court decisions like *Brown v. Board of Education* changed access for people of color's education, but it still isn't equal. So I want to try my best to take advantage of my freedom before they take it away.

One example of what they can't take from me is when I went to visit Lawrence Livermore Laboratory. I saw a lot of technology and we did a science experiment where we put chemicals into a graduated cylinder to produce a chemical compound called elephant toothpaste. The scientists were communicating to each other as they were working on the project, which showed that being a scientist involves a lot of teamwork. The paste kept growing and growing and the color was blue like Colgate. The paste sounded gooey like suctioning slime. I saw the world's largest laser (it was huge) and therefore the building had a lot of security. The buff and bearded security were the FBI of the lab. They were pacing themselves back and forth, waiting for one of us to make a mistake. The Central Park Five were in the same situation, so I had them on my mind. I wondered why there was so much security for a fourteen-year-old African American child. I know because of the color of my skin anything can happen to me. That day at the lab I could've been falsely accused of something because it happened to Yousef and Korey. This is why my freedom is to become a scientist.

I feel like white nationalists try to take away freedom from young African Americans. They try to take away their education, rights, and their will to live. Black youth drop out of school because their teachers tell them they can't be anything. Blacks not only have to do their work, but they also have to tolerate the criticism from the racist, white teachers. I know I could be mistreated, so I prepare for it. At a school like Mission, there's a lot of people of color. The Tulsa Race Riots had a lot of successful black people and they were destroyed by the U.S. because they were making a profit. A racist professor in the class could potentially restrict my education by treating me differently from the other kids in my class.

I want to get an opportunity to work at NASA one day to get a good experience and good pay. I would wake up in the morning with positive energy. I would go to the lab with a Warriors and 49ers logo. I would walk into the automatic doors and go up the elevator to my room and look at the view from my window. I would sit at the desk with my molecules, trying to find a cure for cancer. I would have that sigh of relief, breathing the air of the future.

This is what freedom of education looks like to me. Free to learn whatever you want and not get criticized. I want to see kids get the opportunity like I did and not have their freedom restricted like the Central Park Five. I try to encourage other people to pursue their passion and use education to the best of their ability. I want to have a school named after me just like George W. Carver had a school named after him. Carver's work inspired youth to attend a school that's named after an African American. That work could give a child hope in life and also show how African Americans can be successful. Visiting laboratories and experiencing science experiments has helped me gain a passion for science. I know it could take a lot of work, but it can be achieved by doing what I have to do in school. I want to be the black person to represent the rest of the scientists. I want to get other black people to work on what they want to achieve, and for that they'll need an education.

Tommy Harper was born in San Francisco. He is seventeen years old. He likes to play video games and watch sports. His favorite sports are football and basketball. One day, he hopes to become a scientist. He loves listening to music and his favorite rapper is NBA Youngboy. His favorite food is cheeseburgers and he likes to spend time with his family.

Did the Caterpillar Ever Dream of Becoming a Butterfly?

EZREALLA LAUDENORIO

In the second grade, I did not wear what I wanted to wear nor did I act the way I wanted to act. I came to school in an itchy, wool, grey sweater that looked "good and elegant" in, well, my mom's eyes at least. The car ride to school was quiet. The sound of my soft sniffles and trying to hold my tears back made the tension in the car louder. At school, my friends would wear comfortable hoodies, clothes they chose to put on themselves, and clothing I would much rather wear.

When I first attended Mission High School, it changed my outlook on everything. I started to dress, talk, and act differently, and I can guarantee you it was not my teenage hormones or puberty that affected my relationship towards my mom. Growing up, I was always taught to obey my parents, whether it makes me happy or not; it was like my sickness, the "always listen to your parents" sickness, and I can tell you that nobody wants to listen to their parents. However, this sickness is the reason why I could not speak up to my mom on not wanting to wear that horrible, ugly, grey wool sweater and it is the reason I did not grow up expressing my true self. Although, can you blame me for not having control over the environment I grew up in? James Baldwin, one of my favorite writers said, "When a child is born, if I'm the child's parent, it is my obligation and my high duty to civilize that child. Man is a social animal. He cannot exist without a society." Meaning, as a child, my innocence was being tampered with by ideas that I believed were normal. The way I am raised reflects my actions and decisions I make for myself today. I am who I am, I believe what I believe, and it is because of my history and my past. I cannot say that I am cured from this sickness yet, but I am woke to the fact that I can question and maneuver my way around to being true to my true self.

My mother was born in the Philippines and she migrated here to California her freshman year of high school, along with her grandpa and grandma. The Philippines is a place with high poverty and low employment, and the life you were born into is the life you will have for now and for future generations. It is ironic that a country of poverty also has highways that are bordered with rice fields, tall towering mountains, and whenever I'd go outside, I could feel the hot, beaming sun hit my skin and thick, black hair. By the beaches, the wind blows and the water is nice and warm; you also see insects on the roads and chickens walking all over the place. I know this because I lived there myself for a period of time. I noticed how big the gap is between the rich and the poor, and who goes to college and who doesn't. Luckily, my mother was able to escape the cycle that was built for the people of my country and start a new life here in America. My mother had hopes and dreams of becoming a nurse or a doctor, but she could not achieve those dreams because she had me.

My body sunk into an overused, white couch. As my mom walked into the house, I said with excitement, "Mom, I know what I'm going to major in!" She ignored me when I said it the first time. Her thick, black hair was tied back and her face was red from exhaustion from work. I said it again, but this time a little louder, "I think I want to go into business." My mother looked at me like the many times she did when we had this same conversation.

The room started to feel more tense and I already felt the judgment coming even before I opened my mouth. "What are you going to do with a business degree? You can always own a business when you're a nurse and on top of that, you'll be financially stable," she told me with an angry tone in her voice. Every time we have a conversation of what career I would like to pursue, or anything that has to do with what is best for me, it reminds me of the battle I am having with myself: *Do I want to remain in the same itchy, wool sweater or try on the hoodie?*

I remember a time when we were at a family party. You know those people who you call your aunts and uncles, but are not related to you, they're just your parents' friends? Well, those were the people I was surrounded with and that came along with conversation starters like, "Ezrealla! What happened to you? You're growing so fast," or, "You are so tall! Taller than me," when they literally saw me two weeks ago. One of the only reasons why I liked going to these parties was because of the food. The food's aroma filled up the room, with the kare-kare, pancit, barbecue, and adobo. It gave me a nostalgic feeling of when I used to make food with my grandma back home in the Philippines. After I said hi to everyone in the house, I grabbed my food and sat at a small, faded wooden table. My aunts were sitting at the same table, and I had forgotten that they were all nurses. As soon as I sat down, I realized what I got myself into. My aunt asked, "How's school, Realla?" The key to answering questions like this is to keep it as vague as possible and give them what they want to hear. "Oh, you know, it's going well," I continued to eat the warm, delicious food that I wanted to enjoy quietly. I waited for the next bunch of questions they had for me.

"I heard that you wanted to be a nurse, huh?" My mom had probably told them that. How could it not be her.

"Oh, I don't even know what I'm going to pursue in college. I wrote undeclared for all the schools I applied to."

"Yeah? What are you leaning towards?" She had a confused look on her face, because my mother had told her otherwise.

"I was thinking about business." I stopped and took a bite of my food when I realized that my answer was not vague and something she did not want to hear. I followed it with, "But I was thinking about nursing too."

"Yeah, nursing is a good career path. I mean, look at me and your aunts. We're all stable, have a home, a car."

I took a deep, long breath. Instead of keeping my answers vague, I started to explain to her that I wanted to be outside the stereotype of "all Filipinos being nurses," how we need to see more of our people in different career fields, and not just nursing. Then she explained to me why Filipinos take nursing. "Your mom and I, and everyone in this room, did not grow up wealthy. We grew up with our parents wanting us to work right away, help out with bills. We saw nursing as a way out. We knew that nursing only took four years of college and would give us an income that could provide for our family now, and for future generations." I sat there and hated myself, because she was right.

It makes me indecisive about what career path I would like to take. Since I'm a senior, applying to colleges was difficult. There was an angel on one shoulder, telling me to put nursing as my major, and the devil on the other, telling me otherwise. It is the itchy, wool sweater verses the hoodie all over again, but this time, I am willing to break free from my mom's reality, and pursue my own.

Ezrealla Laudenorio is seventeen years old and was born and raised in San Francisco, CA. She lives with her mom and little sister. She loves to live in the moment and have fun. One day, she hopes to be successful, do what makes her happy, and travel the world.

Free Is in You and Me

■ XOCHITL QUIROZ

What is freedom to you and what is it to me?
To escape this mind control and social conditioning
Human minds or a human mine?
Are we giving each other space to grow or helping the hands in power confine?
Stop yourself and ask if these thoughts you think and believe are even your own
And I promise once you see it, your higher power will begin to atone

What is freedom to you and what is it to me?
To speak unapologetically is one of the many things it can be
Fear and punishment create shame in the brain
We fear disapproval so instead we abstain
From doing what we love or saying how we feel, just so validation we can obtain
And in us, obedience and dependency, they begin to ingrain

What is freedom to you and what is it to me?
To step outside the box and feel comfortable alone
To reclaim my space and not fear the world unknown
To see love and light in others as I see it in myself
Because only then will the individual come to find true happiness and eternal wealth

What is freedom to you and what is it to me?
Escaping psychological locks and letting my wonders run free
To ask for clarification and not be afraid to disagree

To listen to my brothers and sisters and be able to see
That no matter our differences, when you cut us, we will both bleed

I think it's time we break through these barriers and start by planting the seed
Of generational healing and together agree
That freedom is a construct only we can grasp ourselves and help the next person achieve
You and I
In U-N-I-T-Y

Xochitl Quiroz was born and raised in San Francisco. She's seventeen and an Aquarius. Her pronouns are she/her. She enjoys media arts and working with community. She hopes to become a social worker and study sociology in college. Her favorite colors are green and purple, and her name means "flower" in the Aztec language, Nahualt.

Fighting for the Freedom of Women

ANGELICA VILLAFLOR

I can't always please everybody,
Doesn't mean I should change myself.
Women getting the right to marry other women,
Marrying for love, not wealth.

Darling, just wipe those tears away,
Don't listen to what people have to say.
Look in the mirror, you'll see a beautiful girl.
There's no one like you in the entire world.

There's no such thing as "perfect,"
Unless perfect is loving yourself and all your scars.
I smile a lot more than I used to.
I smile for me and not for you.

The color of my skin shouldn't determine my success.
Women should get paid the same amount like the rest.
My gender, my race, shouldn't determine how much I make,
Especially if it's women of color putting their health at stake.

You don't need a man to make you feel loved.
Home is not in the arms of a man who treats you wrong.

Women allowed a no-fault divorce
Shouldn't be seen as weak, but strong.

Women continue to fight the battle for freedom,
Getting catcalled in the streets,
Sexual harassment at work,
Physical abuse in our own homes.
We have to keep fighting; that is what our past has shown,
We are not alone.

Angelica Villaflor is eighteen years old. She's a Filipina girl who was born in San Francisco. She loves listening to music and singing. Her long-term goal is to go to college and learn how to write music. She hopes to one day be a songwriter.

How Deep

▌TAMIYA FIELDS

Dear reader,

I hope that you understand and receive the message that I am trying to give out. I want you to educate yourself and set your mind free, liberate yourself so you can have a story to tell the others when you liberate them. I am liberating you, so let me tell you my story . . .

It took me a long time to realize that to be free, you have to be white. My name is Claudia Smith. I've been on this earth for almost three hundred years now. I am what one calls 'immortal,' I guess. Let me tell you my story . . .

I was born on February 7, 1850, to Glinda Mae and Thomas Mae. They were bought from their last slave owner so they don't have the same last name as me. I have the same last name as Mr. Smith, all of ours' slave master. During that time, of course, I had no idea that I was a slave yet. I was not able to realize that until I was twelve years of age.

Mama and Papa had always talked about this other daughter they had before me, not that I believed them anyways. They said her name was Tatanya, and that I looked just like her: smooth, brown skin and light, brown eyes; not hazel, but right between the two colors of brown and hazel. Beautiful long, sandy brown hair that reached the lower back, but still nappy and kinky like me and Pa. Legs were smooth and strong; we were both quick, and they said we both had a mind that would run wild. I never knew my sister, but we do visit the homemade grave we were allowed to bury her in and make only because Mr. Smith's son, Henry, talked him into allowing it. He's always had a thing for me. Although I did not know her, Ma and Pa told me stories about her all the time, and I always listened and asked questions as if I were in a classroom.

But one question I always asked and never got the answer to was, "How did she die?"

I always got the same response, "That doesn't matter, you just stay away from that Henry. You hear me?" I just stopped asking about it. I didn't realize what they meant until I was twelve years of age.

February 7, 1862. Henry was about five years older than me. That isn't that much older, right? Henry and I would play all day long together. It was sorta weird to see a black girl and a white boy play together, but we did not care. Shortly after, Henry's dad, Mr. Smith, found out that we were in love. Henry loved me like Jay Z loves Beyoncé, and it was vice versa from my end. Mr. Smith soon separated us, and he told us very loudly and very clearly, and I could see the spit leave his mouth as he talked, "YOU TWO ARE TO NEVER SPEAK TO EACH OTHER AGAIN OR I'LL DO TO HER WHAT I DID TO THE LAST ONE!!" Henry quickly left and did not speak to me again. It was my first heartbreak. How could the boy I love just ignore me and never speak to me again? How could he do that to me? Before I knew it, he had a girlfriend. A WHITE girlfriend at that.

All I could think was maybe they were perfect for each other. I mean, they could do things that I would never be able to do with him. They were able to leave this plantation, walk hand in hand together, something I would never do. Over time, I wondered why Mr. Smith wasn't so mad about her. So one night when Henry was alone walking in the woods, as he does every night, I grabbed his arm and pulled him behind a tree. Before he could let out any words, I put my finger to his lips and told him to be quiet.

I only had one question, "Who is the other one, and why does your dad not want us together, Henry?" Without a doubt, Henry knew exactly what I was talking about, and he fell silent with his head down. I pushed harder and harder for an answer, until he finally gave me an answer.

"The other one is . . . it's . . . it's your sister. Back when I was younger, I had a crush on her, a really big one too. I talked about her all the time, and my dad told me that if I did not stop, then something that I would regret would happen." He started to cry for some reason.

"I didn't know, Claudia. I didn't know, I swear." As he continued to cry, I made him finish the story.

"I continued to help her in the field and see her all the time, and Daddy told me he was going to sell her. I cried and cried and I begged him not to. That didn't work, it only made Daddy more mad. He grabbed me by my ear and dragged me to the basement. He made me stay there, and about five minutes later, he came back in the basement with Tatanya with him. He had her by the hair and he came down the stairs with her. I could hear her crying, begging him to let go, and he laughed as he walked towards me down the stairs. He threw her on the table, her feet on the floor and her stomach on the table. He tied a rope to the legs of the table and, on the other end, to her wrists. He eventually began to rape her. It was so vicious the way he did it. He made me watch and he told me if I closed my eyes, he would really sell her. My mom walked in and she just laughed as if this was something of humor, the way he touched her. I watched everything as I cried, and before I knew it, Tatanya was done crying. She had completely stopped crying. He laughed and Tatanya was still. She was still looking at me, she did not blink, her eyes were still filled with water, and her body was still. I didn't even see her breathing. My dad left and I ran to Tatanya. I shook her over and over, but no response. Soon after, I realized she was gone, and I just couldn't stop crying. The story that my dad let everyone believe was that I had killed my first n—."

I was broken. I had no clue about what to do or say. I just hugged him. He had no choice. He was a baby. I could never blame Henry for anything. He doesn't even use the whip when Mr. Smith tells him to.

"Yeah, and you asked one more question, why does my dad not want us together, right?" Henry said as he lifted his head from my shoulder and wiped his eyes.

"It's because you're black. He would never accept it." Those were the final words for me that changed my perspective on everything.

Fast forward to the future . . .

As I've lived throughout this life, I have laid low and observed how far my people have come. I've watched Harriet Tubman become one of the best black historical figures. She freed about three hundred or more enslaved black people, but they are still not free. They just went to the North where color doesn't matter, just know your place. Martin Luther King, "I Have A Dream," preached and preached about the unfair statue of liberty, but was beaten and thrown in jail for such things. I've watched Malcolm X become an extraordinary man. I've kept close eyes on him and Martin actually, but I still don't know who killed them and apparently neither does our government. I've watched Rosa Parks say, "I'm not getting up," and start the civil rights movement when she was put in jail for not leaving a seat. And movements like the Little Rock Nine, they said we could go to school with them, but that isn't right, look at what they do. I've seen the way they treated us, how eventually we became good enough to live in our own homes, but everything was still restricted from us. Was everything restricted from the white people? No. And despite how far we have come in the world, it doesn't take a rocket scientist to know that we still have no justice when it comes to our lives. Emmett Till, must I remind you of the "justice" he got, beaten to death at the age of fourteen? "The two men then beat him nearly to death, gouged out his eye, shot him in the head and then threw his body, tied to the cotton-gin fan with barbed wire, into the river." The men were let go. On September 15, 1963, a bomb was set at 16th Street Baptist Church, Alabama "kills four girls and several others injured," read all about it on the news. Now let's take it to modern-day lynching, sorry, I mean police brutality. Why hasn't it changed? Lynching used to be legal. It was legal to beat and hang a black person. It is not legal anymore, but it's legal for a police officer to shoot when they feel threatened. The question is, when don't they feel threatened by a black person? Trayvon Martin, now we can't wear hoodies, we have to look around everywhere, worried about a police officer or someone else trying to kill us. Oscar Grant, laid on the floor, hands in cuffs behind his back.

Freedom of speech, isn't that what we have as an amendment? He asked about those rights and he continued to ask, but all that asking did was get him shot by a police officer. Hmm, maybe the police officer felt threatened by an educated black man, who knows? Put your hands up and say don't shoot, can I get a surrender like Michael Brown or will they shoot you too? You can still see the same poverty since I was a kid, the difference here is that the government now pities us and provides free money and health care, something we had to settle for. You see all these struggles that black people go through just to get somewhere physically, but still be imprisoned mentally. The system is so big, it's beyond what we fully know. How deep does this go?

Now with that being said, name one white person off the back of your head who has had no justice. You can't do it. It's because they have all the justice and opportunities. They can do whatever they want to do and do not have to face the same cost as me and my people. Throughout all this time, where have the white people been? Living their lives at the top of the pyramid, while us black and other people of color have held it up. So this brings me back to the conclusion, do you see it now . . . you are not free unless you are white.

Sincerely,
A lifetime of
Claudia Smith

Tamiya Fields was born in San Francisco. She is seventeen years old. She likes to dance and read. She is a cheerleader and plays basketball, flag football, and runs track. One day she hopes to be a veterinarian and minor in Greek mythology. She is in the Black Student Union and loves to organize events. Wingstop is her favorite food and she can eat it all day.

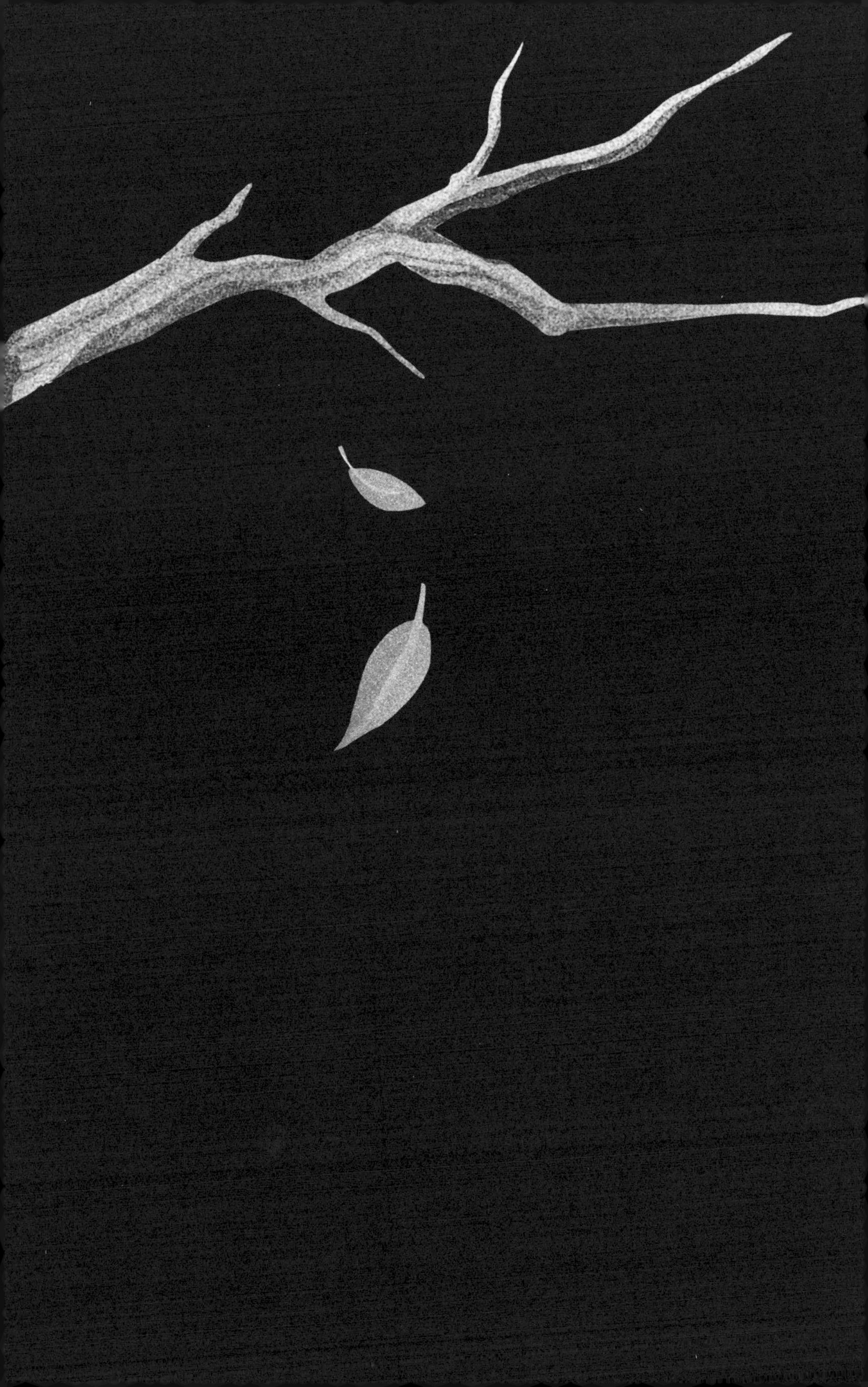

“You see all these struggles that black people go through just to get somewhere physically, but still be imprisoned mentally. The system is so big, it’s beyond what we fully know. How deep does this go?”

Tamiya Fields

Our Best Selves Come from Within

ZAPRIEL WADE

I remember being eleven and going to a new school. It was in Palo Alto, right over the freeway that separates two completely opposite cities. East Palo Alto (EPA), the city I grew up in, was once the murder capital of the world. I was raised in the "G" for gardens, because every street is named after a plant. My siblings and I would ride our bikes around the corner to our grandmother's house, and it felt like a mission. It was only us, our bikes, and the road ahead of us. Growing up in EPA taught me a lot of things, but it could not prepare me for middle school. EPA taught me how to stand up for myself and build a sense of community with others around me. In my upbringing, all of my cousins would come to my house whenever there was a birthday or playdate. We wrestled, played hide-and-seek, and enjoyed being kids without thinking about it. But I was soon hit with a rude awakening. In junior high, I was a fish out of water. My school, only fifteen minutes away from my grandmother's house, felt like a different world. My first day during sixth-grade orientation, I could already tell it would be an eye-opening experience. After setting our backpacks down in our homeroom, the teachers gathered us up and led us to a park. Once there, we all spread out across a field into a big circle. As I looked around, I could see no one else looked like me. There were no brown skin girls with curly hair and dark brown eyes. We proceeded to play games and introduce ourselves, and I met the people who would later become my best friends. Instantly, we formed a connection because we were the only three black kids in our class. Sixth grade just started, and it was already the complete opposite of my childhood. Being in EPA was freeing. I related to the people I grew up with, and most of their struggles were the same as mine. None of us had a lot, but we all had each other. Being at my new school made me feel like an animal at the zoo, constantly being watched, and studied.

I often questioned who I was because I knew I was not like my peers, but I felt as if I did not know myself. I tried to change: straighten my hair, wear different clothes, listen to different music, but there was always an elephant in the room, and I was that elephant. Every. Single. Time. My only concern was to fit in, but my hair and brown skin made that exceptionally difficult. As a twelve-year-old, this only added onto my long list of insecurities. In eighth grade in one of my English classes, our homework was to pick an article, annotate it, and present it to the class. A classmate of mine chose an article about a white kid who was shot and killed by a white policeman. She presented her article and explained why she chose it. While the rest of my classmates and I started to discuss the topic, she said, "I bet if that was a black kid, this would've been all over the news." Just like that, all eyes were on me. I furrowed my eyebrows and looked at her. What she said made zero sense to me. I knew her comment was wrong and hurt my feelings, but I did not know what to classify the outlandish remark as. Was she being blatantly racist or just honestly confused? I raised my hand and she called on me.

I told her, "When black kids are shot by the police, the crimes are racially motivated. This wasn't." She didn't seem to understand, and that's when I knew how much different my life was from my peers because of the color of my skin. My classmates did not have to worry about police brutality or go through the daily racism that people of color face. Again, I was in a predicament where I felt as if I was being trapped. Everyone was waiting for my reaction and my input on the matter; that was my unspoken obligation at school. To be a diversity quota, to speak for all black people. It was draining. After our graduation, I said my final goodbyes and never talked to them again. Then I moved to the City.

San Francisco was different. My family moved here because my stepdad's parents left him their house. There were so many people in such a tiny space, in certain neighborhoods you could not walk five feet without seeing a homeless person or trash flooding the sewers. In others, there were multi-million dollar houses and Google cars. I loved going to Mission High School. I made friends instantly. Mission was diverse and provided me with a sense of freedom that allowed me to be myself. I learned to love the things that once isolated me. My hair that defies gravity, my skin that absorbs the sun, the rap and R&B I listen to, but most importantly that I could talk to people about my struggles and they could relate. Our families were not rich, did not own any Teslas, or go on annual Hawaii trips, but we loved each other. We had each other's backs and always pushed each other to be our best selves.

Now I'm a senior, almost eighteen, about to graduate high school, and start college. I got accepted into over nine historically black colleges and universities (HBCUs), and am looking forward to becoming a freshman at Howard University this fall. With all that life has thrown at me, being a black woman has been nothing but a blessing. I'm authentic, one hundred percent true to myself and my story. When adversity hits, I know that I can handle it. Initially, when asked what freedom meant to me, I was not sure what to write about because all I could think about was how some of my experiences kept me from being who I want and believing in myself. I see now that it comes from within. I will never be completely free, for I live in a society that flourishes because of the disenfranchisement of people of color, but that will never stop me from trying and pushing to become my best self.

Zapriel Wade was born in Phoenix and is seventeen years old. She likes to listen to music and play basketball. Her dream is to become a physician's assistant and give back to under-resourced communities because she believes everyone deserves to be healthy.

Getting the Words Out

BETZABE HERRERA

It was one o'clock and my palms were sweaty. I was finally landing from my trip. I didn't know what was waiting for me at baggage claim, but I was certain that my life was about to change. You see, a few weeks ago my dad had called me to warn me that his family was coming to live with us by the end of the summer. I didn't know how I was going to process this, so instead I left for another trip before the big shift.

I was finally home again. But I knew I was going to regret it because as soon as I stepped into my room, I saw it had been changed by an intruder, Andrea, my older cousin, who I was forced to share my room with. I had to play nice, but luckily school was right around the corner, giving me excuses to avoid conversations.

It had been two months now and the move had been difficult for everyone. We were always arguing over the bathroom, food, or dirty dishes. Even though I didn't like her yet, I was trying my best not to argue with Andrea. I had been finding ways for us to feel comfortable around each other.

Without realizing it, October had finally arrived and I finally realized that Andrea wasn't that bad. But I was still choosing to distract and distance myself from the family. I didn't know what was going on in their lives.

I had been in my own bubble up until tonight, when my sister told me Andrea had bulimia. I was a little confused because I didn't know what bulimia was, so I was waiting for someone to explain what was going on. My sister started to explain to me that for the past few weeks, she had noticed Andrea's eating patterns. She told me Andrea would binge eat or make herself purge. Because I wasn't aware of the dangers of her condition, I didn't know she could be in danger.

Out of love and concern, I spent time making sure Andrea was taking care of herself. I watched what she put into her body and helped her with her relationship with food. I helped find her a therapist and nutritionist. For a while, I noticed she got healthy and happy again. But this slowly changed when her mom arrived from Mexico. It didn't help that she brought her problems with her. We didn't have physical space, but now it had become harder for everyone to breathe with her presence.

I believe it was because of all the diseases my aunt brought with her that Andrea got sick. Andrea would stay in bed all day, refusing to go to school. She either ate too much, refused to eat, or cried. She became fragile glass, and no one knew how to be around her.

Everyone wanted to know why she was sick, but didn't want to see why. Everyone asked what was going on, but her response was always the same, "I just want to be with my dad." From the sidelines, I could tell everyone was smothering her and wouldn't let her breathe. I was tired of having to listen to all the lies and assumptions. There were days when I just wanted to just blurt it all out, "Andrea has bulimia and depression because you left her." But no matter how many times I tried, I could never get the words out without choking. I knew everyone felt tired of fighting. No one was okay.

She came into my room one night crying, telling me she got into a fight with her mom. Out of frustration, my aunt bought her a plane ticket back to Mexico. She was leaving on Thursday.

I spent the next few days trying to convince her to stay. I kept telling her she needed to stay for herself and her health. But she was stubborn and told herself she needed to leave. Luckily we found out that the ticket wasn't real.

The following weekend was a three-day weekend. My parents and sister were both going out of town and decided to leave me alone with my aunt and cousin. So I decided that I needed to step back and not fix other people's problems. But even being at home felt weird because I saw Andrea repacking. I felt confused, but I was too scared to ask why. I just rolled over and fell asleep.

When I finally forced myself to wake up, I got a text from my sister, telling me she had landed. I told her I needed air and my stomach was growling. She came to pick me up and that's when I told her, "We need to tell my dad about Andrea's condition." She told me there was no point anymore since they were leaving tomorrow morning.

They were planning on leaving the country before their visas expired and didn't even plan on telling me. I had spent the whole day trying to comfort Andrea and make her feel better, but she couldn't even be honest with me. Then my sister asked me a question I didn't want to hear or answer, "Do you want to go say goodbye?"

When we arrived at the house, I ran upstairs and dragged Andrea into what used to be our room. I asked her if she had planned on telling me that she was leaving or if she was going to get on the plane the next morning and not say goodbye. We sat on the bed and I told her if she chose to leave, I would only want the best for her and for her to take care of herself. That was our last conversation.

Growing up, the only times I heard about or was introduced to bulimia was through American teenage shows. Girls are portrayed with eating and health conditions. I grew up in a family where mental health isn't real, and you'd never expect someone you care about to be impacted by this. My family only worries about heart attacks, not anxiety attacks. They believe that if you have depression, you can just walk it off. But I saw what this condition was doing to her. It was eating her up inside and she wasn't getting better.

For the past few months, Andrea was living in her own cage. She didn't have physical space or a sense of belonging. Her immigration status limited the options she was going to have in her new country. Her lack of English limited her self-expression. But the biggest barrier of all was having to live in an unwelcoming, toxic household. She felt like she had nowhere to go and no one to turn to. By then it was too late for me to save her.

Betzabe Herrera was born in Ecatepec de Morelos, Mexico. She is seventeen years old. Her family is really big with many different characteristics. She loves to draw and paint. She likes to listen to music and go to the gym. She also loves the outdoors and enjoys doing activities in nature. One day she hopes to graduate from the University of California, Santa Cruz and double major in ethnic studies and psychology. She hopes to become an educator or social worker in the City.

Feeling Free Behind the Wheel

■ DIEGO ALMIRANO VALLE

I remember my first time driving a car. It was my uncle Oracio's car. We were at the parking lot and he was tired of driving, so he decided to rest there. After a few hours, he asked me, "You want to learn how to drive a car?"

And I said, "Yes." And there we were in the parking lot. There were some cars, but they were separated, so I had a big space to learn and not crash his car. He had a Toyota Camry and it was kinda new. I was a kid so that was something that caught my attention. Then we changed seats, and we waited until no cars came because it was my first time driving and I was like a mercenary at the wheel. Well, that's what he told me. I thought that driving a car was easy, but no it wasn't, because you have to be ready to press the brake and make maneuvers when necessary because accidents can pass in any moment and you have to be alert. My grandpa (an old man of fifty-nine years, but in good physical condition) also taught me how to drive. He is like a fan of speed, just like me, so he taught me what he does when he is at the freeway. He called it "look for a window."

I didn't even know what that meant, so I asked him and he said, "If you see you cannot go to any other lane, then wait for the car in front of you to move forward. If this other car that is on your left doesn't go fast enough, then you can go close to the car in front of you, but without crashing, and be ready if he presses the brakes." That was my first time doing that. After that, I gave him the car.

Aight, so I was a kid and I had some curiosities, and one of these was to ask him, "Why did you decide to drive a car?"

And his answer was, " 'Cause I feel kinda free. My mind forgets about the rest that is happening, and I'm only focused on my way and not making an accident. Also I forget that I have a phone 'cause I don't use it when I'm driving."

I use the window not just when I'm driving. Also I use it when I have a problem or I'm feeling stressed, so I look for something that can keep my mind busy so I can forget about all that is happening. Like I said, I look for something to keep my mind busy, so in my case I have my work after school. So when I'm working, I'm only focused on doing all that I have to do in the work and finishing. While I'm there, I forget about all that happened during the day 'cause, like I said, I'm only focused on finishing my job. For some, keeping the mind occupied is more a way of escaping the problems that one has, and then I think that they are not mistaken since everyone hides things and they are not good at all. It depends on each person. Each one looks for a way to feel free to do things that other family members don't leave, or something like that.

In my own words, to "look for a window" means that we have to find a different way to solve our problems and other varieties of things, and not just let the things go without solving them.

Diego Almirano Valle was born in Nicaragua. He is seventeen years old. He likes to listen to music and play baseball. He hopes to be a U.S. soldier. Something that almost nobody knows about him is that he has been in jail more than twice. Something that he likes about himself is his way to be/ forma de ser and the way he expresses what he feels.

The Truth

▮ JAHLI SIMMONS

Fred Hampton: "You don't fight fire with fire. You fight fire with water. We're gonna fight racism with solidarity. We're not gonna fight capitalism with Black Capitalism. We're gonna fight capitalism with socialism. Socialism is the people. If you're afraid of socialism, you're afraid of yourself."

When you hear that quote, what does it make you feel or think? That quote was said by former Black Panther member and leader of the lunch program in Chicago, Fred Hampton. He was assassinated in his home by the police department in Chicago at approximately 3:00 in the morning, with the usage of guns fired 200 times. He was an African American man who wanted to support and build up his community. There was a lack of resources provided for the low-income families in Chicago. Being so young and having to sacrifice his life at the age of twenty-one, he tried to do his best so all African Americans in the country could have the support they needed like every other person, regardless of what race they were. He died because he wanted equal rights. That's what the Black Panther Party only wanted, just fairness towards the black community within this country. When you hear that quote it represents more of a meaning, how the whole system is set up in the United States. People of color are still oppressed, and capitalism continues oppression due to the limited resources people still have. They get stripped away from resources and placed in specific areas that have little opportunity.

Capitalism is not for the people. Capitalism benefits the high class and has a huge impact upon most low-income and some middle-class families in the United States. When I think about the word *capitalism,* I only get a sense for how this was made and how it follows us every step of the way as we get older and proceed to move forward. Thinking about it, I look at capitalism, as I like to say, as the "3-Barrier Gap." When I say that, that is when you have your Higher Class, which is full of money, wealth, and most important of all, POWER. Then you have your Middle Class, which is the daily, typical, normal citizen, with decent-sized houses, upper-class jobs, with an amount of money in the making and a voice to speak. Last and finally, your Lower Class, and this is what I grew up off of for my first eighteen years of life and experience. This class receives welfare from the government, housing stability, public education, financial aid, and plenty more. In my opinion, capitalism has definitely affected me. Just growing up with a single mother who raised three children on her own, it was definitely a struggle, but most important of all, a challenge. This tax system is unfair to those who don't come from anything and makes it so complicated for us to move forward. Growing up, I watched my parents argue a lot. I remember asking my mom why we didn't have a lot of money like the other kids at school and she responded, "That's just the way it is." I carried these words with me, trying to comprehend what she was trying to get to.

My cousin wants to be a businessman, and he likes to design clothes. When you start a company, it's difficult because there are a lot of different purchases you'll need to make in order to start making tons of money. I asked him if he supports capitalism and he said no. He mentioned it's a bad system for people who come from low-income backgrounds. I asked him, "What if you became the largest clothing brand in the country? Would you support capitalism?" If he did he might not have to do taxes and keep all his earnings, or would he still be against it? He wasn't sure. I questioned myself, *Why are people like that? Why do we all want money?* Sometimes to have too much of something good is bad, and this speaks upon its capitalist ways. It's simple; we tend to be greedy with money, and without it, life isn't easy.

Breaking down how we are blinded from how we face oppression and everything in such a quiet and silent way. Brushing off things and not really seeing the bigger picture in how we are oppressed by the oppressors. Cognitive dissonance—the state of having inconsistent thoughts, beliefs, or attitudes, especially as relating to behavioral decisions and attitude change. The system has a funny name but it's how everything is run through and set in. It has a blind eye towards lower-class people and the majority of people of color within the United States. So with it now being 2020, we still tend to suffer in silence because of the ways we have to obey other things. These systems are based on the oppression of people of color and always have been.

Jahli Simmons was born in the Bronx, New York and is eighteen years old. He has a passion for writing and taking the car and going on long drives. He plans to go to college and study for a major in psychology and a minor in kinesiology and hopefully would like to attend school in Atlanta, Georgia, at Morehouse College.

Chained by the Opportunities

MIGUEL ANGUIANO

How do you define this country with a few words? Some people would say freedom . . . the country of freedom, but when it is 10:30 in the night after one day of school and work, sometimes I wonder if I'm free. At this point, what is freedom, and what makes someone feel free? Is freedom the ability to do whatever you want? Think whatever you want? To be able to make your choices and not be subdued by others?

I wonder if I am free, after all.

I'm the only one who decides what to do with my life. I'm the only one who decides to wake up at 5:50 a.m. and then go to school, and then I'm the only one who decided I wanted to work at the age of sixteen and did it. After all, then, am I free?

The truth is, I'm not. I'm not deciding it at all. I'm that leaf taken by the wind, to which direction life decides for it.

Just like that leaf that separates from its tree to follow an invisible path, I am, but instead of that, my parents separated from me and I don't blame them, because they were working and wanted my wellness, and they wanted the best opportunities for me that they could have.

I still don't know what freedom actually means, but I want to tell the history of my family . . . no, our reality, and maybe with this, you can create a definition of what freedom is, or just . . . value what you have.

Many times we don't know where we are, we don't know the ground we step on, and why should we know about that? After all, we only care about our well-being, right?

There is no reason why I'm here today. Perhaps a living being, human or man, needs a reason to want to live well and with dignity.

Why do you risk your life to get here, to the U.S.?

"I don't have reasons, because a man doesn't need a reason to live and to want dignity." This is what my father said when he was eighteen and decided to immigrate to the United States because he wanted to live and he wanted a better life. He didn't have the privilege that many of us have to go to school, because he had to get money to pay the debts. He had to live a modest life with limitation, where he had to think if he was going to be able to eat tomorrow, or when he could buy a pair of shoes. Living with a fear of losing his house, where we grew up, was something he felt afraid of, so he decided to migrate to the U.S. because he wanted to do something about it. He dropped out of high school at the age of seventeen and decided to accompany his father, who migrated a year before to get money and to pay all his debts.

That feeling of losing everything was something that didn't let him sleep and live in peace, that feeling that you never understand unless you live it on your own.

As soon as he arrived to the United States, he went to "El Café," a place where many people go to have an opportunity to work in roofing. Near to that cafeteria exists a store where people buy materials for construction, and they incidentally picked up some people to work. My father used to wake up at six in the morning to get to the bus stop to get there and wait until seven to eight in the morning.

He spent the whole day going to different places to find the opportunity to work. Just imagine spending your days thinking about work, just to earn some money to survive and save a little. Is there freedom there?

My father struggled to find a job because at his age and aspect of a skinny, short, young man, nobody wanted to give him the opportunity. Nobody trusts young people when it is about jobs, I know it very well . . .

When finally he got the opportunity to work, all he did was stick to that opportunity and hold onto it. He started in roofing by bringing materials to his mates on the roof and cleaning the garbage that fell on the ground. Sounds simple, and it is, but the materials are heavy and with the hot sun, it made it harder. Whenever he had some free time, he didn't spend it resting, he spent it learning how to improve and do something different. In his free time, he tried and tried to do some of the work on the roof, but when he tried to help do something by himself, the other people that were there said, "Get out of here, you're not good for this."

Even with that, he did not give up, and he continued with his curiosity and desire to learn more. Years went by until that young man became a foreman in that company, and in that job where tall and strong men are required to work, he managed to stand out among many others. My father usually tells me, to cheer me up, "Seré chaparro, pero mientras no me de cuenta de eso, puedo hacer grandes cosas" (I'll be short, but as long as I don't realize that, I can do great things). So we want to say, forget your insecurities and focus on what you want to do.

My parents spent a lot of time in the U.S. working, my father in roofing and my mother in a factory earning seven dollars per hour (that is curious for me because now in San Francisco, you can earn more than double that). So they decided to make a life here and make a family. My parents had three children in the U.S. One is my older brother, I'm the middle one, and then my little brother.

My parents don't speak English, so I learned to speak Spanish only. In that time, Spanish was not so extended as it is today. Speaking only Spanish was a problem when my parents took me to the parks to play because most of the kids spoke English. That limited me to only play with my brothers, separated from other kids, or just with my parents. Like I said, my parents worked a lot, so they didn't have a lot of time to spend with me and it was my grandparents who took care of me in those times. My father used to work six to seven days per week and without a defined time to leave, because that depended on the climate and how developed the work was. But I never saw my father tired. Any time he had in a day off, he spent the time with his family. My father never liked the limitations of living in the U.S. and the little free time he had, so with all his money, he said he wanted to build a house in Mexico. My grandparents came back to Mexico with my brother and me first, and raised me until, in a few years, my parents could come back. I have a few memories of being in the United States. I remember the time when my father bought me a Nintendo GameCube from the Gamestop on 23rd and Mission Street, also the time when we went to the turtle's lake in Golden Gate Park. The reason my parents came back was freedom. They wanted to be free and to spend more time at home with us, as simple as that.

Some of us could think that was an error of my parents to come back to

Mexico and raise us; that's what some of my uncles in the United States say, but I don't think in the same way. I don't blame my parents for wanting some freedom. I don't blame them for having worked a lot and not having spent enough time with me, because they wanted the best for me. So why should I blame them for "ruining my life by making me live with them in Mexico"?

I don't blame them for that. I have very good memories of being with them in Mexico, and even when things didn't go as my father wanted, I spent a lot of time learning from them and their side. For example, the time my father taught me how to ride our horse. I learned about life in Mexico, their culture and their traditions. I used to go with my family to posadas, acostadas, and levantadas, where I had a lot of good time with them.

When I was fourteen years old, one of my uncles came up with the idea to take my brother to the United States so he could study there and work. With this, he would get better opportunities, but I didn't want him to go, because he was like my best friend. We have a difference of just two years, so we always have been together. I proposed to my parents that I wanted to go too, but they didn't want to let me go because I was too young and I could not work. I remember having made a lot of promises to make them change their minds. I said as soon as I worked and got money, I could send it to support them and also my little brother. I remember having said that I would be back with a new truck for my father. It was too expensive for them to pay for two people, especially because we were under eighteen. I said to my father, "Dame una oportunidad para poder demostrarte de lo que puedo ser capaz" (Give me a chance to show you what I can be capable of). It has always been funny for me that I share a primal part of my father, the name Miguel. I don't know if it seems like a tradition, but I was the second one, and that's my name. My mom used to call me Miguel even before I was born. I don't know why, but I feel I used to be her favorite, before my sister was born, and that was why my mother didn't want to let me go.

Currently, I wonder if it was a good idea to have left my home and parents to find my own path at the age of fourteen. I lost a lot; I lost part of freedom, tradition, and family. I had the opportunity to work at the age of sixteen years old and, as it was for my father, it was difficult because I was too young and nobody puts trust in young people. It was difficult to find a job for my age, however when I found it, once I had the opportunity, I had to hold onto it no matter what because it was the opportunity to get some money to help my parents and siblings in Mexico. I started working in a restaurant as a dishwasher. During my days of work (that was four per week at the beginning), I was met by my lack of experience and speed to work out an obstacle, but my desire of work, and with it to be able to help my family, was the thing that stopped me from giving up. The first days were hard; managing my time between school and work was difficult. After we closed, it used to take me more than an hour to wash all the dishes, take the trash out, and mop the floor.

One thing that I have in common with my father is curiosity: desire to learn and listen to advice from others. It is the same thing that helped me to overcome all the obstacles, and with it, I had to confront an "adult life" that took away my freedom and chained me to a life of school and work. I don't have many friends at school because all my time is spent in five days of school, six on my job, and in my free time, I'm used to doing some homework. Living without my parents gives me more responsibilities, such as buying food or cooking at home for myself, washing my clothes, and paying rent. Now I understand what my father meant when he said that he didn't feel free, even though now I'm used to it. It was his advice that helped me do well at my job and school. Even though he is not with me, he still helps me. It was his advice that helped me to pass from dishwasher to working in the kitchen. It was difficult for me to do that because nobody wanted to teach me, but it was my work and desire to work that made it possible.

The reason why I decided to talk about my father first was as a way to say thank you to that person who gave me the opportunity to be more successful in life, even more than he could be. This story is not about me at all, but it is for all people who make it possible for me to be able to receive an education. Now I'm in high school, in twelfth grade, this is my last year of high school and I am thankful for those people who have made it possible that now I will have the opportunity to go to college.

Miguel Anguiano was born in San Francisco, CA. He is the son of parents from Mexico who emigrated to the United States looking for better opportunities in life. He is eighteen years old now and in his last year in high school. He hopes to attend college. Miguel is very shy, but his work and determination talk for him in terms of school and his job. He is very reserved in food and only eats what his mom and grandmother make, so he calls them to get recipes of what he can eat on his days off. He loves to cook and he loves math class, so now he is confused by what he should study. He also loves nature, wildlife, and the town that he grew up in in Mexico, where he left his pets that are his dog and sheep. He dreams and hopes to be able to get together with all of his family again.

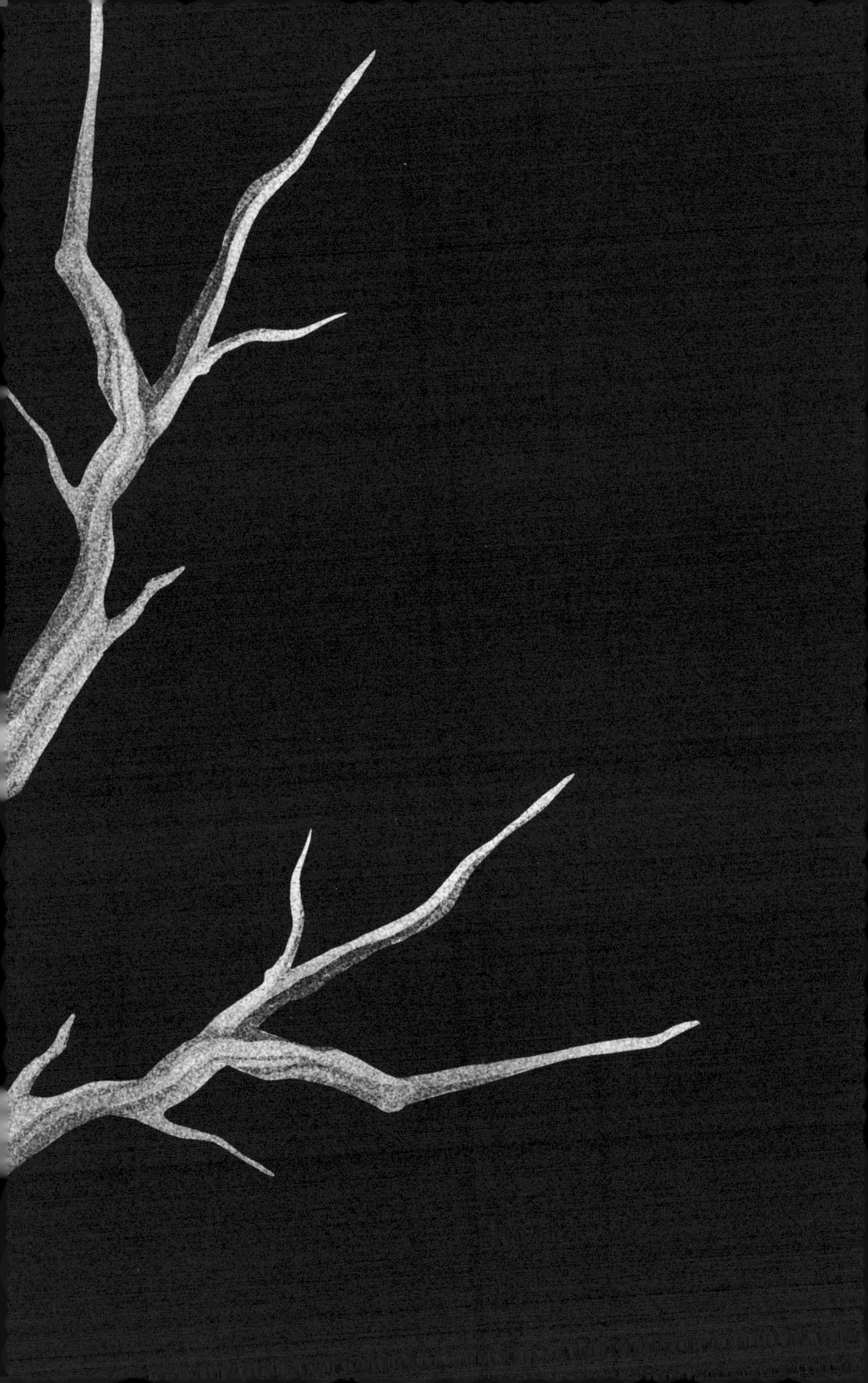

Leaving All Darkness | Goodbye to the Night

A GUIDE FOR EDUCATORS

LEAVING ALL DARKNESS | GOODBYE TO THE NIGHT

A GUIDE FOR EDUCATORS

Created by Ryan Young, Yareli Arreola, and Stina Perkins (826 Valencia) and Catherine Reyes (Mission High School)

■ BACKGROUND

Students read and analyze *The Battle of and for the Black Face Boy* by Nikky Finney and write narratives, letters, and/or poems related to the piece's themes, exploring histories of oppression and imagining paths to freedom. Finney, in the fall 2015 issue of *Oxford American,* describes how her poem came to be:

> "The horrific world of Black slavery of the nineteenth century is reported to have been emancipated, but instead it seems to have been simply modernized, by catastrophic, everyday state-sanctioned violence against millions of Black citizens. Those enslaved human beings and their children, who stepped from slavery into the Civil War, into Reconstruction, into Jim Crow, into the water hoses of the civil rights movement, now step into the streets of Ferguson and Florida, Baltimore and Charleston, holding a two-

hundred-and-fifty-year-old sign that reads an ancient, long-ignored truth: BLACK LIVES MATTER.

The institution of American slavery not only lit the fuse of fighting known as the Civil War, but the question of who could own another human being remained at the heart of this war and remains at the heart of America today. The question of who gets to move like a free person and who gets to move in chains remains ensconced in our everyday American lives one hundred and fifty plus years later. The shooting of young Black men and women has continued ad nauseam. The disregard for Black life has not slowed but surged. I wanted to write a poem that traveled from the horror of one day to the lifting of our chins the next—that paid homage to how we keep moving; keep stepping forward; inventing whatever is next to invent; constructing, fashioning iron chains into wings; how we continue to fold and shape into a future what has been kept from us, regardless of the brutality that still chases us."

"Untitled," from the series Passports, by Keisha Scarville

■ WRITING PROMPT

Nikky Finney believes that history often cuts away things we don't want to see. However, she writes to tell the truth, no matter how hard it is to tell. She urges us to be honest in our own writing, no matter how hard it may be to write, but to also include the beauty that can grow from such hardships. This is the true path to our freedom. This will be your task. ***In the spirit of Finney's poem and Ethnic Studies, what is your truth, what makes you feel free, and "what keeps you moving, stepping forward, inventing whatever is next to invent, constructing,***

fashioning iron chains into wings, continuing to fold and shape a future that has been kept from you, regardless of the brutality that still chases you"?

The writing could take a range of forms and we want to empower students to think and write creatively. Some students will tell personal stories about their communities or their families. Others will write poems or letters that address the poem's themes.

ADDITIONAL PROMPTS AND QUESTIONS

FREEDOM PROMPTS

Freedom of Movement

Where and how are you free to move? Where and how is your movement restricted? What spaces do you feel comfortable and uncomfortable in? Why?

Freedom of Expression

In what ways do you feel free to express yourself (speech, body language, clothing, music, emotions, etc.)? What restricts your self-expression?

Freedom of Belief

How does dreaming, imagining, or innovating relate to freedom? What dreams do you have for your future or for the world? What might be keeping you from these dreams?

Freedom of Knowledge/Story

Who has the freedom to tell their stories? How have you seen yourself, your family, and/or your culture represented in the stories you've read and the history you've learned? What do you want to leave for future generations?

Freedom to Own

Who makes the music, art, or clothes you like? Who profits off of it? How does this relate to systems of power/oppression (histories of slavery, capitalism, school-to-prison pipeline, etc.)?

Write a freedom of your choice.

FREEDOM QUESTIONS

1. What type(s) of freedom are you exploring? What does it look like, feel like, etc.? Who does it impact? Why? Why is it important to you?
2. When did you first become aware of this freedom/restriction? How do you engage in it now?
3. Is this condition permanent? Temporary? Who shaped it? Why is it there?
4. How does this freedom/restriction impact you and who you are in the world?

Interactive Activities to Pair with *Freedom to Live without Fear*

MAKING CONNECTIONS | Choose a piece of writing to read together as a class. As they read, students will actively annotate the text with connections to themselves, other texts, and the world. What does this piece remind you of? Can you relate to the narrator? What images come to mind as you read? How is it similar to other stories you have read, heard, or watched? What local and global issues are raised? How does the narrative connect to history, current events, and the future? Start with modeling and guided practice of the strategy, and then transition to independent work. Student responses can then be synthesized in a discussion or through writing.

SOCRATIC DIALOGUE | Choose a piece of writing to read together as a class and use that as a springboard to explore the questions listed above. Have students then identify textual evidence to support their stance on the selected theme question to prepare for the discussion. The dialogue can occur between a pair of students, as a fishbowl, or you can split the class to present and defend opposing views. The teacher or students can act as facilitators. Establish norms for participation. Consider the following open-ended questions to start, or create your own that are specific to the text: What is the piece saying about "freedom"? How does the piece's outcome support your claim? What are other points of view?

DRAMATIZE IT | Assign a group of students to a scene or scenes, and ask them to write a play based on the narrative. Ask students to create additional text, like character and scene descriptions, stage directions, and design. Invite students to act out their plays, or film their dramatization and share it with others.

WRITE WHAT HAPPENS NEXT | Starting with a piece of writing that ends unresolved, allow students to adopt and extend the narrative. Invite them to pick up where the author left off and write what might happen next, based on what they know about the characters and plot. Students are welcome to write multiple possible endings and reflect on the strengths and limitations of each.

CREATE A PUBLIC SERVICE ANNOUNCEMENT | Begin by showing students examples of public service announcements and discuss persuasive techniques. Students will choose an issue affecting their community or world. This could be a topic appearing in the book (such as gentrification or police brutality), or another topic they are passionate about. Then students will write a script for a public service announcement about an issue affecting their community or the world. Their script should contain a clear purpose, reasons, and relevant facts.

CREATE A GRAPHIC REPRESENTATION | Incorporating a visual element is helpful to both plan and process. In developing the pieces in this book, many students utilized plot maps in order to flesh out their ideas and to stay on track. For this activity, have students choose a narrative to interpret visually—in graphic novel form, via photography, or through another visual medium—in order to see the piece from a fresh perspective and bring it to life in a new way.

DEBATE ABOUT FREEDOMS | Read the foreword and the following excerpt from Nikky Finney's piece from *Oxford American* (Nikky Finney, Issue 90, Fall 2015, September 1, 2015) explaining how "The Battle of and for the Black Face Boy" Came to Be:

> *Nikky Finney:* "The slow dance of the Civil War and the enslavement of Black people in America are my working metaphors for the poem known as 'The Battle of and for the Black Face Boy.'
>
> The barbaric act of restricting a human being by chaining and confining as many as possible in a finite space is founded on the mathematics of profit. Mathematics, which includes adding, subtracting, and division, is one of the main roads used to calculate profit. Profit is the mother and father of war and capitalism. The space and spatial rules and regulations regarding the enslavement of Black people, two hundred and fifty years ago, can be connected to the space and spatial rules and regulations regarding the movement of Black people in modern America.
>
> The world of the enslaved African in America did not include safety, security, or the encouragement to create. Black people had to find

and hold on to those things themselves. The horrific world of Black slavery of the nineteenth century is reported to have been emancipated, but instead it seems to have been simply modernized, by catastrophic, quotidian, state-sanctioned violence against millions of Black citizens. Those enslaved human beings and their children, who stepped from slavery into the Civil War, into Reconstruction, into Jim Crow, into the water hoses of the civil rights movement, now step into the streets of Ferguson and Florida, Baltimore and Charleston, holding a two-hundred-and-fifty-year-old sign that reads an ancient, long-ignored truth: BLACK LIVES MATTER.

In 2013, I was commissioned by the Clarice Smith Center at the University of Maryland to write a libretto in honor of the sesquicentennial end of the Civil War. The university had joined the national celebration that was already scheduling concerts and performances across the country in 2015. 'The Battle of and for the Black Face Boy' became my offering. An incredibly long list of names of young Black men, shot and killed by police and security guards across the country, was kicking me in my heart. The facts of their deaths and lives shook me. Their names and their formerly alive smiling faces, their cornrows, baseball caps, chocolate hoodies, their perfect moon-shaped afros escorted me through my day. The voices of their mothers, speaking of their sweet and funny Black sons, became a somber score that filled my head.

I imagined a radical libretto made of Civil War history, Black history, and modern American headlines. The voice of the historical narrator begins. The voice of the Black Face Boy enters as sonic soliloquy. The narrator and the first-person voice of the Black Face Boy enter into a radical libretto call and response. Great leaps of time are found in each stanza, and a twelve-page album of faces and geographies is set to the music of battles and human discoveries. Nothing is linear because time, history, and truth do not happen in a capsule or a vacuum. At the heart of this radical libretto sits this: The institution of American slavery not only lit the fuse of fighting known as the Civil War, but the question of who could own another human being remained at the heart of this war and remains at the heart of America in 2015. The question of who gets to move like a

> free person and who gets to move in chains remains ensconced in our everyday American lives one hundred and fifty years later.
>
> The shooting of young Black men and women has continued ad nauseam. The disregard for Black life has not slowed but surged. In June, in Mother Emanuel A.M.E. Church, in Charleston, South Carolina, on the edge of the Atlantic Ocean where millions of enslaved Africans first arrived against their will, ninety miles away from where I was born and where I have now returned to teach and write, nine church members attending Bible study were shot by a twenty-one-year-old white male, who had, in the confidence of friends and the Internet, professed a great desire to begin a second Civil War. After being invited into the church by loving, embracing, gracious Black people, who were spiritually, if not literally, children of the Africans who had been violently forced across the Atlantic two hundred and fifty years before in the name of profit. He sat with them and listened to them before he killed them. He must have heard their voices speak of God's undying love as he pulled out his cannon of a gun, raised his Confederate flag over their heads, and pulled the trigger.
>
> I wanted to write a poem that traveled from the horror of one day to the lifting of our chins the next—that paid homage to how we keep moving; keep stepping forward; inventing whatever is next to invent; constructing, fashioning iron chains into wings; how we continue to fold and shape into a future what has been kept from us, regardless of the brutality that still chases us."

Ask students to read Finney's piece and to reflect on the following assertion in the context of their own experiences: "The question of who gets to move like a free person and who gets to move in chains remains ensconced in our everyday American lives one hundred and fifty years later." What spaces do you feel welcome/unwelcome in? Why do you think that is? How might we reimagine these spaces to be more accepting and less restrictive?

Next, allow students to share. Call on students who are discussing different spaces in their community and allow them to explain why they feel welcome/unwelcome. Allow others to share their own experiences. As an extension activity, students may submit their suggestions for more welcoming spaces to leaders in their community (for example, if students have ideas about making their community park a more welcoming space, they may write letters to the Parks and Recreation department).

FORCED CHOICE | Place a sign in each corner of the room: strongly disagree, somewhat disagree, somewhat agree, strongly agree. Read the following statements aloud and direct students to move to the corner representing their opinion about the statement.

- "As long as you are happy, freedom will come no matter what. Freedom is something that will always be deep inside you." (author Larissa Chacon, page 9)
- "It's better to run on a field of thorns than to simply stand in place and never look back." (author Aila Ysabel Alli, page 50).
- "you can't love someone if you don't love yourself" (author Virginia Coello, page 80)
- "The present is a gift, take every moment as it is; a moment you will never get back; one chance to make it count." (author Aaron Villareal, page 122)
- "Freedom is when I can buy anything I want, but I choose to get a burrito from the same spot." (author Jamarion Speed, page 161)

Call on students with different views to explain their stance. Students will then select a statement that they had a strong reaction to (positive or negative) and read the essay it came from. As an extension, students can write a note to the author. What is your reaction? Why? What is or isn't effective about their writing? What questions do you have for the author?

Content Standards

This project-based unit was designed to address a broad array of standards in English Language Arts. The following are key standards:

READING

Key Ideas and Details:

CCSS.ELA-LITERACY.RL.11-12.1

Cite strong and thorough textual evidence to support analysis of what the text says explicitly as well as inferences drawn from the text, including determining where the text leaves matters uncertain.

CCSS.ELA-LITERACY.RL.11-12.2

Determine two or more themes or central ideas of a text and analyze their development over the course of the text, including how they interact and build on one another to produce a complex account; provide an objective summary of the text.

CCSS.ELA-LITERACY.RL.11-12.3

Analyze the impact of the author's choices regarding how to develop and relate elements of a story or drama (e.g., where a story is set, how the action is ordered, how the characters are introduced and developed).

Craft and Structure:

CCSS.ELA-LITERACY.RL.11-12.4

Determine the meaning of words and phrases as they are used in the text, including figurative and connotative meanings; analyze the impact of specific word choices on meaning and tone, including words with multiple meanings or language that is particularly fresh, engaging, or beautiful. (Include Shakespeare as well as other authors.)

CCSS.ELA-LITERACY.RL.11-12.5

Analyze how an author's choices concerning how to structure specific parts of a text (e.g., the choice of where to begin or end a story, the choice to provide a comedic or tragic resolution) contribute to its overall structure and meaning as well as its aesthetic impact.

CCSS.ELA-LITERACY.RL.11-12.6

Analyze a case in which grasping a point of view requires distinguishing what is directly stated in a text from what is really meant (e.g., satire, sarcasm, irony, or understatement).

Integration of Knowledge and Ideas:

CCSS.ELA-LITERACY.RL.11-12.7

Analyze multiple interpretations of a story, drama, or poem (e.g., recorded or live production of a play or recorded novel or poetry), evaluating how each version interprets the source text.

Range of Reading and Level of Text Complexity:

CCSS.ELA-LITERACY.RL.11-12.10

By the end of grade 12, read and comprehend literature, including stories, dramas, and poems, at the high end of the grades 11-CCR text complexity band independently and proficiently.

■ WRITING

Text Types and Purposes:

CCSS.ELA-LITERACY.W.11-12.1

Write arguments to support claims in an analysis of substantive topics or texts, using valid reasoning and relevant and sufficient evidence.

CCSS.ELA-LITERACY.W.11-12.2

Write informative/explanatory texts to examine and convey complex ideas, concepts, and information clearly and accurately through the effective selection, organization, and analysis of content.

CCSS.ELA-LITERACY.W.11-12.3

Write narratives to develop real or imagined experiences or events using effective technique, well-chosen details, and well-structured event sequences.

Production and Distribution of Writing:
CCSS.ELA-LITERACY.W.11-12.4
Produce clear and coherent writing in which the development, organization, and style are appropriate to task, purpose, and audience.

CCSS.ELA-LITERACY.W.11-12.5
Develop and strengthen writing as needed by planning, revising, editing, rewriting, or trying a new approach, focusing on addressing what is most significant for a specific purpose and audience.

CCSS.ELA-LITERACY.W.11-12.6
Use technology, including the Internet, to produce, publish, and update individual or shared writing products in response to ongoing feedback, including new arguments or information.

Research to Build and Present Knowledge:
CCSS.ELA-LITERACY.W.11-12.8
Gather relevant information from multiple authoritative print and digital sources, using advanced searches effectively; assess the strengths and limitations of each source in terms of the task, purpose, and audience; integrate information into the text selectively to maintain the flow of ideas, avoiding plagiarism and overreliance on any one source and following a standard format for citation.

CCSS.ELA-LITERACY.W.11-12.9
Draw evidence from literary or informational texts to support analysis, reflection, and research.

Range of Writing:
CCSS.ELA-LITERACY.W.11-12.10
Write routinely over extended time frames (time for research, reflection, and revision) and shorter time frames (a single sitting or a day or two) for a range of tasks, purposes, and audiences.

SPEAKING AND LISTENING

Comprehension and Collaboration:

CCSS.ELA-LITERACY.SL.11-12.1

Initiate and participate effectively in a range of collaborative discussions (one-on-one, in groups, and teacher-led) with diverse partners on grades 11-12 topics, texts, and issues, building on others' ideas and expressing their own clearly and persuasively.

CCSS.ELA-LITERACY.SL.11-12.2

Integrate multiple sources of information presented in diverse formats and media (e.g., visually, quantitatively, orally) in order to make informed decisions and solve problems, evaluating the credibility and accuracy of each source and noting any discrepancies among the data.

CCSS.ELA-LITERACY.SL.11-12.3

Evaluate a speaker's point of view, reasoning, and use of evidence and rhetoric, assessing the stance, premises, links among ideas, word choice, points of emphasis, and tone used.

Presentation of Knowledge and Ideas:

CCSS.ELA-LITERACY.SL.11-12.4

Present information, findings, and supporting evidence, conveying a clear and distinct perspective, such that listeners can follow the line of reasoning, alternative or opposing perspectives are addressed, and the organization, development, substance, and style are appropriate to purpose, audience, and a range of formal and informal tasks.

CCSS.ELA-LITERACY.SL.11-12.5

Make strategic use of digital media (e.g., textual, graphical, audio, visual, and interactive elements) in presentations to enhance understanding of findings, reasoning, and evidence and to add interest.

CCSS.ELA-LITERACY.SL.11-12.6

Adapt speech to a variety of contexts and tasks, demonstrating a command of formal English when indicated or appropriate.

Educator Resources

***Don't Forget to Write* (2005)** contains fifty-four of the best lesson plans used in workshops taught at 826 Valencia, 826NYC, and 826LA, giving away all of our secrets for making writing fun. Each lesson plan was written by its original workshop teacher, including Jonathan Ames, Aimee Bender, Dave Eggers, Erika Lopez, Julie Orringer, Jon Scieszka, Sarah Vowell, and many others. If you are a parent or a teacher, this book is meant to make your life easier, as it contains enthralling and effective ideas to get your students writing. It can also be used as a resource for the aspiring writer. In 2011, 826 National published a two-volume second edition of *Don't Forget to Write,* also available in our stores.

***STEM to Story* (2015)** contains dynamic lesson plans that use hands-on discovery and creative writing to teach students about science, technology, math, and engineering. These quirky, exploratory lessons are sure to awaken the imagination and ignite passions for both STEM and creative writing. *STEM to Story* is a boon to teachers, parents, and students alike, as each lesson plan is aligned with Common Core and Next Gen Science Standards.

Other Books from 826 Valencia

826 Valencia produces a variety of publications, each of which contains work written by students in our programs. Some are professionally printed and nationally distributed; others are glued together on-site and sold in our stores. These projects represent some of the most exciting work at 826 Valencia, as they enable Bay Area students to experience a world of publishing not otherwise available to them. The following is a selection of publications available for purchase at our stores, online at shop.826valencia.org, or through your local bookstore.

***We All Belong* (2019)** is a collection of writing about physical and metaphorical borders by tenth-grade students of Galileo High School in San Francisco. Inspired by Luis J. Rodriguez's *Always Running,* students set out to define what constitutes a border in the form of personal narratives, fictional short stories, letters, and poems. From reflections about physical boundaries that have impacted them, to internal barriers they've been working to overcome, to divisions between people in their communities, these young authors meditate on their own borders—and how to cross them.

***The Battle Within* (2018)** features writing from the students of Ida B. Wells High School in San Francisco. Inspired by the themes in Khaled Hosseini's *The Kite Runner,* these young authors crafted powerful stories, poems, and letters that get to the heart of what it means to struggle, to regret, to overcome, to love. We invite you to take a moment to step inside each one of their stories, to read their words, and to consider their hopes.

***We Are Here, Walking Toward the Unknown* (2017)** is a collection of narrative essays about adapting, written by students at Phillip & Sala Burton Academic High School. Have you ever been misunderstood or judged? What fears are you working to overcome? Can science and technology go too far? If you had the opportunity to go back, how would you fix a past mistake? While these questions were inspired by the themes in Mary Shelley's *Frankenstein,* a book written in the nineteenth century, they are still as thought-provoking and relevant as ever. In this collection, the seniors of Burton High in San Francisco set out to answer them in the form of personal narratives, fictional short stories, and letters. From intimate reflections about their own lived experiences, to the development of creative and futuristic worlds, these young authors meditate on our past, present, and future—and the results prove illuminating for all.

***Walk the Earth in Our Shoes and Plant Some Seeds Behind You* (2016)** collects personal essays from students at John O'Connell High School. What would we learn if we could interview a whale? Is diversity as advantageous in a social community as it is in a coral reef? How does our environment affect us, and how do we affect our environment? These questions are both age-old and urgent, and in this collection, ninth- and tenth-grade authors set out to answer them. From how their neighborhoods are changing, to what it's like to live in a drought, these young authors share their views and experiences as they investigate the way ecosystems work—and their answers hold insights everyone should read.

***If the World Only Knew* (2015)** features essays written by sixty-six ninth graders at Mission High School. In this book students reflect on their beliefs and where they come from—the people who imparted them, the times when they were most necessary, and the ways in which the world has tested them. The collection is a testament to the power of personal conviction, and a powerful case for why young peoples' voices should be heard—and believed.

***Uncharted Places* (2014)** examines the idea of "place" and what it means to fifty-two young authors in this collection of essays by juniors and seniors at Thurgood Marshall High School. It contains stories about locales real and imagined, internal and external, places of transition and those of comfort. These young writers bravely share their views of the world, giving us a glimpse into the places that are most important to them—those not necessarily found on a map, but in the heart.

***Arrive, Breathe, and Be Still* (2012)** is a collection of monologues and plays exploring the themes of resistance and resilience written by thirty-five students at Downtown High School in San Francisco, with a foreword by playwright Octavio Solis. After a semester of working intensely with actors at American Conservatory Theater and writing tutors from 826 Valencia, the students produced this powerful look into the realities of high school life, the pressures surrounding young people, and the strength it takes to keep going.

***Beyond Stolen Flames, Forbidden Fruit, and Telephone Booths* (2011)** is a collection of essays and short stories, written by fifty-three juniors and seniors at June Jordan School for Equity, in which young writers explore the role of myth in our world today. Students wrote pieces of fiction and nonfiction, retelling old myths, creating new ones, celebrating everyday heroes, and recognizing the tales that their families have told over and over. With a foreword by Khaled Hosseini, the result is a collection with a powerful message about the stories that have shaped students' perspectives and the world they know.

***I Live Real Close to Where You Used to Live* (2010)** is a collection of letters to Michelle, Sasha, Malia, and Bo Obama written by students across the 826 network. These letters are packed with questions, advice, and the occasional request to be invited over to the White House for dinner.

***Show of Hands* (2009)** is a collection of stories and essays written by fifty-four juniors and seniors at Mission High School. It amplifies the students' voices as they reflect on one of humanity's most revered guides for moral behavior: the Golden Rule, which tells us that we should act toward others as we would want them to act toward us. Whether speaking about global issues, street violence, or the way to behave among friends and family, the voices of these young essayists are brilliant, thoughtful, and, most of all, urgent.

***Thanks and Have Fun Running the Country* (2009)** is a collection of letters penned by our After-School Tutoring students to newly-elected President Obama. In this collection, which arrived at inauguration time, there's loads of advice for the president—often hilarious, sometimes heartfelt, and occasionally downright practical. The letters have been featured in the *New York Times*, the *San Francisco Chronicle*, and on *This American Life*.

***Exactly* (2007)** is a hardbound book of colorful stories for children ages nine to eleven. This collection of fifty-six narratives by students at Raoul Wallenberg Traditional High School is illustrated by forty-three professional artists. It passes on lessons that teenagers want the next generation to know.

***Home Wasn't Built in a Day* (2006)** is a collection of short stories based on family myths and legends. With a foreword by actor and comedian Robin Williams, the book comes alive through powerful student voices that explore just what it is that makes a house a home.

Acknowlegments

A Thank You Letter from the Editor

The Young Authors' Book Project (YABP) is an annual labor of love that relies heavily on the generosity and dedication of an incredible number of people. This year was no exception. Our 2020 YABP by the numbers: one school, five weeks, ten sessions, three editorial board meetings, forty-eight volunteers, fifty-nine students, and countless hours of editing. It's been a journey, from start to finish, and we are deeply grateful for all of the support.

We'd first like to thank the school community at Mission High School for being the most incredible collaborator for this project. We'd especially like to thank Mission High Principal Pirette McKamey for her unending support of 826 Valencia and other great resources for students at her school. Thank you also to the staff, administrators, and students who make Mission High a truly special community.

We are honored to have worked with the most amazing partner teacher on this project: Catherine Reyes. Ms. Reyes is an outstanding educator in every way; she knows her students and engages them in the learning process at every turn. Ms. Reyes has cultivated a community that celebrates rich discussion, exploration, and challenge. She inspires her students to speak confidently, to be enthusiastic learners in the classroom and outside of it, and to push beyond accepted histories to strive for truth and equity. For these reasons and more, Ms. Reyes has been a dream collaborator for this project. We look forward to seeing the many ways in which her students will carry the skills and confidence they've gained in her classes with them as they move through the world.

We owe Nikky Finney a tremendous debt of gratitude for her engagement throughout the entire Young Authors' Book Project. From the moment we connected with Nikky, she has greeted every request and every opportunity we have presented with a resounding yes and a relentlessly positive attitude. When she visited the students at Mission High School to launch our project before the first tutoring session, she captivated the room of young authors with her words, her perspectives on doing creative work, and her advice for writers and artists. Ms. Finney provided illuminating, encouraging, and candid responses to all of the questions students posed—from reflections about her writing process, to advice for coming to a creative piece through a "window" rather than the "door," to more philosophical discussions about what freedom means in today's world.

With Nikky Finney's engagement in the project, students saw their school assignment transform into a powerful work of creativity and art. And in her foreword, she captured the energy in all the students' pieces and helped pull together and introduce all the ways they explore the *Freedom to Live without Fear*. We truly cannot thank Nikky enough.

A small group of students and volunteer tutors took their dedication to this book above and beyond by hand-editing each of the narratives collected here and setting the editorial direction for the book. The editorial board showed great professionalism and growth over the course of this process. In just three weeks, these students went from authors to co-editors, and in doing so they gained confidence in their writing skills and became empowered to make the big decisions that made this book a reality. Their hard work shines on these pages. As such, we'd like to extend a special thanks to these students: Virginia Coello, Jackie Hernandez, Ezrealla Laudenorio, and Kimberly Hernandez T., and these volunteers: Tess Canfield, Katie Cugno, Maura Kealey, Anne Sloper, and Tarryn Warn.

Enormous thanks to Molly Schellenger, the designer of this book, for honoring the young authors' words by giving them such a beautiful home! A huge thank you to Azul Quetzalli, the book's illustrator, for bringing the students' voices to light through beautiful cover and interior art. To Brad Amorosino, our Design Director, and Meghan Ryan, our Publications Project Manager, thank you both for your invaluable work on this publication, for amplifying the students' voices with your design expertise, and for keeping us all on deadline. Huge thanks to Christopher Keilman, our copyeditor whose super-human eyes catch every single extra space and misplaced comma, for lending your time to helping our young authors' words shine.

Finally, we are so proud of the young writers collected here. Writers, for sharing your unique and poignant perspectives with us, for your courage in offering your stories and voices to the world, and for never giving up on the writing process, we commend and profoundly thank you.

Ryan Young

Programs Manager and Editor

About 826 Valencia

ABOUT 826 VALENCIA

■ WHO WE ARE AND WHAT WE DO

826 Valencia is a nonprofit organization dedicated to supporting under-resourced students ages six to eighteen with their creative and expository writing skills and to helping teachers inspire their students to write. Our services are structured around the understanding that great leaps in learning can happen with one-on-one attention and that strong writing skills are fundamental to future success.

826 Valencia comprises three writing centers—located in San Francisco's Mission District, Tenderloin neighborhood, and Mission Bay—and three satellite classrooms at nearby schools. All of our centers are fronted by kid-friendly, weird, and whimsical stores, which serve as portals to learning and gateways for the community. All of our programs are offered free of charge. Since we first opened our doors in 2002, thousands of volunteers have dedicated their time to working with tens of thousands of students.

■ PROGRAMS

FIELD TRIPS | Classes from public schools around San Francisco visit our writing centers for a morning of high-energy learning about the craft of storytelling. Four days a week, our Field Trips produce bound, illustrated books and professional-quality podcasts, infusing creativity, collaboration, and the arts into students' regular school day.

IN-SCHOOLS PROGRAMS | We bring teams of volunteers into high-need schools around the city to support teachers and provide one-on-one assistance to students as they tackle various writing projects, including newspapers, research papers, oral histories, and more. We have a special presence at Buena Vista Horace Mann K–8, Everett Middle School, and Mission High School, where we staff dedicated Writers' Rooms throughout the school year.

AFTER-SCHOOL TUTORING | During the school year, 826 Valencia's centers are packed five days a week with neighborhood students who come in after school and in the evenings for tutoring in all subject areas, with a special emphasis on creative writing and publishing. During the summer, these students participate in our Exploring Words Summer Camp, where we explore science and writing through projects, outings, and activities in a super fun, educational environment.

WORKSHOPS | 826 Valencia offers workshops designed to foster creativity and strengthen writing skills in a wide variety of areas, from playwriting to personal essays to starting a zine. All workshops, from the playful to the practical, are project-based and are taught by experienced, accomplished professionals. Over the summer, our Young Authors' Workshop provides an intensive writing experience for high-school-age students.

COLLEGE AND CAREER READINESS | We offer a roster of programs designed to help students get into college and be successful there. Every year, we grant several $20,000 scholarships to college-bound seniors, provide one-on-one support to two hundred students via the Great San Francisco Personal Statement Weekend, and partner with ScholarMatch to offer college access workshops to the middle- and high-school students in our tutoring programs. We also offer internships, peer tutoring stipends, and career workshops to our youth leaders.

PUBLISHING | Students in all of 826 Valencia's programs have the ability to explore, experience, and celebrate themselves as writers in part because of our professional-quality publishing. In addition to the book you're holding, 826 Valencia publishes newspapers, magazines, chapbooks, podcasts, and blogs—all written by students.

TEACHER OF THE MONTH | From the beginning, 826 Valencia's goal has been to support teachers. We aim to both provide the classroom support that helps our hardworking teachers meet the needs of all our students and to celebrate their important work. Every month, we receive letters from students, parents, and educators nominating outstanding teachers for our Teacher of the Month award, which comes with a $1,500 honorarium. Know an SFUSD teacher you want to nominate? Guidelines can be found at 826valencia.org.

826 NATIONAL | 826 Valencia's success has spread across the country. Under the umbrella of 826 National, writing and tutoring centers have opened up in eight more cities. If you would like to learn more about other 826 programs, please visit the following websites.

826 National
826national.org

826 Boston
826boston.org

826CHI
826chi.org

826DC
826dc.org

826LA
826la.org

826michigan
826michigan.org

826 MSP
826msp.org

826 New Orleans
826neworleans.org

826NYC
826nyc.org

826 Valencia
826valencia.org

PEOPLE

STAFF

Bita Nazarian *Executive Director*

Brad Amorosino *Design Director*

Melissa Anguiano *Programs Coordinator*

Yareli Arreola *Programs Coordinator*

Paolo Bicchieri *Volunteer Coordinator*

Nana Boateng *Programs Coordinator*

Angelina Brand *Programs Manager*

Nicole C. Brown *Director of Individual Philanthropy*

Sarah Bruhns *Development Coordinator*

Karla Brundage *Programs Manager*

Ricardo Cruz-Chong *Programs Coordinator*

Lila Cutter *Volunteer Manager*

Precediha Dangerfield *Programs Coordinator*

Allyson Halpern *Advancement Director*

Virdell Hickman *Operations Manager*

Kavitha Lotun *Volunteer Director*

Montana Manalo *Design Associate*

Molly Parent *Communications Manager*

Nick Parker *Finance Director*

Lucie Pereira *Programs Coordinator*

Stina Perkins *Programs Coordinator*

Christina V. Perry *Director of Education*

Ginnie Redmond *Grants and Development Coordinator*

Nesley Rojo *Programs Coordinator*

Meghan Ryan *Publications Project Manager*

Sendy Santamaria *Design Associate*

Ashley Smith *Programs Manager*

Leah Tarlen *Director of Institutional Gifts*

Benita Tsao *Human Resources Manager*

Shelby Urbina *Programs Coordinator*

Jillian Wasick *Programs Director*

Byron Weiss *Stores Director*

Ryan Young *Programs Manager*

AMERICORPS SUPPORT STAFF THROUGH SUMMER 2020

Kanya Abe *Programs Associate, Mission Center*
Ryan Bloom *Programs Associate, Tenderloin*
Kyle Breschini *Programs Associate, Mission Bay*
Sophie Goethals *Communications Associate*
Diego Hernandez *In-School Programs Associate*
Hannah Johnson *In-School Programs Associate*
Natalie Louie *Programs Associate, BVHM*
Daniel Mata *Volunteer Engagement Associate*
Monika Mednick *Programs Associate, Tenderloin*
Fiona Murphy *Programs Associate, Mission Bay*
Peter O'Meara *Programs Associate, BVHM*
Martin Quarto *Programs Associate, Tenderloin*
Alex Turnage *Programs Associate, Mission Center*
Sydney Vogl *Programs Associate, Mission Bay*

STORE STAFF

Devin Angel *Store Coordinator*
Jonathan Kendall *Store Associate*
Andrea Kasprzak *Store Associate*
Steven Peterson Gomez *Store Associate*
Brandon Pipersky *Store Associate*
Tim Ratanpreuskul *Store Coordinator*
Giorgia Sage *Store Associate*
Luis Sepulveda *Store Associate*
Kai Stewart *Store Coordinator*

BOARD OF DIRECTORS

Eric Abrams
Colleen Quinn Amster
Joya Banerjee
Jasmine Berjikly
Lisa Brown
Carolyn Feinstein Edwards
Alex Lerner
Jim Lesser
Julia Matsudaira
Enikia Ford Morthel
Dave Pell
Liza Ramrayka
Joe Vasquez
Rachel Swain Yeaman

CO-FOUNDERS

Nínive Calegari, Dave Eggers

OUR VOLUNTEERS

There's absolutely no way we could create hundreds of publications and serve thousands of students annually without a legion of volunteers. These incredible people work in all realms, from tutoring to fundraising and beyond. They range in age, background, and expertise, but all have a shared passion for our work with young people. Volunteers past and present, you know who you are. Thank you, thank you, thank you.

It's Always a Good Time to Give

WE NEED YOUR HELP

We could not do this work without the thousands of volunteers who make our programs possible. We are always seeking more volunteer tutors, and volunteers with design, illustration, photography, and audio editing skills. It's easy to become a volunteer and a bunch of fun to actually do it. Please fill out our online application to let us know how you'd like to lend your time: **826valencia.org/volunteer**

OTHER WAYS TO GIVE

Whether it's loose change or heaps of cash, a donation of any size will help 826 Valencia continue to offer a variety of free writing and publishing programs to Bay Area youth.
Please make a donation at:
826valencia.org/donate

You can also mail your contribution to:
826 Valencia Street, San Francisco, CA 94110

Your donation is tax-deductible. What a plus! Thank you!